HISTORY OF THE BIBLE IN ENGLISH

GVLIELMVS TINDALE MARTYR

OLIM EX AVLA MAGD

Hac ut luce tuas disper... ... ... fama tenentes
Sponte extorris ero ... ... Sacrificium.

REFERT HÆC TABELLA QVOD SOLVM POTVIT ARS, GVLIELMI TINDALE, HVIVS OLIM AVLÆ ALVMNI, SIMVL
ET ORNAMENTI, QVI POST FÆLICES PVRIORIS THEOLOGIÆ PRIMITIAS HIC DEPOSITAS, ANTVERPIÆ IN NOVO
TESTAMENTO, NEC NON PENTATEVCHO IN VERNACVLAM TRANSFERENDO OPERAM NAVAVIT,
ANGLIS SVIS EO VSQ SALVTIFERAM, VT INDE NON IMMERITO ANGLIÆ APOSTOLAS AVDIRET
MARTYRIO WILFORDÆ PROPE BRVXELLAS CORONATVS A°. 15 36. VIR, SI VEL ADVERSARIO
(PROCVRATORI NEMPE IMPERATORIS GENERALI) CREDAMVS, PERDOCTVS PIVS ET BONVS.

History of the Bible in English

From the earliest versions

F. F. BRUCE

*Formerly Rylands Professor of Biblical Criticism
and Exegesis in the University of Manchester*

New York
OXFORD UNIVERSITY PRESS
1978

OXFORD UNIVERSITY PRESS

Oxford   London   Glasgow

New York   Toronto   Melbourne   Wellington

Nairobi   Dar es Salaam   Cape Town

Kuala Lumpur   Singapore   Jakarta   Hong Kong   Tokyo

Delhi   Bombay   Calcutta   Madras   Karachi

First published in the United States by Oxford University Press, New York,
and in Great Britain by Lutterworth Press, in 1961,
under the title THE ENGLISH BIBLE

Revised edition, 1970

Third edition, 1978

This reprint, 1981

Library of Congress Cataloging in Publication Data

Bruce, Frederick Fyvie, 1910–
History of the Bible in English.

Previous ed. published under title: The
English Bible.
Includes bibliographical references and index.
1. Bible.   English – Versions.   1. Title.
BS455.B74 1978   220.5'2'009   78-16271
ISBN 0-19-520087-X
ISBN 0-19-520088-8 pbk.

First issued as an Oxford University Press Paperback, 1978

Printed in the United States of America

Contents

Preface

THE FIRST edition of this work (issued under the title *The English Bible*) coincided with the publication in 1961 of the New English Bible New Testament. The second (revised) edition followed soon after the publication of the complete New English Bible in 1970. This further edition under a new title endeavours to bring the story up to date, especially by the addition of a chapter which looks at a number of versions which have been produced within the last eight years or so. A few omissions have been repaired and some factual slips corrected. For the rest, the main record remains practically unchanged since 1970.

Traduttore traditore, says an Italian proverb: "the translator is a traitor". An exaggeration certainly; and yet an honest translator is bound to confess that something is lost, something is changed, in the course of translation. Those of us—alas! a diminishing band—who in our earlier years were taught to read Homer in the original know perfectly well that no translation can ever give us the true feel of the authentic Homer. No doubt the Bible suffers less in translation than many other works do, but no Bible translator who knows his business counts himself to have attained perfection. I too have made my own private ventures into the field of Bible translation; and these ventures have at least taught me to deal very leniently with other translators. Not all the Bible translations with which we have been favoured in recent years have been produced by such a well-qualified body of men as the New English Bible; yet one would be slow to pass unmitigated condemnation even on the poorest of them, bearing in mind the difficulties of the task.

Yes, but what of those translations where the translators deliberately introduce their own peculiar ideas of religious belief and practice? Must they not be condemned? Indeed they must; but let those who are themselves sinless in this regard cast the first stones. And by those who are sinless in this regard I do not mean those who have never tried to translate the Bible, but those who have translated it so objectively that their own beliefs, principles and practices have influenced no point of their work. Let us remember, too, that it is usually our unconscious prejudices and preferences that do the most damage; we can recognize our conscious ones for what they are and make allowance for them accordingly. All this suggests that a translation carried through by a body of men representing a wide range of ecclesiastical and theological opinion is more likely to be free from bias in these matters than the work of one individual, or of a committee selected from a more limited field.

One of the earliest of English translators, King Alfred the Great, distinguishes two ways in which translators may go about their work. "I began," he says, "amidst other diverse and manifold cares of the kingdom, to turn into English the book which is called *Cura Pastoralis* in Latin, and in English, *The Shepherd's Book*, sometimes word for word, and sometimes meaning for meaning." The history of the English Bible—indeed the history of Bible translation in general—illustrates the conflict between these two ideals in translation. Because of the special religious character and status of the Bible, there have always been those who felt that only a word-for-word translation could do justice to the implications of its divine inspiration. And some translations in fact have been so extremely literal that they can only be understood by reference to the original.

Now there is a place for such very literal translations. There are, for example, some editions of the Greek New Testament where an interlinear English rendering is provided, in such a way that each Greek word has its English equivalent directly beneath it. This interlinear rendering is not a translation, in the proper sense of the term; it is what schoolboys know as a "crib". Its purpose is to show which Greek word corresponds to which English word, and if it achieves that purpose, good and well. But who would tolerate this if it were offered as a trustworthy translation of the opening words of St John's Gospel?

> In beginning was the Word, and the Word was towards the God, and God was the Word. This was in beginning towards the God. Everything through him became, and apart-from him became not-even one-thing. What has-become in him life was, and the life was the light of-the men. And the light in the darkness shines, and the darkness it not overcame.

What is wrong with that? It is a word-for-word rendering of the Greek text of the 1958 edition published by the British and Foreign Bible Society. There is obviously one thing wrong with it: it is not English. And there is something else wrong with it: it does not faithfully represent the writer's meaning. *Traduttore traditore?* If this is a translation, the translator *is* a traitor. But it is not a translation; it is a "metaphrase".

For certain limited purposes—purposes normally limited to the study and the classroom—a "crib" has its uses.[1] But it can never be an acceptable translation, because the translator's business is, as far as possible, to produce the same effect on readers of the translation as the original text produces or produced on those able to read it. This law of equivalent effect, as it is commonly called nowadays, is not a new-fangled notion; it was known and enunciated centuries ago. There are two versions of the Bible associated with the followers of John Wycliffe. One of these is a very literal rendering of the Latin Vulgate—very literal, it appears, because it was intended to be used as a volume of canon law, where verbal precision is all-important. But that was not the version which people risked their lives and liberties to buy and read. The Wycliffite version which did attain such popularity and excite such devotion was the work of a man who put on record his conviction that the best way to translate from Latin into English was to make the sentence, rather than the individual word, the sense-unit. "Meaning for meaning," in effect, was John Purvey's motto. The translators of the New English Bible have followed the same procedure; how successful they have been it is henceforth for us, the readers, to decide.

[1] Cf. the literal rendering of an Old English Bible story on pp. 4 f. below.

We call the King James Version the "Authorized Version". What makes a version "authorized"? And has the New English Bible been "authorized"?

There is no mystery about the matter. An authorized version is one that has been authorized for stated purposes by competent authority. For example, Roman Catholics in Great Britain have nowadays a variety of "authorized" versions of the Bible in English. The older Douai-Rheims-Challoner version and the more recent version by Mgr Ronald Knox are authorized for public and private use by competent authority—that is to say, by the Roman Catholic archbishops and bishops of England and Wales and of Scotland. The Catholic edition of the Revised Standard Version was "published with ecclesiastical approval" and carried a foreword by Cardinal Heenan in which the work was welcomed "not only because it will lead more of our people to read the Bible, but also because of its ecumenical value". The English edition of *The Jerusalem Bible* was issued with Cardinal Heenan's *imprimatur*.

Similarly, a Bible translation is authorized for the use of members of any other Church if the competent authorities of that Church authorize it. But where a Church is "by law established", the authority of the state may be involved as well. After his breach with Rome, King Henry VIII of England regarded himself as the competent authority in the Church of England as much as in the realm of England. In 1537 his royal licence was granted to two versions of the English Bible—Coverdale's and Matthew's—but that made them permitted rather than fully authorized versions. More explicit authorization was given to the Great Bible of 1539 and following years: the title-page of its second edition describes it as "the Bible appointed to the use of the churches" [i.e. the parish churches of England], and "appointed" means "appointed by royal authority". Later in Henry's reign a ban was imposed on earlier versions (even, and indeed especially, for private use), but the authorization of the Great Bible remained in force. In the reign of Elizabeth I the Bishops' Bible tended to supersede the Great Bible as the version for church use. Convocation of Canterbury directed that it should be made available in many public places, but Queen Elizabeth herself never formally acknowledged it or gave it preferential treatment.

While the Bible of 1611 is a version undertaken under direct royal patronage, and probably approved by the King in Council, its use was not imposed on the churches by Parliament or Convocation. Had it been so imposed, its revision or replacement would have been charged with as much political dynamite as the revision of the Prayer Book. It is something to be thankful for that an Anglican clergyman does not require to have Parliamentary sanction for using in church the Bible version which he thinks fit to use.

In Scotland the Geneva Bible was appointed to be used in churches from the year of its publication onwards. Whether its replacement by the 1611 version was ever formally authorized by competent authority—that is, by the General Assembly of the Church of Scotland—I have not been able to discover.

Authorized or not, the 1611 version found widespread and long-lasting acceptance throughout the English-speaking world because it deserved such acceptance. If any more recent version proves to be deserving of such acceptance, it will not fail to achieve it.

"Man's chief end is to glorify God, and to enjoy him for ever. The word of God, which is contained in the scriptures of the Old and New Testaments, is the only rule to direct us how we may glorify and enjoy him. The scriptures principally teach what man is to believe concerning God, and what duty God requires of man" (*Westminster Shorter Catechism*, Answers 1-3).

"Blessed Lord, who hast caused all holy Scriptures to be written for our learning; Grant that we may in such wise hear them, read, mark, learn, and inwardly digest them, that by patience, and comfort of thy holy Word, we may embrace, and ever hold fast the blessed hope of everlasting life, which thou hast given us in our Saviour Jesus Christ. Amen" (*Book of Common Prayer:* Collect for the Second Sunday in Advent).

Note: Except in extracts from versions of the Bible, the spelling in quotations from older English writers has usually been modernized.

CHAPTER ONE

The Beginnings of the English Bible

THE BIBLE played a central part in English Christianity from its earliest days. But when we speak of the *English* Bible, we are not merely thinking of the Bible in England, but of the Bible in the English language. The Bible which was known and used in the earliest English Church, as in the British and Irish Churches even earlier, was the Latin Bible. From the fifth century onwards, the Latin Bible came to mean the version made by Jerome between A.D. 383 and 405, the version commonly known as the Latin Vulgate. In no part of the western world was this version studied more diligently and copied more lovingly and faithfully than in Great Britain and Ireland. In fact the most reliable extant manuscript of the Vulgate was made in England, at one or other of the twin monastic foundations of Jarrow and Wearmouth. It was copied under the direction of Abbot Ceolfrid, and presented to Pope Gregory II in 716; it is now in the Laurentian Library at Florence. It is known as the *Codex Amiatinus*, because of an inscription on its second page which states that it was presented to the abbey of Monte Amiata.

The Bible in Pictures

From the earliest days of English Christianity the gospel story, which, of course, is based on the Bible, was told to the people of England in their own language. But the preaching of the gospel in English hardly amounts to the beginnings of the Bible in English; for this something less "occasional", something more permanent, is required. One of these more permanent means of teaching people the Bible was the decoration of church buildings with wall-paintings and relief carvings, with which, for example, in the seventh century Wilfrid adorned the church of York and Benedict Biscop the church of Wearmouth. From the same period we have the carved panels, representing incidents from the Gospels, on the Ruthwell Cross—an ancient runic cross near the Solway Firth, on the old pilgrim way between Iona and Lindisfarne. Under each panel is a gospel text from the Latin Vulgate; but wayfarers who could not read the Latin could study the panels and think about the incidents which they depicted. We may compare the strip-cartoons in which, even in our own highly literate generation, Bible stories are portrayed in some of our better-class children's weeklies.

The Ruthwell Cross also contains extracts from one of the greatest of Old English poems, *The Dream of the Rood*, in which a mystic vision of the true cross is described with fervid and tender devotion.

To about the same date belong two other crosses, erected farther east along the pilgrim way—one at Bewcastle in Cumberland, and the other at Hexham Abbey in Northumberland (commonly referred to as Bishop Acca's Cross). All three crosses stand on the 55th parallel of latitude. On the Bewcastle Cross our Lord's name appears with the spelling GESSOS KRISSTOS, which enables interesting inferences to be drawn about the current pronunciation of certain sounds.

Old English Poems

Another way in which people who could not read might learn and remember the contents of the Bible is seen in the Old English poems which tell parts of the Bible story. In this connection it is interesting to recall what Bede, the learned monk of Jarrow, tells us about Caedmon, a labourer attached to the monastery at Whitby in Yorkshire. This man Caedmon was completely ungifted in poetry and song, and one night, when his companions were enjoying themselves at a party, he stole away to the stable in case he would be asked to sing. In the stable he fell asleep, and dreamed that a man came and stood beside him and told him to sing. He replied that he could not sing, but the command was repeated. "What shall I sing?" Caedmon asked, and he was told to sing how all things were first created. So he began to praise the Creator in words which he had never heard before:

> Now must we praise
> The Maker of the heavenly realm,

The Creator's power and wisdom,
The deeds of the Father of glory;
How He, being God eternal,
Was the Author of all wonders,
Who first to the sons of men
Made heaven for the roof of their abode,
And then created the earth,
Almighty Guardian of mankind ...

"And," says Bede, "when he awoke, he remembered everything that he had sung in his dream, and later added further verses in the same strain to the glory of God."

It was recognized that Caedmon had suddenly received a gift from God, and the abbess Hilda, superior of the monastery, persuaded him to join the brotherhood as a monk. He received detailed instruction in the Bible story, and turned what he learned into verse so melodious that (says Bede) "his instructors became his eager listeners. For he sang of the world's creation, the origin of the human race, and all the story of Genesis; he sang of Israel's exodus from Egypt and entry into the promised land, of very many other stories from Holy Writ, of our Lord's incarnation, passion, resurrection and ascension into heaven, of the coming of the Holy Spirit, and the apostles' teaching. Moreover he composed many songs telling of the terror of judgment to come, the horror of the pains of hell, and the bliss of the heavenly kingdom, and very many others of the divine blessings and judgments, in all of which he made it his aim to draw men away from the love of evil deeds and to stir them up to love and zeal for good works."[1]

Thus Caedmon by his songs supplied a sort of people's Bible, in words which they could easily memorize and sing themselves. How many of the Old English poems on these themes can be ascribed to Caedmon is difficult to say, but he may very reasonably be credited with the ultimate authorship of a metrical version of the narratives of Genesis, Exodus and Daniel. The narratives of Exodus in particular are rendered with vivid descriptive power. The Genesis version has had inserted into it a section which did not originally belong to it.

[1] Bede, *Ecclesiastical History of the English Nation*, iv. 24.

This section, known as *Genesis B*, is an Old English translation from continental Old Saxon; it may well have been known to Milton and it anticipates certain features of his *Paradise Lost*, such as the portrayal of a heroic Satan.

Old English—the designation of the earliest known stage of our language, in the centuries before the Norman Conquest—differs so much from Middle English (*c.* 1100–1500) and Modern English (since 1500) as to be a foreign tongue to us, requiring to be translated as much as Norse and German do before we can understand what is meant. Here, for example, is Moses' address to the panic-stricken Israelites before the Red Sea divides in front of them so that they can cross to the other side:

> Ne beoth ge thy forhtran, theah the Faraon brohte
> sweordwigendra side hergas,
> eorla unrim! Him eallum wile
> mihtig drihten thurh mine hand
> to daege thissum daedlean gyfan,
> thaet hie lifigende leng ne moton
> aegnian mid yrmthum Israhela cyn.
> Ne willath eow ondraedan deade fethan
> faege ferhthlocan! fyrst is aet ende
> laenes lifes. Eow is lar godes
> a-broden of breostum: ic on beteran raed,
> thaet ge gewurthien wuldres aldor
> and eow liffrean lissa bidde,
> sigora gesynto, thaer ge sithien!
> This is se ecea Abrahames god,
> frumsceafta frea, se thas fyrd wereth
> modig and maegenrof mid thaere miclan hand.

If we turn this into more recent English line by line, following the ord-order fairly closely, the result will be something like this:

> Be not frightened thereat, though Pharaoh has brought
> sword-wielders, vast troops,
> men without number! To them all will
> the mighty Lord through my hand

4

this very day a recompense give,
that they may not live long
to frighten with distress Israel's kin.
Be not afraid of a dead army,
death-doomed bodies! The term is at an end
of their mortal life. By you the exhortation of God
has been removed from your breasts: I offer better counsel,
that you honour the Prince of glory,
and pray the Lord of life for favour to you,
victory's fruit, wherever you journey!
It is the eternal God of Abraham,
creation's Lord, who this camp protects,
valiant and powerful with that mighty hand.

(One of the most prominent features of Old English poetry that tends to disappear in such a translation is the elaborate alliteration.)

These lines we have quoted are a paraphrase of the words of Moses in Ex. 14 : 13 f., "Fear ye not, stand still, and see the salvation of the LORD, which he will shew to you to day: for the Egyptians whom ye have seen to day, ye shall see them again no more for ever. The LORD shall fight for you, and ye shall hold your peace" (A.V.).

Cynewulf, a gifted poet of the ninth century, has bequeathed a version of the gospel story in his *Crist*—"a noble poem," says Sir Herbert Grierson.[1] From the tenth century we have a metrical version of *Judith*, one of the apocryphal books of the Old Testament. This is all that survives of what was originally a much longer poem. It includes a particularly vivid account of Judith's slaying of the heathen general Holofernes.

Old English Translations of the Bible

When we turn from these metrical paraphrases of the Bible story to straightforward translations of the Bible text, the first name that meets us is that of Aldhelm, first bishop of Sherborne in Dorset. He is said to have translated the Psalter into Old English soon after the year 700. Aldhelm was a pupil of Theodore of Tarsus, Archbishop of Canterbury from 668 to 690, one of the most illustrious alumni

[1] *The English Bible* (London, 1943), p. 7.

of the school which Theodore instituted at Canterbury and one of the most learned men of his day.

But there was a man in England whose reputation for learning throughout Western Europe was greater even than Aldhelm's. This was Bede, the monk of Jarrow whose account of Caedmon has been quoted above. His learned contributions to history and exegesis were written in Latin, but he had a concern for the spiritual welfare of his less learned fellow-countrymen, and gave them some parts of the New Testament in their own tongue. We have, for example, the statement by his disciple Cuthbert (later Abbot of Wearmouth and Jarrow) that during his last illness he was engaged in translating St John's Gospel into English. Bede died on Ascension Eve (May 25) in 735. His translation of the Gospel, unfortunately, has not survived.[1]

Bede himself in a letter to Egbert (who became Archbishop of York shortly before Bede died) exhorts him to take special care to see that ordinands whose Latin was weak or non-existent were conversant with the Apostles' Creed and the Lord's Prayer in the vernacular, adding that he himself "had both these, that is, the creed and the *Pater Noster*, translated into the English tongue, for the sake of many priests, who are often unlearned."

This Egbert, it may be added, was later to render a great service to biblical scholarship by founding the minster-school of York. His most distinguished pupil was Alcuin, who was later attached to Charlemagne's court at Aachen (Aix-la-Chapelle) and made that court the centre of a revival of learning which influenced for good the whole course of mediaeval culture. Alcuin made a special contribution to biblical scholarship by his revision of the text of Jerome's Vulgate, a task undertaken at the commission of Charlemagne himself.

The Court of Alfred

Another court which, while by no means so grandiose as that of Charlemagne, was equally devoted to learning, was that of the English king Alfred (871-901). Most kings whose names have come

[1] A. S. C. Ross, "A Connection between Bede and the Anglo-Saxon Gloss to the Lindisfarne Gospels?" (*Journal of Theological Studies*, October 1969, pp. 482 ff.), raises the question whether Bede's translation may have been used by Aldred (see pp. 7 f.); if so, it would be extant in part.

down in history with the epithet "the Great" appended to them appear to owe this title to the high number of their fellow-men whom they have succeeded in killing; Alfred the Great can base his claim to the title on nobler foundations. It was unusual for a king in those days to be so literate as Alfred was, and he used his literacy and general interest in culture to promote the good of his subjects. He translated (or had translated) into English Bede's *Ecclesiastical History of the English Nation*, Orosius's *Universal History*, and Pope Gregory the Great's *Pastoral Care* (a handbook for parish priests). Towards the end of his life he published a code of laws, and this code was introduced by English versions of the Ten Commandments, followed by further extracts from chapters 21 to 23 of Exodus (the chapters commonly referred to nowadays as "The Book of the Covenant"). The reference to buying a *Hebrew* servant in Ex. 21 : 2 is made more relevant to the English situation in Alfred's day; the phrase appears as "a Christian servant"! These extracts are followed by a translation of the apostolic letter drawn up at the Council of Jerusalem (Acts 15 : 23-29), in a longer text which includes, at the end, the Golden Rule, in its negative form: "Whatever you would not like others to do to you, do not that to others." Thus Alfred's "dooms" (judgments) are preceded by the "dooms" of God. As his last literary work Alfred is said to have translated part of the Psalter into English.

Early Glosses

One form which early translations of biblical texts into English took was that of interlinear "glosses" in Latin manuscripts. In an eighth-century Latin Psalter in the British Museum there appears such an interlinear translation, executed probably in the ninth century. The Lindisfarne Gospels, also in the British Museum, constitute one of the best examples of illuminated manuscript work surviving from Old English times. This manuscript is a Latin copy of the Gospels, written by Bishop Eadfrith of Lindisfarne towards the end of the seventh century. About the middle of the tenth century a priest named Aldred wrote between the lines a literal English rendering of the Latin, in the Northumbrian dialect; and at the end of the manuscript he added a note on its history in which he not only mentions Eadfrith as the man who wrote the manuscript but also names the men responsible for its binding and splendid ornamentation, and adds that he himself, "an unworthy and most miserable priest," was responsible for the gloss. A similar gloss is provided in the Rushworth Gospels, a manuscript copied from the Lindisfarne Gospels, and now housed in the Bodleian Library, Oxford. The Rushworth glosses are practically transcripts of the Lindisfarne glosses so far as the Gospels of Mark, Luke and John are concerned, but in Matthew the Rushworth gloss is an independent rendering in the Mercian dialect by a priest named Farman.

Samples of Old English Versions

From the same period as the Lindisfarne and Rushworth glosses comes the first extant independent Old English version of the Gospels, known as the Wessex Gospels. And a little later, towards the end of the tenth century, Abbot Aelfric of Eynsham in Oxfordshire produced a translation of parts of the first seven books of the Old Testament; he was also the author of homilies which incorporated English renderings from some of the other Old Testament books— Kings, Esther, Job, Daniel and Maccabees.

The following quotation—the Parable of the Sower from Matt. 13 : 3–8—will serve as a sample of the Wessex Gospels:

> Sothlice ut eode se sawere his saed to sawenne. And tha tha he seow, sumu hie feollon with weg, and fuglas comon and aeton tha. Sothlice sumu feollon on staenihte, thaer hit naefde micle eorthan, and hraedlice up sprungon, for thaem the hie naefdon thaere eorthan diepan; sothlice, up sprungenre sunnan, hie a-drugodon and forscruncon, for thaem the hie naefdon wyrtruman. Sothlice sumu feollon on thornas, and tha thornas weoxon, and forthrysmdon tha. Sumu sothlice feollon on gode eorthan, and sealdon waestm, sum hundfealdne, sum siextigfealdne, sum thritigfealdne.

And here is Aelfric's version of the story of the Tower of Babel in Gen. 11 : 1–9:

> Aefter thaem sothlice ealle menn spraecon ane spraece. Tha

tha hie ferdon fram east-daele, hie fundon anne feld on Sennaar-lande, and wunodon thaeron.

Tha cwaedon hie him betweonan: "Uton wyrcan us tigelan, and aelan hie on fyre!" Witodlice hie haefdon tigelan for stan and tierwan for weal-lim. And hie cwaedon: "Uton timbrian us ceastre, and stiepel oth heofon heanne! uton weorthian urne naman, aer thaem the we sien todaelde geond ealle eorthan!"

Witodlice Dryhten astag nither, to thaem thaet he gesawe tha burg and thone stiepel, the Adames bearn getimbrodon. And he cwaeth: "This is an folc, and ealle hie sprecath an laeden, and hie begunnon this to wyrcenne: ne geswicath hie aer thaem the hit gearu sie; sothlice uton cuman and todaelan hiera spraece!"

Swa Dryhten hie todaelde of thaere stowe geond ealle eorthan. And for thaem man nemnde tha stowe Babel for thaem the thaer waeron todaelde ealle spraeca.

The reader who compares these extracts clause by clause with the corresponding passages in his modern English Bible will get some idea of the relation of tenth-century English to the English which he himself speaks.

After the Conquest

The Norman Conquest of 1066 and the following years dealt a heavy blow to Old English culture. English history has sometimes been taught in schools in such a way as to suggest that the Conquest represented a cultural advance, but a comparison of William the Conqueror with Alfred the Great from this point of view points to a different conclusion. A British Museum manuscript of the Wessex Gospels, copied in the early part of the twelfth century, indicates that Old English biblical texts continued to be read by some people at least after the Conquest. But the impact of the Conquest, carried as it was by a new ruling class speaking Norman French, brought about such radical changes in spoken English that before long the Old English versions of the tenth century must have been unintelligible to the great mass of the English people.

Some manuscripts survive of translations of considerable parts of the Bible into the Anglo-Norman speech of the new ruling class, but

9

they do not belong to the history of the Bible in English, but to that of the Bible in French—even if their French is the variety described by Chaucer as "after the scole of Stratford-atte-Bowe".

Early Middle English Versions

From the end of the twelfth century or beginning of the thirteenth comes a work called the *Ormulum*—a poetical version of the Gospels and Acts of the Apostles, accompanied by a commentary, the work of an Augustinian monk named Orm or Ormin. It is extant only in one Bodleian manuscript, which may be the original autograph.

Towards the middle of the thirteenth century the stories of Genesis and Exodus were translated into rhyming English verse; later in the century a metrical version of the Psalter appeared. Two prose translations of the Psalter have survived from the first half of the fourteenth century, one in the dialect of the West Midlands and the other by Richard Rolle, the hermit of Hampole near Doncaster. Rolle's version forms part of a verse-by-verse commentary on the Psalms; it appears to have been a popular work, for it was copied out in other dialects than Rolle's northern one.

Towards the end of the fourteenth century a version of the chief New Testament epistles was made, apparently for the use of monks and nuns; this is suggested by the fact that the translator frequently apostrophizes his reader as "brother" or "sister" (or rather "suster") in prologues and epilogues to the various epistles. This version was subsequently amplified by the addition of Acts and the earlier part of Matthew. The whole is introduced by a prologue in which the Old Testament history is summarized from the Creation to the giving of the Law; in this prologue the garments which Adam and Eve made of fig-leaves are called breeches nearly two hundred years before the Geneva Bible described them by the same term ("for schame", says our translator, "thei maden hem breches of leues to huyden with hure membres"). The section of Matthew which is included in this version comes to an end with the Lord's Prayer (Matt. 6 : 9–13), which runs as follows:

Oure Fader that art in heuene, halewed be thi name. Thi kyng-dom come to us. Thi wylle be don, as in heuene, and in erthe.

THE BEGINNINGS OF THE ENGLISH BIBLE

Oure eche dayes breed yeue us to day. And foryeue us oure
dettys, as we foryeue oure dettourys. And ne lede us not in
temptacyon, but delyuere us of yuel. Amen.

The Epistle to the Hebrews in this version is introduced thus:

And to the children of Israel, suster, he[1] wryteth and saith,
God hath y-spoken in many maneres sumtyme in prophetes to
oure fadres, bote al-ther last in these dayes he hath y-spoken to ous
in his sone, whom he hath y-ordeyned to ben eyr of alle thinges,
by whom also he made the worldes; and he is the brytnesse of his
blisse, and the fygure of his substaunce, berynge alle thinges
thorogh the word of his vertu, and makynge the purgacyoun of
synnes, he syt on the ryght syde of the mageste an hygh in hefne;
so muche y-maad betur than aungeles, in as muche as he hath an-
heryted a different name to-foren hem.[2]

While a version like this might freely be made for the devotional
use of inmates of religious houses, there was as yet no thought of
supplying ordinary layfolk with the Scriptures in the vernacular.
This revolutionary idea was first entertained (so far as mediaeval
England is concerned) by the Wycliffite movement, and to this new
departure we must now turn our attention.[3]

---

[1] That is to say, Paul, whom the translator, like all his contemporaries, assumed to be the
author of Hebrews.

[2] See *A Fourteenth Century English Biblical Version*, edited by Anna C. Paues (Cambridge,
1904).

[3] For a more detailed account of the subject-matter of this chapter see G. Shepherd,
"English Versions of the Scriptures before Wyclif", in *The Cambridge History of the Bible*, 2:
The West from the Fathers to the Reformation, ed. G. W. H. Lampe (Cambridge, 1969), pp.
362–387.

CHAPTER TWO

John Wycliffe and the English Bible

THE FIRST translation of the whole Bible into English is associated with the name of John Wycliffe (c. 1330–1384), the most eminent Oxford theologian of his day. His theological interests were not confined to the purely academic realm; they were related to the crucial ecclesiastical and social issues of contemporary politics. The prestige of the Papacy had fallen very low, partly by reason of the "Babylonian captivity" of the Popes at Avignon, where they maintained their residence from 1309 to 1378, under the control of the French kings, England's hereditary enemies; and partly by reason of the "Great Schism" which followed it, when for nearly forty years (1378–1417) there were two rival Popes, one at Rome and the other at Avignon, one recognized by some European powers and the other recognized by others. In England itself there was much unrest. The tendency for the great offices of state to be occupied by clerics was resented by many of the nobility. The clerical party had a royal champion in the Black Prince, while the anti-clerical party had his brother John of Gaunt as their leader. Wycliffe was a supporter of John of Gaunt, and found in him a loyal protector.

Wycliffe set himself to rethink the whole question of the basis of society, with special reference to the status of the Church. The organization of the Church as a feudal hierarchy seemed to him to be a great mistake, as also did the rich endowments which it enjoyed, a condition of affairs for which he could find no New Testament precedent. Wycliffe propounded the theory of "dominion by grace", according to which each man was God's direct tenant-in-chief, immediately responsible to God, and immediately responsible to obey His law. And by God's law Wycliffe meant not canon law, which he repudiated, but the Bible. The Bible was to him the rule of faith and practice, including ecclesiastical practice, for he did not conceive that the Bible's guidance on questions of church order and organization could be ambiguous.

But if every man was responsible to obey the Bible, as the codification of the law of God, it followed that every man must know what to obey. Therefore the whole Bible should be accessible to him in a form that he could understand. Earlier Bible translations had concentrated on those parts of the Bible which were liturgically relevant or had some specific religious value in the narrower sense of that adjective, but Wycliffe's theory of dominion meant that the Bible as a whole was applicable to the whole of human life, and should therefore be available in the vernacular.

It would be a mistake, however, to think that Wycliffe's interests were wholly, or even primarily, political. He was a keen Bible student, a scholarly commentator on the sacred text, and a preacher of intense moral urgency. He propagated his principles throughout the country by means of travelling preachers, followers and admirers of his, many of them Oxford scholars like himself. But this activity led him into serious trouble. An attempt was made to put him on trial in 1378, but it failed. An attack in 1382 was more successful, for many held him partly to blame for the peasants' revolt of the previous year. Some of his disciples, if not Wycliffe himself, justified the killing of Simon Sudbury, Archbishop of Canterbury, by Wat Tyler's men who invaded London. Wycliffe was attacked in a sermon preached at St Mary's, Oxford, in the summer of 1382, and his followers were for the first time denounced as "Lollards"—a term hitherto reserved for groups of pious Bible students in the Low Countries who, for all their devoutness, were generally marked down as heretics. This sermon led to a furious controversy in Oxford, in the course of which Wycliffe's teachings were pronounced heretical. He was obliged to retire to his rectory at Lutterworth, where he spent the remaining eighteen months of his life.

The Wycliffite Bible

It is doubtful if Wycliffe himself took any direct part in the work of Bible translation, but we need have no qualms about referring to the Wycliffite Bible, for it was under his inspiration and by his friends and colleagues that the work was done.

The standard printed edition of the Wycliffite Bible is Forshall and Madden's text, published at Oxford in 1850. This work distinguishes two Wycliffite versions, an earlier and a later. The earlier one was produced between 1380 and 1384, while Wycliffe was still alive; the later one appeared after his death. Both these versions were based on the Latin Vulgate, and both were copied and recopied by hand; the invention of printing was still to come.

What is generally thought to be the original manuscript of the earlier Wycliffite version belongs to the Bodleian Library in Oxford. It breaks off half-way through the Book of Baruch, at chapter 3, verse 20. (Since it followed the Latin Vulgate, this version translated the apocryphal books in the order in which they appear in the Vulgate; Baruch comes after Jeremiah and Lamentations.) One of the earliest copies of the earlier version has a break at Baruch 3 : 20, with a note saying: "Here ends the translation of Nicholas of Hereford". From this it has usually been inferred that Nicholas of Hereford, a canon of the Abbey of St Mary of the Meadows at Leicester, whom we know to have been an ardent supporter of Wycliffe, was the translator of the earlier version up to this point. It may be that the version had reached this point when the storm broke at Oxford in 1382, and had to be completed by others, since Nicholas of Hereford spent the next five years either on the Continent or in prison.

Who completed the earlier version we cannot be sure. Some have suggested Wycliffe himself, others his secretary John Purvey. Mr Henry Hargreaves of Aberdeen University has recently drawn our attention to an abridged Wycliffite Bible, intermediate between the earlier and the later versions, preserved in a Cambridge manuscript which appears to have taken over some scribal notes from a copy of the earlier version.[1] After Baruch 3 : 19 this note is found: "Here endeth the translation of Her and now beginneth the translation of j and of other men". "Her" is in all probability a contraction of "Hereford"; but what of the letter "j"? It might be intended as the initial of "John"; but if so, should we think of John Wycliffe, John Purvey, or some other John? We cannot be sure, any more than we can be sure of the identity of the "other men" who helped to com-

[1] H. Hargreaves, "An Intermediate Version of the Wycliffite Old Testament", *Studia Neophilologica* 28 (1956), pp. 130 ff.

plete this version; but they themselves would have thought the perpetuation of their names as translators a matter of no importance.

A literal translation

The earlier Wycliffite version is an extremely literal rendering of the Latin original. Latin constructions and Latin word-order are preserved even where they conflict with English idiom. This reflects one theory about Bible translation, according to which the sacred quality of the text could be preserved in translation only by the most painstaking word-for-word procedure. But a translation of this kind would have been of little value for ordinary people. Professor Margaret Deanesly suggests that this version was made in accordance with Wycliffe's conception of the Bible as the codification of God's law, something that ought to take the place of contemporary canon law as the basis of church order and authority.[1] In the formulation of law verbal accuracy is of the utmost importance. While men of learning could still use the Latin Bible as their law-book, the less learned clerics and the lay leaders of John of Gaunt's anti-clerical party would have at their disposal a strictly literal rendering of that law-book. Besides, if recourse were had to the standard glosses or commentaries on the biblical text, in which each individual word was annotated, the relevance of these glosses to the English translation would be more apparent if the translation corresponded to the Vulgate word for word.

The first paragraph of the Epistle to the Hebrews will serve as a sample of this first English version of the complete Bible:

Manyfold and many maners sum tyme God spekinge to fadris in prophetis, at the laste in thes daies spak to us in the sone: whom he ordeynede eyr of alle thingis, by whom he made and the worldis. The which whanne he is the schynynge of glorie and figure of his substaunce, and berynge alle thingis bi word of his vertu, makyng purgacioun of synnes, sittith on the righthalf of mageste in high thingis; so moche maad betere than aungelis, by how moche he hath inherited a more different, *or excellent*, name bifore hem.

[1] *The Significance of the Lollard Bible* (London, 1951), pp. 8 f.

15

If we compare this with the Latin text, we see how faithfully it follows its original. The first two verses in Latin run as follows:

> Multifariam multisque modis olim Deus loquens patribus in prophetis, nouissime diebus istis locutus est nobis in filio: quem constituit heredem uniuersorum, per quem fecit et saecula.

Word for word the Wycliffite version corresponds to the Latin, even at the expense of natural English word-order, as in the last clause of verse 2, "by whom he made and the worldis" (the idiomatic Latin *et* before *saecula* being represented literally by the unidiomatic English *and* before *the worldis*). Again, when a participle occurs in the Latin text, it is rendered by a participle in English, although English idiom very often prefers a subordinate clause to a participial construction. Thus in verse 1 "God spekinge" is the literal equivalent of *Deus loquens*, but the familiar wording of the Authorized Version, "God, who ... spake", is much more in keeping with English usage; and in fact the later Wycliffite version shows an appreciation of this, for in it the Epistle to the Hebrews begins with the words "God, that spak".

The later Wycliffite version shows a feeling for native English idiom throughout. Here is how it presents the first paragraph of the same epistle:

> God, that spak sum tyme bi prophetis in many maneres to oure fadris, at the laste in these daies he hath spoke to vs bi the sone; whom he hath ordeyned eir of alle thingis, and bi whom he made the worldis. Which whanne also he is the brightnesse of glorie, and figure of his substaunce, and berith alle thingis bi word of his vertu, he makith purgacioun of synnes, and syttith on the right-half of the maieste in heuenes; and so myche is maad betere than aungels, bi hou myche he hath eneritid a more dyuerse name bifor hem.

John Purvey and his Prologue

Wycliffe himself died at the end of 1384, but he left many ardent disciples. Of these none rendered a greater service to the cause which his master had at heart than his secretary, John Purvey. He found refuge at Bristol and undertook a thorough revision of the earlier Wycliffite version, producing an English Bible which was bound to make a much greater appeal to his fellow-countrymen than a word-for-word rendering of the Vulgate could make. It is Purvey who must receive the credit for the later Wycliffite version, in which the latinate constructions of its predecessor are to a great degree replaced by native English idiom. The revision is particularly thorough in that part of the earlier version which is attributed to Nicholas of Hereford.

The principles directing the production of the later version are set forth in a tract commonly called the *General Prologue*. This tract was evidently composed in 1395 or 1396, and it implies that the work of revision is already complete. It consists of fifteen chapters, in which all men, great and small, learned and unlearned, are urged to make themselves acquainted with God's law—that is to say, the Bible, and not least the Old Testament. The fifteenth chapter defends the circulation of the Bible in the vernacular tongue. It is the desire, and the right, of the common people to have Holy Writ in a form which they can readily understand.

> For these reasons and other, with common charity to save all men in our realm, which God would have saved, a simple creature hath translated the Bible out of Latin into English. First, this simple creature had much travail, with divers fellows and helpers, to gather many old Bibles, and other doctors, and common glosses, and to make one Latin Bible some deal true; and then to study it anew, the text with the gloss, and other doctors, as he might get, and specially Lyra on the Old Testament, that helped full much in this work; the third time to counsel with old grammarians and old divines, of hard words and hard sentences, how they might best be understood and translated; the fourth time to translate as clearly as he could to the sentence, and to have many good fellows and cunning at the correcting of the translation.

The author's description of himself as "a simple creature" is a well-attested mannerism of Purvey's; elsewhere he speaks of himself as "this coward sinful caitiff", "this poor scribbler", and the like. But in fact, as the passage just quoted makes plain, he was no mean scholar, and had a remarkably sure grasp of what was required in preparing an accurate version of the Bible. Since the Latin text was to form the basis of his version, it was necessary to establish as pure a Latin text as possible. Many contemporary copies of the Latin Bible were sadly marred by scribal errors. Indeed, Purvey's judgment of the more recent copies is stated plainly later in this chapter of the *General Prologue*:

> the common Latin Bibles have more need to be corrected, as many as I have seen in my life, than hath the English Bible late translated—

"the English Bible late translated" being no doubt the earlier Wycliffite version, which he had just finished revising.

In order to establish a purer Latin text than was provided by more recent copies, Purvey tells us that he and his colleagues made a careful comparative study of many older and more reliable copies. In this textual work, as well as in the elucidation of the text, he tells us that he received help from the writings of commentators and other biblical scholars, among whom he makes special mention of Lyra— Nicholas of Lyra, the great Franciscan scholar of the fourteenth century, who represents the culmination of a long mediaeval tradition of Hebrew and rabbinical study. And it is interesting to trace in this version examples of Purvey's indebtedness to Lyra's commentary. Some notable examples are recorded in an interesting article on "The Latin Text of Purvey's Psalter" which Mr Henry Hargreaves contributed to *Medium Aevum* in 1955.[1]

In Psalm 8 : 4—rendered in A.V. "What is man, that thou art mindful of him? and the son of man, that thou visitest him?"—the second question appears in the earlier Wycliffite version as "or the sone of man for thou visitest hym." But the later version has the remarkable reading: "ethir the sone of a virgyn for thou visitist hym". Here at least it is the earlier version that preserves the true reading. But where did Purvey get the reading "the sone of a virgyn"? Probably from Lyra's comment on this phrase:

[1] Vol. 24, pp. 73 ff.

or the son of man: that is, the son of a virgin; for man is of common stock, and so Christ's human nature, considered in itself, is lower than the nature of angels.

and yet thou visitest him: by assuming that nature over and above that which was his as the Word, so that thus one and the same person should be son both of a virgin and of God.

But Lyra's gloss has here become Purvey's text.

The first clause of Psalm 132 : 6 runs "Lo, we heard of it at Ephratah" (A.V.). Purvey's text is longer: "Lo, we herden that *arke of testament* in effrata, *that is in silo.*" Where did these additional (italicized) words come from? Certainly not from any manuscript of the Vulgate. But Lyra again supplies the answer to our question. His commentary on this clause is as follows:

> *Lo, we heard of it:* namely, that the ark had been placed at first *in Ephratah*—that is Shiloh, which is in the allotted territory of Ephraim, and therefore Ephratah is not to be understood here of the city of Bethlehem, which is called by the alternative name Ephratah, e.g. in Genesis 25, because the ark is never said to have been in Bethlehem.

In this place Lyra's gloss does not replace the biblical text in Purvey's version, but expands it.

But the establishment of the authentic text and the use of the best aids in understanding that text, while indispensable for the work of translation, are not sufficient in themselves. The actual technique of translation must be considered carefully, in order that the meaning of the original be reproduced as faithfully as possible in the version. So Purvey goes on:

> First, it is to be known that the best translating out of Latin into English is to translate after the sentence[1] and not only after the words, so that the sentence be as open,[2] or opener, in English as in Latin, and go not far from the letter; and if the letter may not be followed in the translating, let the sentence ever be whole and open, for the words ought to serve to the intent and sentence, or

---

[1] I.e., "meaning".   [2] I.e., "plain".

else the words be superfluous or false. ... And whether I have translated as openly or openlier in English as in Latin, let wise men deem, that know well both languages, and know well the sentence of holy scripture. And whether I have done this or no, no doubt they that con well the scripture of holy writ and English together, and will travail, with God's grace thereabouts, may make the Bible as true and open, yea and openlier in English than it is in Latin.

In other words, the translation must be intelligible without reference to the original. And if it is to be intelligible, it must be idiomatic, sufficiently idiomatic to convey the sense without difficulty to a reader whose only language is English. Yet the translator must bear in mind that it is Holy Writ that he is translating; therefore he will not depart from the letter of the original more than is necessary to convey the true and plain sense.

Moreover, the translation of the Bible is a task that imposes a salutary discipline on the translator.

A translator hath great need to study well the sense both before and after, and then also he hath need to live a clean life and be full devout in prayers, and have not his wit occupied about worldly things, that the Holy Spirit, author of all wisdom and knowledge and truth, dress him for his work and suffer him not to err. By this manner, with good living and great travail, men can come to true and clear translating, and true understanding of holy writ, seem it never so hard at the beginning. God grant to us all grace to know well and to keep well holy writ, and to suffer joyfully some pain for it at the last.

The Constitutions of Oxford

This last prayer was no merely pious sentiment on Purvey's part; he and his fellow-translators knew that their work was frowned upon by those in high places who disapproved of Lollardy and all its works. Both he and Nicholas of Hereford endured terms of imprisonment for their activities, and both of them in due course were obliged to abjure their Lollard principles. Some of their associates

died at the stake in accordance with the statute *de heretico comburendo*
passed in 1401. So closely was the translation and circulation of the
Bible in the common tongue connected in the mind of the rulers
with the less desirable features of Lollardy that in 1408 a synod of
clergy at Oxford, summoned by Thomas Arundel, Archbishop of
Canterbury, forbade anyone to translate, or even to read, a vernacular version of the Bible in whole or in part without the approval
of his diocesan bishop or of a provincial council. This prohibition
was one of thirteen provisions passed by the synod against Lollardy;
they are generally known as the "Constitutions of Oxford", and they
remained in force until the establishment of the Reformed religion
in England.

But Purvey's version made such an appeal to the hearts and minds
of the English people that it could not be suppressed, in spite of the
severe penalties attached to its circulation. Something of its appeal
may be appreciated if we quote its rendering of the parable of the
Good Samaritan (Luke 10 : 25-37).

And lo, a wise man of the lawe ros vp, temptynge hym, and
seiynge, Maister, what thing schal Y do to haue euerlastynge lijf?
And he seide to hym, What is writun in the lawe? how redist
thou? He answeride and seide, Thou schalt loue thi Lord God of
al thin herte, and of al thi soule, and of alle thi strengthis, and of
al thi mynde; and thi neighbore as thi silf. And Ihs̄ seide to hym,
Thou hast answerid rightli; do this thing, and thou schalt lyue.
But he willynge to iustifie hym silf, seide to Ihū, And who is my
neighbore?

And Ihs̄ biheld, and seide, A man cam doun fro Ierusalem
in to Ierico, and fel among theues, and thei robbiden hym, and
woundiden hym, and wenten awei, and leften the man half alyue.
And it bifel, that a prest cam doun the same weie, and passide
forth, whanne he hadde seyn hym. Also a dekene, whanne he was
bisidis the place, and saigh hym, passide forth. But a Samaritan,
goynge the weie, cam bisidis hym; and he sigh hym, and hadde
reuthe on hym; and cam to hym, and boond togidir hise woundis,
and helde in oyle and wynne; and leide hym on his beest, and ledde
in to an ostrie, and dide the cure of hym. And another dai he

broughte forth twey pens, and yaf to the ostiler, and seide, Haue the cure of hym; and what euer thou schalt yyue ouer, Y schal yelde to thee, whanne Y come aghen.

Who of these thre, semeth to thee, was neighbore to hym, that fel among theues? And he seide, He that dide merci in to hym. And Ihͣs seide to hym, Go thou, and do thou on lijk maner.

During the first half of the fifteenth century this version of the Bible was augmented by the inclusion of the spurious "Epistle of Paul to the Laodiceans". In Col. 4 : 16 Paul directs the Colossians, when they have read his letter to them, to pass it on to the Church of Laodicea, and to see that they in turn have an opportunity to read "the epistle from Laodicea". This "epistle from Laodicea" has always provided commentators with an interesting problem, as no document bearing this title occurs in the New Testament. But before the end of the fourth century someone obligingly composed an epistle in Paul's name, addressed to the Laodiceans, and this un-authentic composition survived and circulated for many centuries. But any lingering inclination to accept it as Paul's own work received its deathblow with the revival of learning towards the end of the fifteenth century.

There was nothing in Purvey's version in itself to indicate that it was the product of a movement that had been condemned as here-tical. This evidence was contained in the General Prologue, in the prologues to individual books of the Bible, and in the marginal glosses. But copies of the version were made without these additions, and in spite of the Constitutions of Oxford such copies were acquired and read with impunity in many English homes. In due course the Wycliffite origin of the version was forgotten, and it was looked upon as a perfectly orthodox work.

In 1529 Sir Thomas More, soon to become Lord Chancellor of England, published a work[1] in which he launched a fierce attack upon the English version of the New Testament lately completed by William Tyndale. In the course of this attack he refers to the "great arch-heretic Wycliffe", who undertook "of a malicious purpose" to translate the Bible into English and "purposely corrupted the holy

---

[1] *A Dialogue Concerning Heresies.*

text". It was Wycliffe's activity, he says, that led to the ban on unauthorized versions of the Bible in the Constitutions of Oxford. But it was by no means intended that all Bible versions should be indiscriminately banned. For, he goes on, "myself have seen, and can shew you, Bibles fair and old written in English, which have been known and seen by the bishop of the diocese, and left in lay-men's hands, and women's, to such as he knew for good and catholic folk. But of truth, all such as are found in the hands of heretics, they use to take away."

Now it is almost certain that these Bibles which Sir Thomas More had seen—probably in noblemen's houses and the like—were copies of the later Wycliffite version. There was nothing in them that smacked of Lollardy either to himself, to the owners, or to the bishop who sanctioned their use. If the owners were orthodox and practising Catholics, no one would forbid them to read these books.

But by the time that Sir Thomas More wrote his *Dialogue*, a new situation had begun to develop in the history of the English Bible which rendered all the Wycliffite and other early versions obsolete. This was the production of the first *printed* English Bibles, which were translated not from the Latin but from the original tongues.

Yet it is held by some,[1] that when the citizens of London welcomed the first Elizabeth as their queen in 1558 and presented her with "The Word of Truth", the volume which she so gratefully received was a copy of the Wycliffite Gospels. We cannot be sure of this, but that would indeed have been a fitting climax to the history of the first English Bible.[2]

[1] Cf. J. P. Smyth, *How We Got Our Bible* (reprinted, London, 1938), p. 121.
[2] See further H. Hargreaves, "The Wycliffite Versions", in *The Cambridge History of the Bible*, 2: *The West from the Fathers to the Reformation*, ed. G. W. H. Lampe (Cambridge, 1969), pp. 387–415.

CHAPTER THREE

The English New Testament in Print

The Printing Press

THE THREE QUARTERS of a century from 1450 to 1525 were momentous years in the history of Europe. Mid-century witnessed the invention of printing—an invention which seems so simple to us who are acquainted with it that it may seem surprising that no one had thought of it before, or at any rate had thought of it as a means for multiplying the output of books. Few inventions, apart from the invention of writing itself, have had such far-reaching implications for human life and culture. Henceforth, where formerly each individual copy of any work had to be laboriously transcribed by hand, hundreds or even thousands of identical copies could be produced at one printing. The credit for the discovery goes to Johann Gutenberg of Mainz in the Rhineland. The first dated printed work is a Latin Psalter of the year 1454; the first major work to emerge from the press was the Latin Bible of 1456—commonly called the Mazarin Bible, because of the interest excited by a copy of it belonging to the great library of the seventeenth-century French statesman Cardinal Jules Mazarin, but more justly known as the Gutenberg Bible.

The Pentateuch in Hebrew was printed at Bologna in North Italy in 1482, and the complete Hebrew Bible at Soncino, near Cremona, in 1488. The New Testament was first printed in Greek in 1514 at Alcala in Spain, under the direction of Cardinal Ximenes. This printing formed part of the *Complutensian Polyglot* (so called from Complutum, the Latin name for Alcala). In this the New Testament appeared with the Greek text and the Latin Vulgate in parallel columns; in the Old Testament section of the work the Latin Vulgate was flanked by the Hebrew and the Septuagint Greek (like our Lord on the cross between the two thieves, commented the editor as though disguising his enthusiasm for the new learning). But while the New Testament part of the enterprise was printed in 1514, it was not published until some years later, when the whole work, running to six volumes, was complete. The first Greek Testament to be *published*, therefore, was the first edition prepared by the Dutch humanist Desiderius Erasmus, printed at Basel and published in March 1516. This first edition was followed in rapid succession by others in 1519, 1522, 1527 and 1535. It was one or another of the editions of Erasmus which formed the basis for Luther's German New Testament, first printed in 1522, and for William Tyndale's English New Testament, first printed in 1525.

William Tyndale's translation was the first English New Testament to be printed. Surprise has sometimes been expressed that no attempt had been made to print the earlier English New Testament, the second Wycliffite version, which enjoyed a wide circulation in manuscript throughout the fifteenth century. William Caxton set up his printing-press towards the end of 1476 at the sign of the Red Pale in the Almonry at Westminster (on the site of the modern Tothill Street). The output of his press was voluminous, including a number of his own translations, for he was an able linguist. Among his major editions were the works of Chaucer and Sir Thomas Malory's *Morte d'Arthur*. Had he been minded to print the Bible in Purvey's version, his press was certainly equal to the task, and the work would have been sure of an even readier sale than Chaucer and Malory. But the Constitutions of Oxford were still in force, and it would probably have been difficult to secure episcopal permission for such wholesale production and distribution of the English Bible.

Caxton did, however, print some portions of the biblical text in English in his translation of *The Golden Legend*. This work, originally compiled in Latin by one Jacobus de Voragine who later became Archbishop of Genoa, consisted mainly of lives of the saints, including the biblical patriarchs and apostles. The biographies of the biblical characters were to a large extent transcripts of the relevant biblical texts, and so Caxton's printing of this work included fairly literal renderings not only of parts of the New Testament but also of most of Genesis and part of Exodus. In 1509 a printed edition of sermons by Bishop John Fisher was prefaced by an English translation of the penitential psalms.

The Revival of Learning

It was a happy coincidence that the discovery and rapid development of printing should have been followed so quickly by the Revival of Learning—or was it altogether a coincidence? Another important event which made its contribution to the Revival of Learning was the Turkish capture in 1453 of Constantinople, which for eleven hundred years and more had been the capital of the Eastern Roman Empire, the centre of Byzantine culture. The fall of the Eastern Empire led many Greek scholars to migrate to the West, together with their manuscripts; thus the study of Greek, and in particular the study of the New Testament in Greek, received a powerful impetus.

So far as the history of the English Bible is concerned, three representatives of the Revival of Learning are specially worthy of mention. Erasmus (1466–1536) and Sir Thomas More (1480–1535) have already been mentioned, but when we think of them we must not forget a man who influenced them both—John Colet (c. 1467–1519), who became Dean of St Paul's in London in 1505 and founded St Paul's School five years later. Colet in 1496 returned from a prolonged continental visit to his own University of Oxford, and there delivered a course of lectures on the Pauline Epistles (primarily the Epistle to the Romans) which made a deep impression on many who heard them. In his principles of biblical interpretation he made a clean break with the methods of the mediaeval scholastics, and expounded the text in accordance with the plain meaning of the words viewed in relation to their historical context. Erasmus spent some time in Oxford in 1499, and met Colet and More. To Colet he owed much of his insight into the true methods of biblical interpretation, as contrasted with the scholastic way.

Erasmus paid a second visit to England in 1506, and a third in 1511. His third visit was his longest; it was spent mainly in Cambridge, where he served both as Professor of Greek and as Lady Margaret Professor of Divinity. During his years at Cambridge he gave himself especially to the study of Jerome and of the New

Testament, and laid the foundations of his edition of the Greek Testament that was to appear very soon afterwards. It has sometimes been suggested that one of his pupils at Cambridge was William Tyndale; unfortunately the evidence is against this. Erasmus left Cambridge in 1514, and Tyndale probably did not arrive there before 1516 at the earliest. But the influence of Erasmus remained even when the man himself had returned to Europe.

Luther and his influence

In November 1515 Martin Luther, Augustinian monk and Professor of Sacred Theology in the University of Wittenberg, began to expound Paul's Epistle to the Romans to his students. As he prepared his lectures, he came more and more to grasp the crucial character of Paul's teaching about justification by faith. When at last he understood what Paul was getting at, and applied it to himself, then, he says, "I felt myself to be reborn and to have gone through open doors into paradise. The whole of Scripture took on a new meaning, and whereas before 'the righteousness of God' had filled me with hate, now it became to me inexpressibly sweet in greater love. This passage of Paul became to me a gateway to heaven." But no greater challenge to Paul's teaching about justification by faith, as understood by Luther, could be conceived than the views of justification in God's sight popularized at that time by Johann Tetzel, commissioner for the collection of money for the indulgences which the Papacy had been issuing since 1506 to defray the expense of building the new St Peter's in Rome. Justification by grace through faith—or justification by the purchase of a papal indulgence? To Luther the issue seemed clearcut, and in October 1517 he nailed to the doors of the castle church in Wittenberg his Ninety-Five Theses—points intended for academic debate, bringing out various corollaries of the New Testament doctrine of justification and exposing the abuses of the indulgence system. Thus: "every Christian who feels true repentance has as of right full remission of penalty and guilt, even without letters of pardon."

Luther himself did not foresee what his action would lead to, but in the light of the sequel we look back to that action as the one which more than any other sparked off the Reformation. And the progress of the Reformation in the years that followed is closely bound up with the history of the first printed Bibles in the vernaculars of western Europe, including the first printed Bibles in English. This, then, brings us to William Tyndale, to whom we owe the first printed English Bible.

Tyndale's Earlier Years

William Tyndale (who sometimes used the alternative family name of Hutchins) was born in Gloucestershire in 1494 or 1495. He went up to Magdalen Hall, Oxford at what would now seem an impossibly tender age, became Bachelor of Arts in 1512 and Master in 1515. Every Master of Arts was required to lecture in the schools for a year after taking his degree, so Tyndale presumably remained at Oxford until 1516 at least. Then he moved to Cambridge—too late, as has been said, to sit at the feet of Erasmus. But Cambridge was then more advanced than Oxford as a home of the new learning; in 1518 Richard Croke, who had spent several years on the Continent and occupied the Chair of Greek at Leipzig, returned to Cambridge and began to give lectures on Greek. Tyndale's competence in the Greek language may well owe much to Croke's lectures at Cambridge.

From Cambridge Tyndale went in 1522 to Little Sodbury in Gloucestershire as tutor to the children of Sir John Walsh, twice high sheriff of the county. While there he translated Erasmus's *Enchiridion Militis Christiani* ("The Christian Soldier's Handbook"), a short treatise on the Christian's spiritual equipment and discipline which the Dutch scholar had written in 1502. This work insists on the duty of studying the New Testament, and making it the court of appeal in questions of life and doctrine. Tyndale's employer and his wife were greatly impressed by reading Tyndale's translation of the little book, but the ecclesiastical authorities of the county were less favourably disposed towards him, the more so as some of them had experienced his powers in debate at his master's dining-table. He was summoned before the Chancellor of Gloucester diocese to answer a charge of heresy, but the charge was not sustained.

Such experiences, however, led Tyndale to the conviction that the root cause of much confusion in people's minds on the matters then under debate was ignorance of the Scripture. If this ignorance could be corrected, the eyes of all would be opened and the truth made clearly known. And the ignorance was not confined to the humbler laity; it was shared by many of the clergy. A first-hand account of Tyndale's career at this time, which John Foxe later incorporated in his *Book of Martyrs*, reports one conversation which shows the direction of his mind.

> Soon after, Master Tyndall happened to be in the company of a learned man, and in communing and disputing with him drove him to that issue, that the learned man said: "We were better be without God's law than the Pope's." Master Tyndall, hearing that, answered him: "I defy the Pope and all his laws"; and said: "If God spare my life, ere many years I will cause a boy that driveth the plough shall know more of the Scripture than thou dost."

In these words we may certainly recognize an echo of words appearing in Erasmus's preface to his Greek New Testament of 1516:

> I totally disagree with those who are unwilling that the Holy Scriptures, translated into the common tongue, should be read by the unlearned. Christ desires His mysteries to be published abroad as widely as possible. I could wish that even all women should read the Gospel and St Paul's Epistles, and I would that they were translated into all the languages of all Christian people, that they might be read and known not merely by the Scots and the Irish but even by the Turks and the Saracens. I wish that the farm worker might sing parts of them at the plough, that the weaver might hum them at the shuttle, and that the traveller might beguile the weariness of the way by reciting them.

Erasmus's desire was shortly to be translated into fact by Tyndale, so far as the needs of the English people were concerned.

No room in England

Perhaps the knowledge that Luther had given his countrymen the German New Testament in 1522 was a further stimulus to Tyndale to do the like service for *his* countrymen. But it would not be politic to mention Luther's name in this connection. Luther was disapproved of in the highest quarters in England; in 1521 King Henry VIII had published his *Assertion of the Seven Sacraments* against Luther, and received thereby from Pope Leo X the title "Defender of the Faith", which his successors have borne to this day. And the very fact that Luther had issued the New Testament in the vernacular might well arouse suspicion against anyone else who proposed to do the same.

In any case, the Constitutions of Oxford were still in force, and Tyndale could not carry out his heart's desire anywhere in England without episcopal licence. To which bishop should he apply? Cuthbert Tonstall had recently become Bishop of London; he was reputed to be favourably disposed to the new learning; Erasmus spoke well of him. To him, then, Tyndale decided to go. So, taking leave of Sir John Walsh, and bearing a letter of introduction from him to the controller of the king's household, Tyndale went to London in the summer of 1523, and in due course obtained an interview with the bishop.

His hope was that the bishop would look kindly on his project and not only authorize the work of translation but provide him with a residential chaplaincy while he was engaged on it. In order to show the bishop his quality as a translator from Greek, he had transmitted to him a speech of the Athenian orator Isocrates which he had translated into English. But the bishop was not very encouraging; he told Tyndale that he had no vacancies in the palace at the time, and advised him to find suitable employment elsewhere in London.

No doubt Tyndale could have found employment suitable to his attainments, but what he wanted was leisure to permit him to translate the Bible. Fortunately, he found a friend in Humphrey Monmouth, a wealthy cloth-merchant, who took him into his house for six months, a kind action which brought Monmouth himself into serious trouble some years later. But it became increasingly evident that he would have to go abroad in order to carry out his work of translation; as he puts it later in the preface to his translation of the Pentateuch (printed in 1530), he "vnderstode at the laste not only that there was no rowme in my lorde of londons palace to translate the new testament, but also that there was no place to do it in all englonde, as experience doth now openly declare."

Tyndale's first New Testament

In April or May 1524, therefore, Tyndale sailed for the Continent, taking with him no doubt all the books which he required for his translation project. He spent the best part of a year at Wittenberg, then returned to Hamburg, from which he sent for some money which he had left with Humphrey Monmouth in London, and made his way to Cologne about August 1525. By this time his English New Testament was practically complete, and Cologne suggested itself as a likely place to have it printed in. The work was entrusted to a printer named Peter Quentel, and ten sheets (80 quarto pages) were printed, when information was laid with the city senate and the printer was forbidden to proceed with the work. Tyndale was able to secure the printed sheets before they were seized, and took ship up the Rhine for Worms. Here the work of printing was set afoot from the beginning again, and was completed without mishap. The first complete printed New Testament in English appeared towards the end of February 1526, and copies were beginning to reach England about a month later.

The Worms New Testament is an octavo edition, of which two copies are still in existence—one, complete except for the loss of its title-page, in the Baptist College at Bristol, and the other, imperfect at the beginning and end, in the library of St Paul's Cathedral.

The Cologne Quarto

But what happened to the sheets of the quarto edition which Tyndale rescued from Quentel's printing house in Cologne? It is probable that he sent some copies of these to England in advance of the Worms edition, to whet people's appetite for the complete New Testament when it was ready. They contained a prologue of fourteen pages, the complete Gospel of Matthew, and the beginning of Mark. For long this fragmentary version was thought to have disappeared completely, but in 1834 the first 64 pages of it (except for the title-page) were identified in a volume where they were bound up with another work. This unique treasure was bought by Thomas Grenville, and later bequeathed by him, with the rest of his library, to the British Museum. A facsimile edition, with an introduction of 70 pages, was issued by Edward Arber in 1871.

The first folio, containing the title-page, is missing; apart from that, we have here the first eight of the original sheets. The prologue of 14 pages is followed by a list of New Testament books; then comes a woodcut showing St Matthew dipping his pen into an ink-well which an angel is holding out to him. This identical woodcut, slightly cut down, was reproduced in a commentary on St Matthew's Gospel published by Quentel in 1526; this is a most conclusive proof that (despite the loss of the title-page) the fragment with which we are dealing is indeed the part of Tyndale's New Testament which Quentel printed at Cologne before the ban was imposed on the continuation of the work. After the woodcut comes the text, beginning at Matt. 1 : 1 and going on to Matt. 22 : 12, where the king says to the man who came to his feast without a wedding garment, "frende / howe camyst thou in hydder / and"—and there it breaks off. The first words on the following page (if we supply them from later editions of Tyndale's New Testament) would have been: "hast not on a weddyng garment?"

When we say that it breaks off at Matt. 22 : 12, we do not mean that it was divided into verses; another quarter of a century went by before the New Testament was first divided into verses. Chapter divisions are marked; both Testaments had been divided into chapters in the thirteenth century by Cardinal Hugh de St. Cher.

The prologue to the Cologne fragment is the work which Tyndale later expanded and issued as a separate tract entitled *Pathway into the Scripture*. The first page and a half offer his apology for the work: he tells his "brethern and susters moost dere and tenderly beloued in Christ" why he has undertaken to translate the New Testament, and begs them "yf they perceyve in eny places that y have not attayned the very sense of the tonge / or meanynge of the scripture / or haue not geven the right englysshe worde / that they put to there handes to amende it / remembrynge that so is there duetie to doo." For a further page and a half he gives a straightforward translation of part of Luther's prologue to his 1522 German New Testament, explaining that the gospel is God's news of deliverance from bondage and the fulfilment of the promises made to Abraham. The remaining eleven pages are devoted to a discussion of the relation between law and gospel. This discussion is characterized by an evangelical fervour which, however heart-warming we find it to-day, must have smacked too much of Lutheranism to be acceptable to the civil and ecclesiastical rulers in England of that day. Luther's name is not mentioned, not even where he is quoted for a page and a half, but anyone familiar with his teaching must have recognized it in Tyndale's prologue. Tyndale may have realized that a prologue of this character was apt to prejudice the minds of some readers against his translation from the start; it was omitted from the octavo edition printed at Worms in 1526.

The list of New Testament books which follows the prologue in the Cologne fragment is particularly interesting. It takes this form:

The bokes conteyned in the
newe Testament

i.   The gospell of saynct Mathew.
ii.   The gospell of S. Marke
iii.   The gospell of S. Luke.
iiii.   The gospell of S. Jhon.
v.   The actes of the apostles written by S. Luke.
vi.   The epistle of S. Paul to the Romans.
vii.   The fyrst pistle of S. Paul to the Corrinthians.
viii.   The second pistle of S. Paul to the Corrinthians.
ix.   The pistle of S. Paul to the Galathians.
x.   The pistle of S. Paul to the Ephesians.
xi.   The pistle of S. Paul to the Philippians.
xii.   The pistle of S. Paul to the Collossians.
xiii.   The fyrst pistle of S. Paul vnto the Tessalonians.
xiiii. The seconde pistle of S. Paul vnto the Tessalonians.
xv.   The fyrst pistle of S. Paul to Timothe.
xvi.   The seconde pistle of S. Paul to Timothe.
xvii.   The pistle of S. Paul to Titus.
xviii. The pistle of S. Paul vnto Philemon.
xix.   The fyrst pistle of S. Peter.
xx.   The seconde pistle of S. Peter.

xxi.   The fyrst pistle of S. Jhon.
xxii.   The seconde pistle of S. Jhon.
xxiii. The thryd pistle of S. Jhon.

> The pistle vnto the Ebrues.
> The pistle of S. James.
> The pistle of Jude.
> The revelacion of Jhon.

The last four books are separated from the first twenty-three by a space, by special indentation, and by the lack of serial numbers. Why is this? The answer is clear to anyone who looks at the list of New Testament books supplied in Luther's German New Testament of 1522. For Luther separates Hebrews, James, Jude and Revelation from the other books by a space and gives them no serial number such as he gives to the first twenty-three. But Luther had his reasons for this; he did not think that these four books had the same high canonical quality as the "capital books", and expresses his opinion vigorously in his prefaces to the books in question. There is no particular reason to suppose that Tyndale shared Luther's estimate of the "deuterocanonicity" of Hebrews, James, Jude and Revelation; he simply followed Luther's arrangement of the list of books, as also did his successors, until the Great Bible of 1539 reverted to the more usual order.

The New Testament text itself is equipped with an apparatus of marginal notes—references to parallel passages in the inner margin, and comments on the text in the outer margin. Of the cross-references the great majority are taken over from Luther's edition; about half of the comments on the text are based on Luther's comments. But the fierceness of some of Luther's comments is absent from Tyndale's. Tyndale's most polemical comment comes at the point where Jesus replies to Peter's confession at Caesarea Philippi with the words: "Thou art Peter ..." (Matt. 16 : 17–19).

> Peter in the greke sygnieth a stoone in englysshe. This confession is the rocke. Nowe is simon bariona, or simon ionas sonne, called Peter, because of his confession. whosoever then this wyse

confesseth of Christe, the same is called Peter. nowe is this confession come too all that are true christen. Then ys every christen man & woman peter. Rede bede, austen & hierom, of the maner of lowsinge & bynding and note howe hierom checketh the presumcion of the pharises in his tyme, which yet had nott so monstrous interpretacions as oure new goddes have feyned. Rede erasmus annotations. Hyt was noot for nought that Christ badd beware of the leven of the pharises. noo thynge is so swete that they make not sowre with there tradicions. The evangelion, that ioyfull tidynges, ys nowe biterer then the olde lawe, Christes burthen is hevier then the yooke of moses, our condicion and estate ys ten tymes more grevious then was ever the iewes. The pharises have so levended Christes swete breed.

But many of the notes are purely calculated to make the sense of the text plainer; thus, against the words "Doo not the publicans even so?" (Matt. 5 : 46), there is the useful comment:

Publicans gadred rentes, toll, custume, & tribute for the romans, & were comenly hethen men ther vnto appointed of the romans.

It cannot fairly be said that the opposition to Tyndale's New Testament was aroused by the objectionable character of the notes rather than by the text itself.

Here is the form of the Lord's Prayer in this earliest printed fragment of the English New Testament:

O oure father, which art in heven halowed be thy name. Let thy kyngdom come. Thy wyll be fulfilled, as well in erth, as hit ys in heven. Geve vs this daye oure dayly breade. And forgeve vs oure treaspases, even as we forgeve them whych treaspas vs. Lede vs nott in to temptacion. but delyvre vs from yvell, Amen.

The incidental resemblances between Tyndale's New Testament and Luther's have led some people to suppose that Tyndale did little more than translate Luther's version into English. This is far from being the truth. Tyndale's version was indeed stigmatized as "Lutheran"; but this epithet was applicable to Tyndale's personal outlook and the principles which led him to translate the New Testament into English rather than to the translation itself. Tyndale did have Luther's German New Testament at his hand for reference, and also the Latin Vulgate, but his work is a translation not of Luther's version but of Erasmus's third printed edition of the Greek Testament, which came out in 1522. Tyndale was a better Greek scholar than Luther, and his rendering is in general closer to the Greek text than Luther's is. On the other hand, there is nothing pedantic about Tyndale's translation; he turns the Greek text into good English, not into a painfully literal rendering of the original idiom.

The Worms Octavo

The octavo New Testament, printed at Worms after Tyndale had been compelled to leave Cologne, lacked the prologue of the Cologne fragment, as we have seen. Instead, a short epistle to the reader is appended at the end, in which he is exhorted to come to the reading of the sacred words with a pure mind and a single eye, so as to reap the spiritual blessing which they impart, and not to be over-critical of any defects in the translation, which is a first attempt. The translator promises to issue it in a revised and improved form if God grants the opportunity, and meanwhile bespeaks his readers' prayers.

NOTE. Some reviewers have cast doubt on the propriety of quoting sources like John Foxe and William Fulke in what purports to be "a *history* of translations" (one reviewer describes the story related at the top of p. 29 as "a blatant fairy tale"). The trustworthiness of Foxe, especially in his account of Tyndale, has been vindicated by recent research; cf. J. F. Mozley, *John Foxe and his Book* (London, 1940); G. Rupp, *Six Makers of English Religion* (London, 1964), pp. 53 ff. As for Fulke, his narrative commands respect where it is consistent with the course of events already established.

CHAPTER FOUR

Tyndale's Later Years

Now that the whole of the New Testament was safely in print, it had to be got into England, in order that it might be read by the people for whom it was intended. There was ample opportunity to pack copies along with other merchandise, for there was an active trade in many commodities between England and the Continent, and there were several merchants of the calibre of Humphrey Monmouth, who would do their best to help what they believed to be a good work. Nevertheless it was necessary to use caution. Lutheranism was held by the authorities in England, from King Henry downward, to be of the very devil. Tyndale and his associates were known to be infected with Lutheranism, and there could be no question of allowing their books, Bible translations or otherwise, to be imported freely.

The Burning of the Books

Cuthbert Tonstall, Bishop of London, was specially disturbed by the importation and distribution of Tyndale's New Testament, because naturally his diocese was more affected than anywhere else in the country. In October 1526 he took steps to gather up as many copies as he could within his diocese, ordering their owners to hand them over on pain of excommunication or worse, and those which he collected were publicly burned at St Paul's Cross. But this procedure, though spectacular, could do little to check the circulation of the books, and the bishop conceived the plan of buying them up in large quantities on the Continent, and thus making sure that they would not come to England except to be burned.

A quaint account of this matter is given in the *Chronicle* of Edward Halle, who tells how Bishop Tonstall, during a visit to the Continent, met in Antwerp a London merchant named Augustine Packington, who was well disposed to Tyndale. The bishop told Packington how eager he was to buy up as many copies of Tyndale's New Testament as he could, and Packington assured him that, if the bishop provided money to pay for the New Testaments, he could buy them in large quantities, for he was well acquainted with the merchants who were handling them. Then Halle goes on:

The bishop, thinking that he had God by the toe, when indeed he had (as after he thought) the devil by the fist, said: "Gentle Master Packington, do your diligence and get them, and with all my heart I will pay for them, whatsoever they cost you; for the books are erroneous and naughty, and I intend surely to destroy them all, and to burn them at Paul's Cross." Augustine Packington came to William Tyndale and said: "William, I know thou art a poor man, and hast a heap of New Testaments and books by thee, for the which thou hast both endangered thy friends and beggared thyself; and I have now gotten thee a merchant, which with ready money shall dispatch thee of all that thou hast, if you think it so profitable for yourself." "Who is the merchant?" said Tyndale. "The bishop of London," said Packington. "Oh, that is because he will burn them," said Tyndale. "Yea marry," quoth Packington. "I am the gladder," said Tyndale; "for these two benefits shall come thereof: I shall get money of him for these books, to bring myself out of debt, and the whole world shall cry out upon the burning of God's word. And the overplus of the money, that shall remain to me, shall make me more studious to correct the said New Testament, and so newly to imprint the same once again; and I trust the second will much better like you than ever did the first." And so forward went the bargain: the bishop had the books, Packington had the thanks, and Tyndale had the money.

It is a good story, and no doubt basically true, even if Halle has added some colour and vivacity to the details. The bishop certainly did buy up many of Tyndale's books to destroy them and thus prevent them from doing any harm, but (as might have been expected) the money with which he paid for the books was used for the production of further copies. Halle tells us how the bishop met

Packington later in London and complained that copies of Tyndale's New Testament were coming into the country in greater quantities than ever. Packington assured him that he had kept his side of the bargain, but suggested that it might really be necessary for the bishop to buy up the standing type as well, if he wanted to prevent the circulation of the books effectively.

The bishop had probably discussed the idea of buying up the offending books with some of his friends and colleagues, and there is evidence that one at least of these told him what the result would be. For, to quote Halle's *Chronicle* again:

> Shortly after, it fortuned one George Constantine to be apprehended by Sir Thomas More, which then was lord chancellor of England, of suspicion of certain heresies. And this Constantine being with More, after divers examinations of divers things, among other Master More said in this wise to Constantine: "Constantine, I would have thee plain with me in one thing that I will ask of thee, and I promise thee I will show thee favour in all the other things, whereof thou art accused to me. There is beyond the sea Tyndale, Joye, and a great many more of you. I know they cannot live without help: some sendeth them money and succoureth them; and thyself, being one of them, hadst part thereof, and therefore knowest from whence it came; I pray thee, who be they that thus help them?" "My lord," quoth Constantine, "will you that I shall tell you the truth?" "Yea, I pray thee," quoth my lord. "Marry I will," quoth Constantine. "Truly," quoth he, "it is the bishop of London that hath holpen us; for he hath bestowed among us a great deal of money in New Testaments to burn them, and that hath been, and yet is, our only succour and comfort." "Now by my troth," quoth More, "I think even the same, and I said so much to the bishop, when he went about to buy them."

More and Tyndale

But burning was not the only form of attack that was launched against Tyndale's New Testament. Sir Thomas More issued his *Dialogue* (1529), in which he "treated divers matters, as of the veneration and worship of images and relics, praying to saints and going on pilgrimage, with many other things touching the pestilent sect of Luther and Tyndale, by the tone begun in Saxony, and by the tother labored to be brought into England." In the course of this *Dialogue* he attacked Tyndale's New Testament. Tyndale replied in 1531 with *An Answer unto Sir Thomas More's Dialogue*, and this brought forth from More in the following year a larger work, entitled *The Confutation of Tyndale*.

It affords no pleasure to us to-day to contemplate two great Englishmen, men of principle who were both to suffer death for conscience' sake, engaging in bitter controversy of this kind. But the issue was one in which the lives of men—and, as both Tyndale and More believed, the souls of men—were at stake; and both men would probably have thought that the urbanities of modern theological debate betokened a failure to appreciate the seriousness of the issue. Yet More was no bigoted obscurantist; he was a leading humanist and patron of the new learning, and a warm friend of Erasmus, whose Greek New Testament Tyndale had now turned into English. One might have thought that he would at least have appreciated the cultural value of Tyndale's work, however much he deplored Tyndale's theological position.

But no: Tyndale's New Testament, said More, was not the New Testament at all; it was a cunning counterfeit, so perverted in the interests of heresy "that it was not worthy to be called Christ's testament, but either Tyndale's own testament or the testament of his master Antichrist." To search for errors in it was like searching for water in the sea; it was so bad that it could not be mended, "for it is easier to make a web of new cloth than it is to sew up every hole in a net."

We may well rub our eyes at these charges. Tyndale's New Testament lies before us, and Erasmus's Greek Testament of which it is a translation, and we can only be surprised that a scholar like More should go to such lengths in denouncing so good an achievement. True, there were things in it which were capable of improvement, as Tyndale himself acknowledged, but it was a pioneer work; the New Testament had never been turned from Greek directly into English before. Tyndale complained that if his printer so much as failed to dot an *i*, it was solemnly noted down and reckoned as a heresy.

When More's charges are examined, they amount to nothing more than a complaint that Tyndale translated certain ecclesiastical terms by English words which lacked ecclesiastical associations. Thus he used "congregation" and not "church", "senior" (in later editions, "elder") and not "priest" (where the Greek had *presbyteros*), "repentance" and not "penance", "love" and not "charity", and so forth. But no fault can be found with Tyndale in this regard from the standpoint of pure scholarship; in fact, his translations at times are more accurate than those which More preferred. And indeed Tyndale could point to Erasmus, More's great friend, for a precedent. For Erasmus had not only edited the New Testament in Greek; he had also translated it afresh into Latin. And in Erasmus's Latin translation the Greek word *ekklesia* ("church") appeared at times as *congregatio*, Greek *presbyteros* appeared as *senior* or *presbyter* (and not as *sacerdos*, which in the Latin Bible was traditionally reserved for "priest" in the Jewish or pagan sense), and so forth. Why should such translations be branded as heretical in Tyndale's English version when they were tolerated in Erasmus's Latin version? Because, said More, he found no such "malicious intent" in Erasmus as he found in Tyndale. In short, it was not the translation but the translator that More really objected to.

Old Testament translation

It was not only Bible translation that Tyndale engaged in during these years. He took a vigorous part in the theological and political disputation of the day; one of his works, *The Obedience of a Christian Man* (1528), finding considerable favour with no less illustrious a reader than Henry VIII. We may wish that he had given himself exclusively to his Bible translation, because then he might have come near to translating the whole Bible; but we must allow him his own judgment of what the times demanded in the way of earnestly contending for the faith. By 1530 he had completed and published the translation of the first five books of the Old Testament from Hebrew; he followed this up the following year with an edition of Jonah—"Jonas made out by Tyndale," wrote Sir Thomas More, "a book that whoso delight therein shall stand in peril that Jonas was never so swallowed up by the whale as by the delight of that book a man's soul may be swallowed up by the devil that he shall never have the grace to get out again." A translation of the historical books of the Old Testament, from Joshua to 2 Chronicles, is also most probably to be attributed to him; it was not published during his lifetime, but was incorporated in "Matthew's Bible", which appeared in 1537.

Tyndale's Old Testament translation is free, bold and idiomatic; he indulges to the limit his preference for translating the same original word by a variety of English synonyms. The serpent says to Eve in Genesis 3 : 4, "Tush, ye shall not die"; in Genesis 39 : 2 we read that "the Lorde was with Ioseph, and he was a luckie felowe"; in Exodus 15 : 4 Pharaoh's "jolly captains" are drowned in the Red Sea, and in verse 26 of the same chapter God introduces Himself as "the Lord thy surgeon". Some of the marginal notes make amusing reading to-day, though we can understand why they were not universally appreciated at the time. Against Exodus 32 : 35, where we read of the pestilence that broke out among the Israelites after their worship of the golden calf, he remarks: "The Pope's bull slayeth more than Aaron's calf." On Exodus 36 : 5–7, where the people are asked not to bring any more offerings for the building of the tabernacle, because they have already contributed more than enough, he says: "When will the Pope say 'Hoo! [Hold!]' and forbid an offering for the building of St Peter's church? And when will our spirituality say 'Hoo!' and forbid to give them more land? Never until they have all." On Leviticus 21 : 5, where the priests of Israel are forbidden to "make tonsures upon their heads" (R.S.V.), he notes: "Of the heathen priests, then, our prelates took the example of their bald pates."

The New Testament revised

A revision of Genesis was published in 1534. But a more urgent task demanded Tyndale's attention. The situation in England was changing; King Henry had quarrelled with the Pope, Sir Thomas More had resigned his office of Lord Chancellor on conscientious grounds, and Thomas Cromwell was rapidly rising to a position of high favour and influence with the king. Cromwell was a warm advocate of the circulation and reading of the Bible in the vernacular. The demand for copies of the Bible, or at least the New Testament, in English was rising, and pirate printings of Tyndale's New Testament began to appear on the market. The fact that they were pirate printings was not the worst thing about them; the text was deliberately changed in places, and not changed for the better. The chief offender in this matter was George Joye, a former associate of Tyndale. Tyndale was naturally indignant at this conduct. In the postscript to his New Testament of 1526 he had promised that he would endeavour to revise his work, "as it were to set it better, and to make it more apt for the weak stomachs: desiring them that are learned, and able, to remember their duty, and to help thereunto; and to bestow unto the edifying of Christ's body (which is the congregation of them that believe) those gifts which they have received of God for the same purpose." He was now actively engaged with this work of revision, and did not take it kindly that Joye had forestalled him. When Tyndale's revised New Testament did make its appearance, in November 1534, the prologue contained the following sharp admonition to Joye and others like him:

Wherefore I beseech George Joye, yea and all other too, for to translate the scripture for themselves, whether out of Greek, Latin or Hebrew. Or (if they will needs) ... let them take my translations and labours, and change and alter, and correct and corrupt at their pleasures, and call it their own translations, and put to their own names, and not to play bo-peep after George Joye's manner. Which whether he have done faithfully and truly, with such reverence and fear as becometh the word of God, and with such love and meekness and affection to unity and circumspection that the ungodly have no occasion to rail on the verity, as becometh the servants of Christ, I refer it to the judgments of them that know and love the truth. For this, I protest that I provoke not Joye nor any other man (but am provoked and that after the spitefullest manner of provoking) to do sore against my will and with sorrow of heart that I now do. But I neither can nor will suffer of any man, that he shall go take my translation and correct it without name, and make such changing as I myself durst not do, as I hope to have my part in Christ, though the whole world should be given me for my labour.

Tyndale was particularly annoyed at Joye's foolish alteration of "resurrection" to "life after this life" or the like. Had Joye put out this mistranslation under his own name, he would have been welcome to the credit that it brought him; but Tyndale naturally did not like it to be assumed that he himself had authorized this and similar changes.

However, with the publication of *The Newe Testament dylygently corrected and compared with the Greke by Willyam Tindale* the pirate editions were seen for what they were. Although Tyndale produced a further revision in 1535—*The New Testament yet once again corrected by Willyam Tindale*—it is the 1534 edition that is to be regarded as his definitive version of the New Testament. Bishop Westcott describes this version as "altogether Tyndale's noblest monument". It is no superficial revision; the whole work has been gone over in scrupulous detail, and nearly always the changes are for the better, reflecting mature judgment and feeling.

When we talk of Tyndale's version of the New Testament as being basic to the successive revisions which have appeared between his day and ours—more particularly the Authorized Version, the Revised Version and the Revised Standard Version—it is his 1534 edition that is meant. "Tindale's honesty, sincerity, and scrupulous integrity," says Professor J. Isaacs, "his simple directness, his magical simplicity of phrase, his modest music, have given an authority to his wording that has imposed itself on all later versions. With all the tinkering to which the New Testament has been subject, Tindale's version is still the basis in phrasing, rendering, vocabulary, rhythm, and often in music as well. Nine-tenths of the Authorized New Testament is still Tindale, and the best is still his."[1] More than that: in a number of places where the Authorized Version of 1611 departs from Tyndale's wording, the Revisers of 1881 return to it. For example, the A.V. of John 10 : 16 makes Jesus say that when He has called His "other sheep ... which are not of this fold"—that is, not of the Jewish people—"there shall be one fold, and one shepherd." But this rendering misses the point of His statement by using the word "fold" to translate two quite different Greek words; it is a defect which goes back to the Latin version. Tyndale had already

[1] *The Bible in its Ancient and English Versions*, ed. H. W. Robinson (Oxford, 1940), p. 160.

given the correct rendering: "and other shepe I have, which are not of this folde. Them also must I bringe, that they maye heare my voyce, and that ther maye be one flocke and one shepeherde." And the Revisers of 1881 follow him almost word for word: "And other sheep I have, which are not of this fold: them also I must bring, and they shall hear my voice; and they shall become one flock, one shepherd."

There is a general prologue, entitled "W.T. unto the reader," which begins with the words: "Here thou hast (most dear reader) the new Testament or covenant made with us of God in Christ's blood." There are special prologues to the Epistles of the New Testament, of which that to the Epistle to the Romans is the longest; it is, in fact, a treatise in itself, of about equal length with the epistle which it introduces. To Tyndale, as to Luther, the Epistle to the Romans was "the principal and most excellent part of the New Testament, and most pure Euangelion, that is to say glad tidings and that we call gospel, and also a light and a way into the whole scripture." Towards the end of the prologue he says:

> Wherefore it appeareth evidently, that Paul's mind was to comprehend briefly in this epistle all the whole learning of Christ's gospel, and to prepare an introduction unto all the Old Testament. For without doubt whosoever hath this epistle perfectly in his heart, the same hath the light and the effect of the Old Testament with him. Wherefore let every man without exception exercise himself therein diligently, and record it night and day continually, until he be full acquainted therewith.

And finally:

> Now go to, reader, and according to the order of Paul's writing, even so do thou. First behold thyself diligently in the law of God, and see there thy just damnation. Secondarily turn thine eyes to Christ, and see there the exceeding mercy of thy most kind and loving Father. Thirdly remember that Christ made not this atonement that thou shouldest anger God again: neither died he for thy sins, that thou shouldest live still in them: neither cleansed he thee, that thou shouldest return (as a swine) unto thine old puddle

again: but that thou shouldest be a new creature and live a new life after the will of God and not of the flesh. And be diligent lest through thine own negligence and unthankfulness thou lose this favour and mercy again.

Is not this the very heart of the Reformation message?

This is the rendering of the Lord's Prayer in the 1534 New Testament:

> O oure father which arte in heven, halowed be thy name. Let thy kyngdome come. Thy wyll be fulfilled, as well in erth, as it ys in heven. Geve vs thisdaye oure dayly breede. And forgeve vs oure treaspases, even as we forgeve oure trespacers. And leade vs not into temptacion: but delyver vs from evell. For thyne is the kyngedome and the power, and the glorye for ever. Amen.

If we compare this rendering with that from the Cologne fragment of 1525 (quoted on p. 35), we notice that the doxology is added in this version,[1] and also that the phrase "them whych treaspas vs" has now been replaced by "oure trespacers". As for the considerable variations in spelling, that simply shows how free and easy a matter spelling was in Tyndale's day.

The parable of the Good Samaritan appears as follows in the 1534 version:

> A certayne man descended from Hierusalem in to Hierico, and fell in to the hondes of theves, which robbed him of his rayment and wounded him, and departed levynge him halfe deed. And by chaunce ther came a certayne preste that same waye, and when he sawe him, he passed by. And lykewyse a Levite, when he was come nye to the place, went and loked on him, and passed by. Then a certayne Samaritane, as he iornyed, came nye vnto him, and when he sawe him, had compassion on him, and went to and bounde vp his woundes, and poured in oyle and wyne, and put him on his awne beaste, and brought him to a commen ynne, and made provision for him. And on the morowe when he departed,

---

[1] The doxology is absent from the best Greek MSS. and the Latin Vulgate, but it appears in the majority of later Greek MSS.

he toke out two pence and gave them to the host, and sayde vnto him. Take cure of him, and whatsoever thou spendest moare, when I come agayne, I will recompence the. Which now of these thre, thynkest thou, was neighbour vnto him that fell into the theves hondes? And he sayde: he that shewed mercy on him. Then sayde Iesus vnto him. Goo and do thou lyke wyse.

How closely the A.V. follows Tyndale's wording here needs no emphasizing.

The opening paragraph of Hebrews is rendered as follows by Tyndale in this edition:

God in tyme past diversly and many wayes, spake vnto the fathers by Prophetes: but in these last dayes he hath spoken vnto uv by his sonne, whom he hath made heyre of all thinges: by whom also he made the worlde. Which sonne beynge the brightnes of his glory, and very ymage of his substance, bearinge vp all thinges with the worde of his power, hath in his awne person pourged oure synnes, and is sitten on the right honde of the maiestie an hye, and is more excellent then the angels, in as moche as he hath by inheritaunce obteyned an excellenter name then have they.

Here the A.V. has departed farther from Tyndale, but it is plain to whom we are indebted for the final clause of this paragraph in the A.V., "as he hath by inheritance obtained a more excellent name than they"—except that the rather clumsy comparative "excellenter" has been replaced by "more excellent".

There are marginal notes in this New Testament, but they lack the polemical pungency of those appearing in Tyndale's Pentateuch. That is really all to the good; however much enjoyment later generations of readers—Roman Catholics and Protestants alike—may derive from reading comments about the Pope's bull slaying more than Aaron's calf and so forth, notes and comments which reflect particular points of view inevitably limit the usefulness of Bible translations, good as those translations may be in themselves. In his 1534 New Testament Tyndale contents himself for the most part with supplying notes which explain, summarize or apply the text in a generally helpful manner. In the Gospels marginal references to parallel passages are given.

The Old Testament Epistles

As an appendix to the New Testament, this edition contains Tyndale's translation of the Old Testament "Epistles" prescribed to be read in church on certain days in the year according to the use of Sarum. Some of these "Epistles" are taken from the poetical and prophetical books of the Old Testament, and as we read them in Tyndale's translation we find ourselves wishing that he could have lived long enough to translate the whole of the Old Testament. For Tyndale did not translate these from the Latin of the service-book, but from the Hebrew (or from the Greek, in the case of readings from the Apocrypha). Here is the fifty-third chapter of Isaiah, appointed for the Wednesday after Palm Sunday:

Esaias sayde, lorde, who beleueth oure sayinges, and the arme of the lorde, to whome is it opened? He came vp as a sparow before him, and as a rote oute of a drye lande. There was nether fassyon or bewtie on him. And when we looked on him, there was no godlynes that we shuld lust after him. He was despised and cast oute of mennes companye, and one that had soffered sorowe, and had experynce of infirmitie: and we were as one that had hid his face from him. He was so despisable, that we estemed him not.

Truly he tooke vpon him oure deseases, and bare oure sorowes. And yet we counted him plaged, and beaten and humbled of God. He was wounded for oure transgression, and brused for oure iniquities. The correccion that brought vs peace was on him, and with his strypes we were healed. And we went astraye as shepe, and turned euery man his waye: and the lorde put on him the wyckednes of vs all.

He soffered wronge and was euell entreated, and yet opened not his mouth: he was as a shepe ledde to be slayne: and as a lambe before his sherer, he was domme and opened not his mouth. By the reason of the afflyccion, he was not estemed: and yet his generacion who can nombre? When he is taken from the erth of lyuynge men: for my peoples transgression he was plaged. He put his sepulchre with the wycked, and with the ryche in his deth: because he dyd none iniquitie, nether was gyle founde in his mouth.

And yet the lorde determyned to bruse him with infirmities. His soule gevynge hirselfe for transgression, he shall se seed of long continuaunce, and the will of the lorde shall prospere in his hande. Because of the laboure of his soule, he shall se and be satisfied. With his knowledge, he beynge iust, shall iustifie my saruauntes and that a great nombre: and he shall beare their iniquities. Therfore I will geue him his parte in many and the spoyle of the ryche he shall deuyde: because he gaue his soule to death, and was nombred with the trespasers, and he bare the synne of many, and made intercession for transgressors.

This translation has had a less direct influence on the familiar Authorized Version wording of Isaiah 53; yet now and again we recognize a familiar cadence, and could well believe that Tyndale's rendering of this and other liturgical "Epistles" was consulted by those who completed his work by translating the prophets into English. "He came up as a sparow" at the beginning of verse 2 is an odd rendering; "tender plant" or "young plant" is what the Hebrew word means here, and the Latin Vulgate translates accordingly. But the same word can mean "suckling" in an appropriate context, and the Greek Septuagint accordingly mistranslates it as a "young child". Most probably, however, "sparow" here is a misprint for "spraye" (meaning tender twig or shoot). In verse 11 the singular "servant" becomes the plural "saruauntes" and is object instead of subject. This could be the meaning of the Hebrew word if one had regard to the consonants only and not to the vowel-signs (which were added later, about the ninth century A.D.), but it is ruled out by the context. However, Tyndale's rendering at the beginning of verse 10, "And yet the lorde determyned to bruse him with infirmities", conforms more closely than either A.V., R.V. or R.S.V to what scholars nowadays generally consider the original Hebrew to have said; Dr Christopher R. North, for example, in his rendering of the clause adopts the same construction as Tyndale: "Yet Yahweh was pleased to crush him with sickness."[1]

Here is another of these Epistles, this time from the second chapter of the Song of Songs, verses 1–4 and 10–14, prescribed for the feast of the Visitation of the Virgin:

> I am the floure of the felde, and lylyes of the valeyes. As the lylye amonge the thornes so is my loue amonge the daughters. As the apple tre amonge the trees of the wood so is my beloued amonge the sonnes, in his shadow was my desyer to syt, for his frute was swete to my mouth. He brought me into his wyne seller: and his behauer to mewarde was louely. Beholde my beloued sayde to me: vp and hast my loue, my doue, my bewtifull and come, for now is wynter gone and rayne departed and past. The floures apere in oure contre and the tyme is come to cut the vynes. The voyce of the turtle doue is harde in oure lande. The fygge tre hath brought forth hir fygges, and the vyne blossoms geue a sauoure. Vp hast my loue, my doue, in the holes of the rocke and secret places of the walles. Shew me thy face and let me here thy voyce, for thy voyce is swete and thy fassyon bewtifull.

Something seems to have fallen out here at the end of verse 13; either the translator's eye or the printer's has skipped a few words. The expression "wyne seller", which seems less appropriate than A.V. "banqueting house", follows the Latin closely; so also the Douai version says "He brought me into the cellar of wine" (but the Knox version says "banqueting-hall"). The Hebrew expression means literally "house of wine".

A de luxe copy of this New Testament, bound in vellum, with gold edges, was presented to Queen Anne Boleyn, probably by an Antwerp merchant to whom she had done a service in time of need. The words *Anna Regina Angliae* can be faintly discerned in red on the gold edges of the volume, which is in the British Museum.

Imprisonment and death

Antwerp, which was Tyndale's residence in his closing years, was

[1] C. R. North, *The Suffering Servant in Deutero-Isaiah* (Oxford, 1948), p. 122.

a free city; but the surrounding territory was under the control of Charles V, Holy Roman Emperor. Tyndale's enemies could take no legal action against him in Antwerp, but in the emperor's domains it would be easy to proceed against him for heresy. On May 21, 1535, he was treacherously kidnapped, conveyed out of Antwerp, and imprisoned in the fortress of Vilvorde, some six miles north of Brussels, where he remained until October of the following year. Thomas Cromwell made an energetic attempt to procure his release, and even Henry VIII bestirred himself somewhat in Tyndale's cause, however little he approved of his Lutheranism. But Charles V was in no mood to respond to such overtures; he was nephew to Katharine of Aragon, whom Henry had recently divorced, so that he had personal and political as well as religious reasons for allowing the law against heretics to take its tedious course with Tyndale.

The most interesting piece of information about Tyndale's imprisonment came to light about the middle of last century in the form of a letter written in his own hand to someone in authority, probably the Marquis of Bergen. It is undated, but was written evidently at the beginning of the last winter of Tyndale's life. It is in the Latin language; here is the English translation:

I believe, right worshipful, that you are not unaware of what may have been determined concerning me. Wherefore I beg your lordship, and that by the Lord Jesus, that if I am to remain here through the winter, you will request the commissary to have the kindness to send me, from the goods of mine which he has, a warmer cap; for I suffer greatly from cold in the head, and am afflicted by a perpetual catarrh, which is much increased in this cell; a warmer coat also, for this which I have is very thin; a piece of cloth too to patch my leggings. My overcoat is worn out; my shirts are also worn out. He has a woollen shirt, if he will be good enough to send it. I have also with him leggings of thicker cloth to put on above; he has also warmer night caps. And I ask to be allowed to have a lamp in the evening; it is indeed wearisome sitting alone in the dark. But most of all I beg and beseech your clemency to be urgent with the commissary, that he will kindly permit me to have the Hebrew bible, Hebrew grammar, and

Hebrew dictionary, that I may pass the time in that study. In return may you obtain what you most desire, provided that it be consistent with the salvation of your soul. But if any other decision has been taken concerning me, to be carried out before winter, I will be patient, abiding the will of God, to the glory of the grace of my Lord Jesus Christ, whose Spirit (I pray) may ever direct your heart. Amen.   W. Tindalus.

The resemblance has often been noted between this letter and another letter from prison, Paul's last letter in which he urges his friend Timothy to do his best to visit him before winter, and to bring when he comes "the cloak that I left with Carpus at Troas, also the books, and above all the parchments" (2 Tim. 4 : 13).

Evidently Tyndale was anxious to continue his work of translating the Old Testament. It would be pleasant if we could believe that his request was granted, and that he was not only able to keep himself a little warmer, but permitted to have his Hebrew books with him in his cell. But his surveillance must have been strict if he found it necessary to approach so exalted a dignitary in order to have the use of his own warmer clothes, and the authorities may have judged it to be out of the question to grant him access to literature which he could only use in further heretical activity. In August 1536 Tyndale was found guilty of heresy, degraded from his priestly office, and handed over to the secular power for execution, which was carried out on October 6. In the words of John Foxe, "he was brought forth to the place of execution, was there tied to the stake, and then strangled first by the hangman, and afterwards with fire consumed, in the morning at the town of Vilvorde, A.D. 1536; crying thus at the stake with a fervent zeal and a loud voice: 'Lord, open the King of England's eyes'."

Tyndale probably did not know that, some months before his death, a version of the Bible in English, which drew largely upon his own work, was circulating in his native land with King Henry's permission. In the sense which Tyndale intended, the King of England's eyes were already opening when he voiced his dying prayer.[1]

---

[1] No student of Tyndale's life and work can afford to neglect J. F. Mozley's excellent study, *William Tyndale* (London, 1937).

CHAPTER FIVE

The Complete English Bible Printed and Licensed

Myles Coverdale

NEXT TO Tyndale, the man to whom lovers of the English Bible owe the greatest debt is Myles Coverdale (1488–1569). Coverdale was not the scholar that Tyndale was, but the best part of his life was devoted to the task of making the Bible accessible to his fellow-countrymen in their own tongue. In addition to the version regularly known as "Coverdale's Bible", which appeared in 1535, he edited the Great Bible of 1539 and had some part in the preparation of the Geneva Bible before its publication in 1560. In addition to these major enterprises, he produced diglots or bilingual editions in Latin and English—of the New Testament in 1538, and of the Psalter in 1540. These diglots, however, do not play the part in the main line of development of the English Bible that is played by the great versions in which Coverdale had so active a share.

Coverdale was a native of York, a graduate of Cambridge, and an Augustinian friar. He left his order, however, after coming under the influence of the Reformation movement. In 1528 he was compelled to seek safety on the Continent, where he spent some time as assistant to Tyndale in Hamburg and as a proof-reader in Antwerp. In 1535 he returned to England, where for a short time he enjoyed the patronage of Anne Boleyn and Thomas Cromwell. But with Anne's execution, Cromwell's fall from power and a change in the king's ecclesiastical policy in 1540, Coverdale found it necessary to return to the Continent, and he remained there until the king's death in 1547. Soon after the accession of Edward VI he came back to England, and became Bishop of Exeter in 1551.

Coverdale did not enjoy his episcopal office for long; he was deposed when Mary Tudor ascended the throne in 1553, and it was only through the intervention of the King of Denmark that he did not go to the stake as so many other leading Reformers went in her reign, but was allowed to go into exile for a third time. He spent the latter part of his third exile in Geneva, where he became an elder of the English church, and stood as godfather to the minister's second son. The minister was John Knox. This was not Coverdale's only connection with Scotland; his wife, Elizabeth Macheson, was a Scotswoman.[1]

Coverdale returned to England for the last time in 1559, and shortly after his arrival he took part in the historic consecration of Matthew Parker as Archbishop of Canterbury. But for the last ten years of his life he did not figure much in public affairs. Not only were the infirmities of old age beginning to tell on him, but his strong Puritan convictions could not be reconciled to many features of the Elizabethan religious settlement.

Coverdale's Bible

It was apparently at the instance of Jacob van Meteren, a merchant of Antwerp, that Coverdale undertook to produce a version of the Bible in English. The printing was finished in October 1535, and the work was published under the title: *The Bible: that is, the holy Scripture of the Olde and New Testament, faithfully and truly translated out of Douche and Latyn into Englishe*. This was the first *complete* printed Bible in English. It was printed on the Continent (probably at Cologne) but it was quickly imported into England; a dedication to Henry VIII, printed (it appears) in Southwark, was inserted in those copies which were so imported.

The dedication speaks in severely critical terms of the Pope, who is compared to Caiaphas; yet even as Caiaphas spoke better than he knew when he prophesied that Jesus would die for the nation, so the Pope did better than he knew when he conferred the title "Defender of the Faith" on King Henry. For King Henry has proved himself a worthier Defender of the Faith than the Pope envisaged.

And the truth of our Balaam's prophecy is, that Your Grace in

---

[1] Elizabeth's sister Agnes married a Scots scholar named John Macalpine, who regularly latinizes his surname as Maccabaeus. He became Professor of Divinity at Copenhagen in 1542 and was one of the translators of the Danish Bible. This helps to explain the Danish king's exertions on Coverdale's behalf.

very deed should defend the Faith, yea even the true faith of Christ, no dreams, no fables, no heresy, no papistical inventions, but the uncorrupt faith of God's most holy Word, which to set forth (praised be the goodness of God, and increase your gracious purpose) Your Highness with your most honourable council applieth all his study and endeavour.

Coverdale evidently shared a widely held belief that King Henry had come round to the view that an authorized English translation of the Bible should be made available to the people. Indeed, when Thomas Cranmer became Archbishop of Canterbury in 1533, the Church of England acquired a Primate who lent all the weight of his high office to this and similar causes, and in December 1534 Convocation of Canterbury petitioned the King to decree "that the holy scripture should be translated into the vulgar English tongue by certain good and learned men, to be nominated by His Majesty, and should be delivered to the people for their instruction."

King Henry probably responded to this petition by telling Cranmer to set about preparing a suitable version; at any rate there is evidence that Cranmer himself, with a few other divines, took steps to revise an existing translation of the New Testament books. (The existing translation was almost certainly Tyndale's.) However, nothing came of this enterprise. For one thing, not all the bishops of the province of Canterbury were so enthusiastic about it as Cranmer was; for another thing, the work of revision was still incomplete when Coverdale's whole Bible appeared, with a dedication to the King.

King Henry VIII and Coverdale's Bible

Thomas Cromwell's interest was enlisted in the new translation, and it was he no doubt who drew his royal master's attention to it. The king, if he followed his usual custom, would submit the matter to various advisers, and then, after hearing their opinions, make his mind up for himself. Evidently he took this course with the new Bible, and when the bishops whom he directed to read it and report on it seemed to him to be a long time in coming to a decision he summoned them to his presence. They had various criticisms to make of it on the score of translation and the like. "Well," said he, "but are there any heresies maintained thereby?" They had to admit that they could find none. "If there be no heresies," said he, "then in God's name let it go abroad among our people."[1] To our present-day taste the flattering language with which Coverdale began his dedication to the king may appear over-fulsome; but it no doubt helped towards this desirable issue. The king's approval was given only by word of mouth, and no formal royal permission could be recorded on the title-page; but no doubt Cromwell and others interested in the circulation of the Bible knew when it was advisable to be grateful for small mercies.

Coverdale's dedication to the king ended with the following paragraph:

Considering now (most gracious prince) the inestimable treasure, fruit and prosperity everlasting, that God giveth with his Word, and trusting in his infinite goodness that he would bring my simple and good labour herein to good effect, therefore as the Holy Ghost moved other men to do the cost thereof, so was I boldened in God to labour in the same. Again, considering Your Imperial Majesty not only to be my natural sovereign liege Lord and chief Head of the Church of England, but also the true defender and maintainer of God's laws, I thought it my duty and to belong unto my allegiance, when I had translated this Bible, not only to dedicate this translation unto Your Highness, but wholly to commit it unto the same: to the intent that if anything therein be translated amiss (for in many things we fail, even when we think to be sure) it may stand in Your Grace's hands to correct it, to amend it, to improve it, yea and clean to reject it, if your godly wisdom shall think it necessary. And as I do with all humble-ness submit mine understanding and my poor translation unto the spirit of truth in Your Grace, so make I this protestation (having God to record in my conscience) that I have neither wrested nor altered so much as one word for the maintenance of any manner of sect: but have with a clear conscience purely and faithfully trans-

[1] This story, for which we are indebted to William Fulke's *Defence of the Translations of the Holy Scriptures into the English Tongue* (London, 1583) is often thought to refer to the Great Bible of 1539; but see J. F. Mozley, *Coverdale and His Bible* (London, 1953), pp. 112–114.

lated this out of five sundry interpreters, having only the manifest truth of the scripture before mine eyes: trusting in the goodness of God, that it shall be unto his worship; quietness and tranquillity unto Your Highness, a perfect stablishment of all God's ordinances within Your Grace's dominion, a general comfort to all Christian hearts, and a continual thankfulness both of old and young unto God, and to Your Grace, for being our Moses, and for bringing us out of this old Egypt from the cruel hands of our spiritual Pharaoh. For where were the Jews (by ten thousand parts) so much bound unto King David, for subduing of great Goliath and all their enemies, as we are to Your Grace, for delivering us out of our old Babylonical captivity? For the which deliverance and victory I beseek our only mediator Jesus Christ, to make such means for us unto his heavenly Father, that we never be unthankful unto him nor unto Your Grace: but that we ever increase in the fear of him, in obedience unto Your Highness, in love unfeigned unto our neighbours, and in all virtue that cometh of God. To whom for the defending of his blessed Word (by Your Grace's most rightful administration) be honour and thanks, glory and dominion, world without end. Amen.

Coverdale's Sources

The original title-page describes this version as being "faithfully and truly translated out of Douche [*i.e.*, German] and Latyn into Englishe." Coverdale's dedication speaks of his having "purely and faithfully translated this out of five sundry interpreters". In the translator's prologue to the "Christian reader", which follows the dedication to the king, this is amplified in the first paragraph:

> Considering how excellent knowledge and learning an interpreter of scripture ought to have in the tongues, and pondering also mine own insufficiency therein, and how weak I am to perform the office of a translator, I was the more loath to meddle with this work. Notwithstanding when I considered how great pity it was that we should want it so long, and called to my remembrance the adversity of them which were not only of ripe knowledge, but would also with all their hearts have performed that they began, if

they had not had impediment: considering (I say) that by reason of their adversity it could not so soon have been brought to an end, as our most prosperous nation would fain have had it: these and other reasonable causes considered, I was the more bold to take it in hand. And to help me herein, I have had sundry translations, not only in Latin, but also of the Dutch interpreters: whom (because of their singular gifts and special diligence in the Bible) I have been the more glad to follow for the most part, according as I was required. But to say the truth before God, it was neither my labour nor desire to have this work put in my hand: nevertheless it grieved me that other nations should be more plenteously provided for with the scripture in their mother tongue than we: therefore when I was instantly required, though I could not do so well as I would, I thought it yet my duty to do my best, and that with a good will.

Coverdale makes no pretence of being expert in "the tongues"—that is to say, in Hebrew and Greek. In this regard he compares himself, to his own disadvantage, with others who have both the linguistic ability and the hearty desire to carry out the task of Bible translation. But these men, because of some "impediment", have not been able to finish what they began. Who are these men? To one at least, and that the most outstanding of all, we can readily give a name: William Tyndale, after translating the New Testament, had made a good beginning with the Old; but at the time when Coverdale's Bible was published Tyndale had already spent five months in prison at Vilvorde—sufficient "impediment" to the completion of a work so well begun. It was not politic to mention Tyndale's name, either in the prologue to the reader or in the dedication to the king, but of the "five sundry interpreters" mentioned in the latter document as Coverdale's sources one was undoubtedly Tyndale. It is easy to show Coverdale's dependence on Tyndale's work in the New Testament, the Pentateuch and Jonah. Why then is mention made only of Latin and "Dutch" (German) versions on the title-page and in the prologue to the reader? Perhaps Coverdale's intention was to indicate simply the non-English versions on which he relied; as an honest man, he wished to make it plain that he could not translate directly from Hebrew and Greek: Latin and German were the foreign languages to which he had to confine himself. But possibly later reflection suggested to him that the mention of Latin and German versions only might be unfair to Tyndale; at any rate, when new preliminary sheets were printed for the copies of his Bible which were to circulate in England, the Latin and German versions were not mentioned on the title-page, which now simply described the version as "faithfully translated into English".

If Tyndale's version was one of the five on which Coverdale depended, what were the other four? Two were apparently Latin— the Vulgate, of course, and also a new Latin translation from the original texts made by the Dominican scholar Sanctes Pagninus in 1528. Of the German versions Luther's is obviously one; the other has been proved to be one in which Luther's text was adapted to the Swiss dialect of German, published at Zurich in 1524–29. It was on this last version that Coverdale principally relied in the Old Testament, although he made extensive use of Tyndale's work for those Old Testament books which had been published in Tyndale's translation. Coverdale's New Testament was basically Tyndale's version revised in the light of the German versions, and not noticeably improved thereby. He not only translates characteristic German compound words literally (like "unoutspeakable" in Rom. 8 : 26), but evidently likes this sort of thing so well that he even coins similar compounds where they do not appear in the German versions (like "burntofferingaltar" in 1 Maccabees 4 : 53).

Various features of Coverdale's Bible

Coverdale's Bible was the first to introduce chapter-summaries as distinct from the terse chapter-headings found in copies of the Vulgate. These summaries are sometimes summaries and nothing more, as when St Matthew's fourth chapter is summarized:

> Christ fasteth and is tempted: he calleth Peter, Andrew, Iames and Ihon, & healeth all the sicke.

But an explanatory or hortatory note may be included, as when the following chapter is summarized thus:

In this chapter and in the two next folowinge is conteyned the most excellent and louynge Sermon of Christ in the mount: which sermon is the very keye that openeth the vnderstondinge in to the lawe. In this fifth chapter specially he preacheth of the VIII beatitudes or blessinges, of manslaughter, wrath and anger: of aduoutrie, of swearinge, of suffringe wronge, and of loue euen towarde a mans enemies.

Again, Coverdale's Bible was the first to separate the books of the Apocrypha from the other Old Testament books and print them by themselves as an appendix to the Old Testament—a precedent followed by English Protestant Bibles ever since (in so far as they include the Apocrypha at all). In the first edition of Coverdale Baruch retained its traditional place between Lamentations and Ezekiel, but in an edition of 1537 Baruch, too, was relegated to the appendix. Coverdale introduced this appendix with a special note entitled "The Translator unto the Reader", which is interesting enough to reproduce in full:

These books (good reader) which be called Apocrypha, are not judged among the doctors to be of like reputation with the other scripture, as thou mayest perceive by S. Jerome *in epistola ad Paulinum*. And the chief cause thereof is this: there be many places in them, that seem to be repugnant unto the open and manifest truth in the other books of the Bible. Nevertheless I have not gathered them together to the intent that I would have them despised, or little set by, or that I should think them false, for I am not able to prove it. Yea I doubt not verily, if they were equally conferred with the other open scripture (time, place and circumstance in all things considered) they should neither seem contrary, nor be untruly and perversely alleged. Truth it is: a man's face cannot be seen so well in a water as in a faire glass: neither can it be shewed so clearly in a water that is stirred or moved as in a still water. These and many other dark places of scripture have been sore stirred and mixed with blind and covetous opinions of men, which have cast such a mist afore the eyes of the simple, that as long as they be not conferred with the other places of scripture,

they shall not seem otherwise to be understood than as covetous-
ness expoundeth them. But whosoever thou be that readest
scripture, let the Holy Ghost be thy teacher, and let one text
expound another unto thee. As for such dreams, visions and dark
sentences as be hid from thy understanding, commit them unto
God, and make no articles of them.[1] But let the plain text be thy
guide, and the Spirit of God (which is the author thereof) shall
lead thee in all truth.

As for the prayer of Salomon (which thou findest not herein),
the prayer of Azarias, and the sweet song that he and his two
fellows sang in the fire, the first (namely the prayer of Salomon)
readest thou in the eighth chapter of the third book of the Kings,[2]
so that it appeareth not to be *Apocryphum*: the other prayer and
song (namely of the three children) have I not found among any
of the interpreters, but only in the old Latin text,[3] which reporteth
it to be of Theodotion's translation.[4] Nevertheless, both because
of those that be weak and scrupulous, and for their sakes also that
love such sweet songs of thanksgiving, I have not left them out:
to the intent that the one should have no cause to complain, and
that the other might have the more occasion to give thanks unto
God in adversity, as the three children did in the fire. Grace be
with thee. Amen.

Despite his fondness for ungainly compounds, Coverdale's style is
racy and idiomatic. It is to Coverdale that we owe such colloquial
expressions as "Good luck have thou with thine honour" (Ps. 45 : 5)
and "Tush, say they, how should God perceive it?" (Ps. 73 : 11).[5]
Indeed, he tends to overdo the use of "Tush", inserting it for the sake
of vividness where the original gives no warrant for it, as in 1 Thess.

[1] That is, base no doctrines upon them.
[2] Our 1 Kings is called 3 Kings in Coverdale's Bible (following the Latin Vulgate). The
prayer of Solomon at the dedication of the temple (1 Kings 8 : 23–53) was sometimes included
as a separate document, over and above its occurrence in the proper context.
[3] That is, the Vulgate (as contrasted with the newer Latin texts such as those of Erasmus,
Beza, Pagninus and Castalio).
[4] Theodotion's translation of Daniel into Greek is the text of Daniel which usually appears
in the Septuagint. In the Septuagint the Prayer of Azariah and the Song of the Three Holy
Children come between verses 23 and 24 of Daniel 3.
[5] Both these renderings are preserved in the Prayer Book Psalter, based on the Great Bible.
See pp. 81 f.

5 : 3, "For whan they shal saye: Tush, It is peace, there is no daunger, then shall soden destruccion come upon them."

In an impressive number of places it is Coverdale's wording that has survived in successive versions of the English Bible. It is to him that we owe the "lordly dish" in which Jael brought forth butter to Sisera (Judges 5 : 25), and "enter thou into the joy of thy lord" in the master's commendation of his faithful stewards in the Parable of the Talents (Matt. 25 : 21, 23). On the other hand, a number of his renderings have become immortal for their quaintness, such as "there is no more *triacle* at Galaad" (Jer. 8 : 22) and "thou shalt not nede to be afrayed for eny *bugges* by night" (Ps. 91 : 5)—although we should realize that "treacle" and "bugs" had a different meaning for Coverdale's contemporaries from what they have for us. Even in his book titles he can strike out on a line of his own, as when he calls the Song of Songs "Salomons Balettes".

Sample passages from Coverdale's Bible

The Lord's Prayer in Coverdale's version runs as follows:

O oure father which art in heauen, halowed be thy name. Thy kyngdome come. Thy wyll be fulfilled vpon earth as it is in heauen. Geue vs this daye oure dayly bred. And forgeue vs oure dettes, as we also forgeue oure detters. And lede vs not in to temptacion: but delyuer vs from euell. For thyne is the kyngdome, and the power, and the glorye for euer. Amen.

This rendering does not differ markedly from Tyndale's, except in the petition for forgiveness. It is from Coverdale that the A.V. of Matt. 6 : 12 has derived the wording, "And forgive us our debts, as we forgive our debtors"; the more familiar liturgical form, "And forgive us our trespasses, as we forgive them that trespass against us", is essentially Tyndale's rendering.

Coverdale renders the parable of the Good Samaritan thus:

A certayne man wente downe from Ierusalem vnto Iericho, and fell amonge murthurers, which stryped him out of his clothes, and wounded him, and wente their waye, and left him half deed. And by chaunce there came downe a prest the same waye: and whan he sawe him, he passed by. And likewyse a Leuite, whan he came nye vnto the same place and sawe him, he passed by. But a Samaritane was goynge his iourney, and came that waye, and whan he sawe him, he had compassion vpon him, wente vnto him, bounde vp his woundes, and poured oyle and wyne therin, and lifte him vp vpon his beast, and brought him in to the ynne, and made prouysion for him. Vpon the next daye whan he departed, he toke out two pens, and gaue them to the oost, and sayde vnto him: Take cure of him, and what so euer thou spendest more, I will paye it the, whan I come agayne. Which of these thre now thinkest thou, was neghboure vnto him, that fell amonge the murtherers? He sayde: He that shewed mercy vpon him. Then sayde Iesus vnto him: Go thy waye then, and do thou likewyse.

Here too Coverdale for the most part follows Tyndale; his main deviation is the substitution of "murderers" for "thieves", and this is an obvious instance of the influence of the German Bible, according to which the Jericho-bound traveller *"fiel unter die Mörder"*. Later sixteenth-century versions, and the A.V., preferred "thieves", which indeed goes back to the Wycliffite versions. The Greek word really means "brigands" or "bandits".

And this is the rendering of Heb. 1 : 1–4 in Coverdale's Bible:

God in tyme past dyuersly and many wayes, spake vnto the fathers by prophetes, but in these last dayes he hath spoken vnto vs by his sonne, whom he hath made heyre of all thinges, by whom also he made the worlde. Which (sonne) beynge the brightnes of his glory, and the very ymage of his substaunce, bearinge vp all thinges with the worde of his power, hath in his owne personne pourged oure synnes, and is set on the right hande of the maiestie on hye: beynge euen as moch more excellent then the angels, as he hath optayned a more excellent name then they.

This is little more than a transcript of Tyndale, the main deviation being the omission of the phrase "by inheritance" before "obtained" in the last clause. Here, as we have noticed above, the A.V. (with the other principal versions of the English Bible between 1535 and 1611) reverts to Tyndale's fuller rendering.

Anne Boleyn and Coverdale's Bible

Even if Coverdale did not expressly and publicly acknowledge his indebtedness to Luther and Tyndale, the "Lutheran" affinities of his version were plain to see, and this explains why some church authorities in England were lukewarm towards it, and others positively hostile to it. Among those who are said to have shown their hostility to it was John Stokesley, who had become Bishop of London when Cuthbert Tonstall was translated to the see of Durham. Why then should so energetic an opponent of Lutheranism as King Henry have taken such a tolerant line with it? The answer may be found in the influence exercised over him by Queen Anne Boleyn, until her fall from favour and execution in May 1536. The queen certainly manifested a keen interest in Coverdale's version, and but for her sad fate, this version might have been approved before long for setting up in the parish churches of England. But with her death, Coverdale's Bible ceased to play any major part in English life, although it was reprinted twice in 1537, once in 1550, and once again in 1553.

Matthew's Bible and the Royal Licence

In 1537 there appeared a folio volume bearing the title *The Byble, which is all the holy Scripture: in whych are contayned the Olde and Newe Testament, truly and purely translated into Englysh by Thomas Matthew.* "Thomas Matthew" is best regarded as a pen-name; the editor was one John Rogers, a former associate of Tyndale's, who later was the first of the Marian martyrs to be burned at the stake in 1555. But the most interesting feature of the title-page of this volume is not the title itself, but the words at the bottom of the page: "Set forth with the kinges most gracyous lycence".

We have seen how Archbishop Cranmer, two or three years previously, had begun to superintend a revision of the English Bible which it was hoped might circulate with royal authority. But he evidently had little hope of a speedy completion of this work, for when Matthew's Bible appeared—thanks to the generosity of two London merchants and printers, who financed its production—Cranmer wrote to Thomas Cromwell urging him to use his influence with the king to obtain the royal licence for this new version, permitting it to "be sold and read of every person, without danger of any act, proclamation or ordinance heretofore granted to the contrary, until such time that we, the bishops, shall set forth a better translation, which I think will not be till a day after doomsday".

The royal licence was procured, not only for Matthew's Bible, but also for the second 1537 edition of Coverdale's Bible, which bears on its title-page the words: "Set forth with the kinges most gracyous licence". Both the 1537 editions of Coverdale's Bible were printed in England by James Nicholson of Southwark, the earlier one being a folio and the latter a quarto. Nicholson's folio, incidentally, has the distinction of being the first edition of the whole English Bible to be printed in England.[1] It may be that Nicholson had some idea of printing Matthew's Bible as well (its first printing was probably in Antwerp); Cromwell forbade him to do so, by way of protecting the rights of the original printer, but consoled him by obtaining the royal licence for his next reprint of Coverdale's Bible, which came out without delay before the end of the year.

So now two versions of the Bible in English were circulating freely in England, by formal and avowed permission of the king, in the year after Tyndale's death.

Matthew's Bible mainly Tyndale's

But what was Matthew's Bible? On examination it is seen to be substantially Tyndale's Pentateuch, Tyndale's version of the historical books of the Old Testament as far as 2 Chronicles, which he had completed in manuscript but never got into print, Coverdale's version of the other Old Testament books and Apocrypha, and Tyndale's New Testament of 1535. It was a signal act of justice—ordinary justice and poetic justice too—that the first English Bible to be published under royal licence should be Tyndale's Bible (so far as Tyndale's translation had reached), even if it was not yet advisable to associate Tyndale's name with it publicly.

On the other hand John Rogers, who edited this edition of the Bible, would not associate his own name with it; it was not *his* translation, although he may well have assisted Tyndale in the translation of the books from Joshua to 2 Chronicles and in the production of

[1] Tyndale's New Testament had been printed the previous year by a London printer named Thomas Godfray.

his 1535 New Testament. If the manuscript of the translation from Joshua to 2 Chronicles remained in his custody after Tyndale's arrest, then he would regard it as his duty to publish it as soon as possible. The initials "W.T." appear at the end of Malachi, as though to indicate to the discerning that W.T. was the chief (although not the sole) author of the Old Testament translation. As for the pen-name Thomas Matthew, we cannot be sure what suggested it to Rogers' mind; it may, as Dr Mozley says, have been "some quite trivial thing". Nor should we say that Thomas Matthew is John Rogers' own pen-name; "rather Matthew stands for Tyndale plus Coverdale plus (to a very small degree) Rogers."[1]

The preliminary pages of the Matthew Bible contained a church calendar and almanac, a collection of biblical passages constituting "An Exhortation to the Study of the Holy Scripture", a summary of the chief doctrines contained in the Bible, adapted from Jacques Lefèvre's French Bible of 1534, a dedication to King Henry, an alphabetic concordance to the subjects dealt with in the Bible, translated from Pierre Robert Olivetan's French Bible of 1535, as is also a following preface "to the Christian reader". Then comes a list of the books of the Bible and a chronological table.

As in Coverdale's Bible, the books of the Apocrypha were placed by themselves in an appendix to the Old Testament. It was in the Matthew Bible that the apocryphal "Prayer of Manasseh" was first published in English: it was translated from the French of Olivetan's Bible.

In the New Testament the order of books is the same as in Luther's and Tyndale's versions, with Hebrews, James, Jude and Revelation at the end. Tyndale's prologue to the Epistle to the Romans is reprinted, and so (at the end of the New Testament) is Tyndale's table of liturgical epistles and gospels according to the Sarum use.

The text of Matthew's Bible is copiously equipped with notes and parallel references; these are largely borrowed from the French versions of Lefèvre and Olivetan. The actual renderings of these French versions have also influenced Matthew's text here and there.

[1] J. F. Mozley, *Coverdale and his Bibles*, p. 141.

CHAPTER SIX

The Great Bible

The Bible in Church

WITH TWO VERSIONS of the English Bible now fortified by the royal licence, there was no obstacle to its circulation throughout the land. Many bishops, even some who were by no means friendly to the principles of the Reformation, encouraged their clergy to possess and study the English Bible. Some went further than that: Nicolas Shaxton, bishop of Salisbury, required his clergy, early in 1538, to see to it that by Whit Sunday of that year an English Bible should be chained to the desk in every parish church throughout the diocese, in order that literate parishioners might read, and illiterate ones hear, "wholesome doctrine and comfort to their souls". All these measures had the support of Cromwell, and indeed of the king himself. No particular edition of the English Bible was specified in these injunctions, but while some would prefer Coverdale's quarto edition as being cheaper, others would prefer Matthew's folio edition as being more legible—and it was certainly the more convenient edition for chaining to church desks. But the outspoken Protestantism of its notes and other accessories did not commend itself to the more conservative bishops and clergy, and it was decided—apparently by Cromwell—that a revision of the Matthew Bible should be undertaken to render it more generally acceptable. The work of revision was entrusted to Coverdale, and the printing began in Paris about May 1538. This was the genesis of what came to be known as the Great Bible.

As early as the summer of 1536 Cromwell had entertained the idea of having a copy of the English Bible made publicly accessible in every parish church in England, and an injunction to this effect was actually printed, but withdrawn for political reasons before it was issued. Two years later, however, the situation was much more favourable, and the injunction was taken out of cold storage and published in the king's name on September 5, 1538. It charged the clergy:

> That ye shall provide, on this side the feast of All Saints next coming, one book of the whole Bible of the largest volume in English, and the same set up in some convenient place within the said church that ye have cure of, whereas your parishioners may most commodiously resort to the same and read it; the charges of which book shall be rateably borne between you, the parson, and the parishioners aforesaid, that is to say, the one half by you and the other half by them.
>
> Item, that ye shall discourage no man privily or apertly from the reading or hearing of the said Bible, but shall expressly provoke, stir and exhort every person to read the same, as that which is the very lively Word of God, that every Christian person is bound to embrace, believe, and follow, if he look to be saved; admonishing them nevertheless to avoid all contention and altercation therein, but to use an honest sobriety in their inquisition of the true sense of the same, and to refer the explication of obscure places to men of higher judgment in scripture.

What was meant by "one book of the whole Bible of the largest volume in English"? Cromwell doubtless had the Great Bible in mind; it was being printed in Paris for the very purpose specified in the injunction. But there was little likelihood that the Great Bible would be ready by the beginning of November, and in that case those clergy who were anxious to obey the injunction to the letter had no option but to procure a copy of Matthew's Bible, which (at the time when the injunction was published) was unquestionably the "Bible of the largest volume in English". There is no lack of evidence that, before the first edition of the Great Bible could have been generally available for placing in parish churches, the Bible was being avidly read in many of them, so much so that the king found it necessary to issue a proclamation (towards the end of April 1539) forbidding the reading of the English Bible aloud in church during divine service. Evidently, even while divine service was going on, there were many people who found it much more interesting, and possibly more edifying as well, to listen to the Bible being read by one of their literate fellow-parishioners than to listen to what the parson was saying. Archbishop Cranmer, for all his good will to the free circulation of the English Bible, had to make it clear that the injunction of September 1538 was never intended to permit divine service to be interrupted by unauthorized reading of the Bible, or to permit all and sundry to make its reading (during service or at any other time) an occasion for public exposition of the sacred text by people not duly qualified.

The printing of the Great Bible was delayed by the action of the French inquisitor-general at the end of 1538. He forbade the printers to continue with their work, and the sheets already printed were confiscated. Diplomatic representations were made at the French court, and permission was granted to transport the type, paper and printers to England so that the printing could be done there, but the confiscated sheets were not released. Practically all the Bible apart from the Apocrypha had been printed, so that most of the work had to be done over again. The Great Bible at length made its first appearance in April 1539.

Taverner's Bible

Probably a short time before the appearance of the Great Bible, another revision of Matthew's Bible was published in England. The reviser was a layman called Richard Taverner. He was a good Greek scholar, and the main feature of his revision is the improvement of the New Testament from the standpoint of Greek scholarship, special attention being paid to the accurate rendering of the Greek definite article. Taverner's Bible was almost immediately eclipsed by the Great Bible, and had but little influence on subsequent versions of the English Bible; one notable phrase with which it provided the A.V. comes in Heb. 1 : 3, where the Son of God is called the "express image" of His person.

The Great Bible

The Great Bible of 1539 bears the title: "The Byble in Englyshe, that is to saye the content of all the holy scripture, both of the olde and newe testament, truly translated after the veryte of the Hebrue and Greke textes, by the dylygent studye of dyuerse excellent learned men, expert in the foresayde tonges. Prynted by Rychard Grafton and Edward Whitchurch. Cum priuilegio ad imprimendum solum.[1] 1539." This title is surrounded by a woodcut (which was formerly ascribed to Holbein, on no sufficient grounds), in which King Henry from his throne delivers the Word of God with his right hand to Cranmer and with his left to Cromwell, while Cranmer and Cromwell in their turn deliver it to the clergy and laity respectively. Below a motley crowd of men, women and children cry "God save the king", while the Almighty Father looks down approvingly on the whole scene, proclaiming "My word that goeth forth out of my mouth shall not return to me void, but shall accomplish that which I please" (Isa. 55 : 11) and "I have found a man after my own heart, who shall perform all my desire" (Acts 13 : 22).

Although the title of the Great Bible suggests that it was the product of consultation between "divers excellent learned men", it was actually Coverdale's revision of Matthew's Bible. In other words, it was Coverdale's revision of John Rogers' revision of Tyndale's Bible, so far as Tyndale's Bible went. The "divers excellent learned men" are simply the translators, editors and other scholars whose works Coverdale consulted.

Coverdale did not remain content with the first edition of the Great Bible; he continued his work of revision, and when the second edition appeared in April 1540 it represented a considerable advance over the first edition in the matter of revision, especially in the poetical sections of the Old Testament. This second edition contains a preface by Cranmer, which was reprinted in subsequent editions of the Great Bible; and it has the added words at the foot of the title-page: "This is the Byble apoynted to the use of the churches". These added words made explicit what was intended from the first, that the injunction of 1538 commanding that an English Bible be set up in every parish church envisaged the Great Bible as the one to be used in this way. Five further editions were published between July 1540 and December 1541.

[1] That is to say, "with exclusive right of printing it".

Cranmer's preface

The Great Bible (from the second edition onwards) is sometimes called "Cranmer's Bible" because of the preface which he wrote for it. In this preface he commended the widespread reading of the Scriptures, and appealed to the authority of the ancient fathers, Chrysostom and Gregory of Nazianzus, in support of his plea that the Bible was the sufficient rule of faith and life:

Here may all manner of persons: men, women; young, old; learned, unlearned; rich, poor; priests, laymen; lords, ladies; officers, tenants, and mean men; virgins, wives, widows; lawyers, merchants, artificers, husbandmen, and all manner of persons, of what estate or condition soever they be; may in THIS BOOK learn all things, what they ought to believe, what they ought to do, and what they should not do, as well concerning Almighty God, as also concerning themselves, and all others.

A New Title-page

The woodcut around the title continued to be reproduced in edition after edition of the Great Bible, but after Thomas Cromwell's rapid fall from favour in 1540 his arms were removed from it. In the fourth and sixth editions (November 1540 and November 1541) the title is completely rewritten, and appears as follows:

The Byble in Englishe of the largest and greatest volume, auctoryed and apoynted by the commandemente of our moost redoubted Prynce and soueraygne Lorde Kynge Henry the VIII., supreme heade of this his churche and realme of Englande: to be frequented and used in every churche in this his sayd realme, accordynge to the tenour of his former Injunctions giuen in that behalfe.

Oversene and perused at the commaundment of the Kynge's Hyghnes, by the ryghte reuerende fathers in God Cuthbert Bysshop of Duresme, and Nicolas Bisshop of Rochester. Printed by Edward Whitchurch. Cum priuilegio ad imprimendum solum.

This makes the former direction, "This is the Byble apoynted to the use of the churches", more explicit still. But the most striking feature of the new title is the reference to Cuthbert, Bishop of Durham. For this is no other than Cuthbert Tonstall, formerly Bishop of London, to whom Tyndale had applied in vain for facilities to prosecute his work of Bible translation in 1523, and who bought up as many copies of Tyndale's New Testament as he could lay his hands on, in order to burn them at St Paul's Cross. Now he appears as lending the authority of his high office to a Bible translation which is Tyndale's production more than anyone else's! We may suppose that Tonstall knew only too well how far the translation which he had "overseen and perused" was Tyndale's, but "the commandment of the King's Highness" brooked no resistance.

Comparative quotations

A few Old Testament quotations will help to show the relations between the editions of Coverdale and Matthew and the Great Bible.[1]

Coverdale (1535)	Matthew (1537)	Great Bible (1540)
Gen. 8 : 11. And she returned unto him aboute the euen tyde: and beholde she had broken of a leafe of an olyve tre and bare it in her nebb.	And the doue came to hym agayne about euentyde; and beholde there was in hyr mouth a lefe of an olyve tree, whyche she had plucked.	And the doue came to hym in the euen tyde, and lo in her mouthe was an olyue leafe that she had plucte.
Gen. 39 : 2. And the Lord was with Joseph, in so moch that he became a luckye man.	And the Lorde was with Joseph, and he was a luckie felowe.	And God was with Joseph and he became a luckye man.
Gen. 42 : 36. It goeth all ouer me.	All these things fall upon me.	All these thynges are agaynst me.
Gen. 49 : 4. Thou passeth forth swiftly as the water. Thou shalt not be the chefest.	As unstable as water wast thou, thou shalt therefore not be the chefest.	Unstable as water thou shalt not be the chefest.
Lev. 19 : 27. Ye shal shave no crowns upon your heade, nether shalt thou clyppe thy berde cleane off.	Ye shall not rounde the lockes of your heades, nether shalt thou marre the tuftes of thy bearde.	Ye shall not rounde the lockes of your heades, neyther shalte thou marre the tuftes of thy bearde.
Deut. 32 : 10. He founde him in the wildernesse, euen in the drye deserte, where he roared.	He found hym in a deserte land, in a voyde ground, and a rorynge wilderness.	He found hym in a deserte lande, in a voyde grounde, and in a rorynge wildernesse.

[1] From A. Edgar, *The Bibles of England* (Paisley, 1889), pp. 128 ff.

Coverdale (1535)	Matthew (1537)	Great Bible (1540)
Deut. 34 : 7. His eyes were not dymme, and his chekes were not fallen.	His eyes were not dym nor hys chekes abated.	Hys eye was not dymme, nor hys naturall coloure abated.
Judg. 5 : 12. Arise, Barak and catch him that catched thee, thou sonne of Abinoam.	Up Barak, and take thy praye thou sonne of Abinoam.	Aryse Barak, and leade the captiuitie captiue, thou sonne of Abinoam.
Judg. 5 : 15. Because Ruben stode hye in his awne consayte, and separated him selfe from us.	But in the devysions of Rueben were great ymaginations of herte.	When in the departyng awaye of Ruben there were great men and wyse of hert.
Judg. 15 : 5. And thus he brent the stoukes and the standynge corne.	And burnt up bothe the reped corne, and also the standynge.	And burnt up bothe the reped corne and also the standyng.
Judg. 15 : 8. He smote them sore both upon the shulders and loynes.	He smote them legge and thighe with a mighty plage.	He smote them legge and thygh with a mightye plage.

1 Sam. 2 : 30-33. Therefore sayeth the Lorde God of Israel: I have spoken that thy house and thy father's house shoulde walke before me for ever. But now sayeth the Lorde, That be farre fro me. But who so honoureth me, him will I honoure also, as for those that despyse me they shall not be regarded. Behold the tyme shal come, that I wyll break thyne arm in two, and the arm of thy father's house, so that there shal no oldeman be in thy house. And thou shalt see thine adversaries in the habitacion, in all the good of Israel, and there shal neuer be olde man in thy father's house. Yet wyll I not rote out euery man of the fro myne altare but that thyne eyes may be consumed, and that thy soul may be sory: and a great multitude of thy house shal dye, when they are come to be men.

Wherefore the Lorde God of Israel sayth, I sayde that thyne house and the house of thy father shulde haue walked before me for ever. But now the Lorde sayeth, That be farre from me: for them that worshippe me I will worshippe, and they that despyse me shalbe despysed. Beholde the dayes will come that I will cut of thine arme, and the arme of thy father's house, that there shall not be an elder in thine house. And thou shalt see thine enemy in the tabernacle, in all that shall please Israel, and there shall not be an elder in thine house while the world standeth. Nevertheless I will not destroye all thy males from my aultare to dase thy sight withal and to make thyne hert melte. And all the multitude of thyne house shall dye younge.

Wherefore the Lord God of Israel sayeth I sayde, that thy house and the house of thy father shoulde walke before me for ever. But now the Lord sayth That be farre from me: for them that worship me I wyl worship and they that despyse me shall come to shame. Behold the dayes come that I wyll cutte of thine arm, and the arm of thy father's house that there shall not be an olde man in thine house: and thou shalt se thyne enemy in the tabernacle (of the Lord) and in all the wealth which (God) shall give Israel, and there shall not be an elder in thyne house for ever. Neverthelesse I wyll not destroy all the males that come of the fro myne altar. But to make thyne eyes base, and to make thyne herte melte. And all they that be multyplyed in thyne house shall dye, yf they be men.

| 1 Sam. 3 : 13. He knewe how shamefully his children behaued themselves and hath not once loked sowerly thereto. | For the wickednesse whyche he knoweth, how his sonnes are ungraciouse and he was not wroth therewith. | When the people cursed hys sonnes, for the same wyckednes, he hath not corrected them. |

Coverdale (1535)	Matthew (1537)	Great Bible (1540)
1 Sam. 17 : 4. Then stepte there forth from amonge the Philistynes a stoute bolde man, named Goliath.	And then came a man, and stode in the myddes out of the tents of the Philistines, named Goliath.	And there came a man betwene them both out of the tentes of the Philistines named Goliath.
1 Sam. 18 : 6. The women wente out of all the cities of Israel with songes and daunses to mete kynge Saul with tymbrels, with myrth and with fyddels.	Women came out of all cyties of Israel synging and daunsynge agaynst Saul, with tymbrelles, with joye and with fydilles.	Women came oute of all cyties of Israel syngynge and daunsynge agaynste Kynge Saul, and with tymbrels, with ioye and with instruments of musyke.
1 Sam. 21 : 13. And Dauid ... shewed himselfe as he had bene madd in their handes, and stackered towarde the dores of the gate, and his slauerynges ranne downe his beard.	And he ... raved in their handes, and scrabbled on the doores of the gate, and let his spittel falle downe upon his bearde.	And Dauid ... fayned hym selfe mad in theyre handes and scrabbled on the dores of the gate, and let his spettle fall downe upon his beerde.
1 Kings 4 : 26. And Salomon had fortye thousande cart horses.	And Salomon had fourtie thousand stalles of horses for charettes.	And Salomon had XLM stalles of horses for charrettes.
1 Kings 18 : 28. And they cried loude and prouoked themselues with knyues and botkens, as their maner was, tyll the bloude folowed.	And they cryed lowde and cut themselues, as their manner was with knyues and launcers tyll the bloude folowed on them.	And they cryed loude, and cutte themselues as theyr maner was with knyues and launcers tyll the bloode folowed on them.
1 Kings 19 : 12. And after the fyre came there a styll softe hyssinge.	And after the fyre came a styll small voyce.[1]	And after the fyre came a small styl voyce.
1 Kings 22 : 34. A certayne man bended his bowe harde, and shott the kynge of Israel betwene the mawe and the longes.	And a certen man drew a boowe ignorantly, and smote the kinge of Israel betwene the ribbes of his harnesse.	A certaine man drue a bowe ignorantly, and (by chance) smote the kynge of Israel betwene the rybbes and hys harnesse.
2 Kings 12 : 12. Namely, to the dawbers and masons, and to them that boughte tymber and fre stone.	To masons and hewers of stone to bye tymbre and fre stone.	To masons and hewers of stone. And they bought tymbre and fre stone.

A study of these passages makes it abundantly plain that, although Coverdale had produced a version of his own in 1535, it was not that version but Matthew's (that is to say Tyndale's) that he used as the basis for the Great Bible for the first half of the Old Testament. For the second half of the Old Testament (from Ezra to Malachi) and

---

[1] Thus it is to Tyndale (via Matthew's Bible) that the A.V. of this verse owes the "still small voice".

for the Apocrypha, of course, Tyndale was not available, and since Matthew's Bible had followed Coverdale in these books, they showed much less divergence as between Coverdale's Bible and the Great Bible. Thus, in Coverdale's Bible and the Great Bible alike Hezekiah shows the king of Babylon's messengers "all that was in his cubburdes" (Isa. 39 : 2; A.V. "... treasures"), and the divine oracle to Zerubbabel promises that "he shall brynge up the fyrst stone, so that men shal crye unto hym, Good lucke, good lucke" (Zech. 4 : 7; A.V. "he shall bring forth the headstone thereof with shoutings, crying, Grace, grace unto it"). And both have the same perversion of the sense in Malachi 2 : 16, "Yf thou hatest her put her awaye, sayeth the Lord God of Israel, and geue her a clothinge for the scorne, sayeth the Lorde of hoostes" (A.V., "For the LORD, the God of Israel, saith that he hateth putting away: for one covereth violence with his garment, saith the LORD of hosts").

In other places in the second half of the Old Testament, however, the Great Bible represents a correction of Coverdale's Bible. Thus Coverdale had rendered Eccl. 12 : 12, "Therefore, beware (my sonne) that aboue these thou make the not many and innumerable bokes, nor take dyuerse doctrynes in hande, to weery thy body withal." But the Great Bible says: "Therefore, beware (my sonne) of that doctryne that is besyde thys: for, to make many bokes it is an endlesse worke; and too loude criynge weryeth the bodye." This last version is nearer the sense of the passage (cf. A.V., "And further, by these, my son, be admonished: of making many books there is no end; and much study is a weariness of the flesh"), except for the "too loud crying" in the last clause; there the 1535 version was better. Second thoughts are not always wiser, as may appear further in Psalm 77 : 2. Here Coverdale's 1535 Bible said: "In the tyme of my trouble I sought the Lorde, I helde vp my hondes vnto him in the night season, for my soule refused all other comforte." But in the Great Bible he changed "I held up my hands unto him in the night season" to "my sore ran and ceased not in the night season" (cf. Prayer Book Version); and this correction was taken over by the Geneva Bible of 1560 and by the A.V. But the literal rendering of the Hebrew supports Coverdale's first version, as may be seen from the R.V. ("My hand was stretched out in the night, and slacked not") and R.S.V. ("in the night my hand is stretched out without wearying").

New Testament passages

A few samples may now be given of the New Testament rendering of the Great Bible. Here is the Lord's Prayer, from Matt. 6 : 9-13:

> Oure father which art in heauen, halowed be thy name. Let thy kingdome come. Thy will be fulfilled, as well in erth, as it is in heuen. Geue vs this daye oure dayly bred. And forgeue vs oure dettes, as we forgeue oure detters. And leade vs not into temptation: but delyuer vs from euyll. For thyne is the kyngdom and the power, and the glorye for euer. Amen.

Here the Great Bible has followed Coverdale's "forgeue vs oure dettes, as we also forgeue oure detters" instead of Tyndale's "forgeve vs oure treaspases, even as we forgeve them whych treaspas vs". "Debts" and "debtors" are certainly the literal equivalents of the Greek terms found in Matt. 6 : 12, but these Greek terms go back to the original language used by Jesus—Aramaic—in which the words meaning "debts" and "debtors" were used idiomatically in the sense of "sins" and "sinners". What Jesus really taught His disciples to pray was: "forgive our sins, as we forgive those who sin against us".

The parable of the Good Samaritan is rendered thus in the Great Bible:

> A certayne man descended from Hierusalem to Hierico, and fell among theues, whych robbed him of hys rayment and wounded hym, and departed, leauynge hym halfe deed. And it chaunced, that ther came downe a certayne Preste that same waye: and when he sawe him, he passed by. And lyke wyse a Leuite, when he went nye to the place, came and loked on him, and passed by. But a certayne Samaritane, as he iorneyed, came vnto hym: and when he sawe hym, he had compassyon on hym: and went to, and bounde vp his woundes, and poured in oyle and wyne, and set hym on his awne beaste, and brought hym to a commen ynne,

and made prouisyon for him. And on the morow, when he
departed, he toke out two pence, and gaue them to the host, and
sayd vnto him: Take cure of him, and whatsoeuer thou spendest
moare, when I come agayne I will recompence the. Whych now
of these thre thynkest thou, was neyghbour vnto hym that fell
among the theues? And he sayde: he that shewed mercy on hym.
Then sayde Iesus vnto hym: Go, and do thou lyke wyse.

Here Coverdale has abandoned his 1535 rendering "murderers",
preferring Tyndale's "thieves".

The opening words of the Epistle to the Hebrews in the Great
Bible follow Tyndale's rendering closely:

God in tyme past diuersly and many wayes, spake vnto the
fathers by Prophetes: but in these last dayes he hath spoken vnto
vs by hys awne sonne, whom he hath made heyre of all thinges by
whom also he made the worlde. Whych (sonne) beinge the
brightnes of hys glory, and the very ymage of hys substance
rulynge all thynges wyth the worde of hys power, hath by his
awne person pourged oure synnes, and sytteth on the right hande
of the maiestye on hye: beynge so moch more excellent then the
angels, as he hath by inherytaunce obteyned a more excellent
name then they.

In the last clause Coverdale has reinserted Tyndale's "by inheritance" before "obtained" (he omitted it, as we have seen, in his own
edition of 1535), and by retaining his change of Tyndale's "excellenter" to "more excellent" he has given this clause, in the Great
Bible, the exact form in which it was later perpetuated in the A.V.

Other features of the Great Bible

A few notes were retained in the Great Bible, but only such as
might make the meaning of certain words and expressions plainer to
the reader; the controversial notes of Matthew's Bible were dropped.
A number of marginal signs and the like (principally in the form of
pointing hands) appeared in the earlier editions of the Great Bible;

these were intended to draw the reader's attention to an appendix of "certain godly annotations" by Coverdale himself. This appendix, however, although it was probably compiled, was never published; even if Coverdale's "godly annotations" were couched in the most moderate language, they could not but express his Lutheran views, which would have been objectionable to many of the clergy, not to mention the king himself.

In the title-page to the Apocrypha these books are mistakenly referred to as the "Hagiographa" (*i.e.* "holy writings")—a term which properly denotes those canonical books of the Old Testament which are not included in the Law or the Prophets.

In the New Testament the Lutheran order of the books (followed by Tyndale, Matthew, and Coverdale himself in his 1535 Bible), which places Hebrews, James, Jude and Revelation at the end in a category by themselves, is discontinued; the order adopted in the Great Bible is that given by Erasmus in his Greek Testament, and followed by the A.V. and other principal English versions after 1539.

Years of Reaction

The closing years of the reign of Henry VIII were years of reaction so far as the Reforming movement was concerned. This had an effect in various ways upon the fortunes of the English Bible. For example, in the spring of 1543 Parliament passed an act "for the advancement of true religion and for the abolishment of the contrary", which banned "the crafty, false and untrue translation of Tyndale", made it a crime for any unlicensed person to read or expound the Bible publicly to others, and went so far as to forbid even the private reading of the Bible by people belonging to the lower classes of society. It is to the period following this enactment that the famous inscription of the Gloucestershire shepherd Robert Williams belongs. Robert Williams belonged to those categories of Englishmen who were forbidden to read the English Bible for themselves; yet he was so literate and cultured a man that when Thomas Langley's *Abridgement of Polydore Vergil*[1] appeared in 1546 he bought a copy for himself, and wrote in it:

[1] Polydore Vergil was an Italian humanist; it was his Latin treatise *On Inventors of Things* (1499) that Langley abridged in English.

At Oxforde the yere 1546 browt down to Seynbury by John
Darbye pryse–14d when I kepe Mr Letymers shype I bout thys
boke when the testament was obberagatyd that shepe herdys
myght not red hit I prey God amende that blyndnes. Wryt by
Robert Wyllyams keppynge shepe uppon Seynbury hill 1546.

It was in this year 1546 that a proclamation by King Henry himself went further even than the Act of Parliament of 1543. It ordained
that after the last day of August in that year "no man or woman, of
what estate, condition, or degree, was ... to receive, have, take, or
keep, Tyndale's or Coverdale's New Testament." In the diocese of
London large quantities not only of Tyndale's and Coverdale's New
Testaments but of their Old Testament translations as well were
collected and burned at St Paul's Cross. Edmund Bonner, Bishop of
London, was a protagonist of the conservative reaction.

The ban on the Bibles of Tyndale and Coverdale was a monu-
mental piece of absurdity, when all the time the Great Bible maintained its prominent position in every parish church in the land. To
be sure, the Great Bible itself was not immune from attack; the
Upper House of Convocation of Canterbury in 1542 decided that
the Great Bible could not be retained as the authorized version of the
realm "without scandal and error and open offence to Christ's faithful people" unless it were revised and corrected in conformity with
the Latin Vulgate. The work of revision and correction of the two
Testaments was entrusted to two committees of bishops, each committee including a representative from the Province of York. But
the work came to nothing; the king suddenly decided that it should
be undertaken by the two Universities and not by the bishops, and
the Universities do not appear to have done anything about it. We
cannot be sorry that the work came to nothing; a revision which
rendered the heavenly voice at our Lord's baptism as "This is my
dilect son in whom complacui" (for this is how Stephen Gardiner,
Bishop of Winchester, would have worded it) could scarcely have
commended itself to English readers. One member of the Convocation of Canterbury who shed no tears over the failure of the scheme
was the archbishop himself. Cranmer would not have denied that the
Great Bible was capable of improvement, but such a revision as it

was in a fair way to receive from his more conservative colleagues in the 1540's would not have been an improvement in his eyes.

Thus, when King Henry died on January 28, 1547, the Great Bible was still the version "appointed to the use of the churches" throughout England.

CHAPTER SEVEN

The Elizabethan Bible

The English Prayer Book

WITH THE ACCESSION of Edward VI the reactionary swing of his father's closing years was reversed; the Reforming movement was now in the ascendant. The first year of the new reign saw a repromulgation of the royal injunction of 1538, ordering that within three months from July 31 "one book of the whole Bible of the largest volume in English" should be installed in every parish church. This repromulgation was no doubt necessary because during the preceding years many church Bibles had been removed or allowed to fall into disrepair. The injunction of 1538 had not been abrogated, but the trend of those latter years was not favourable to its full observance, in letter or in spirit. The Great Bible was reprinted twice under Edward VI—in 1549 and again in 1553. The former of these two years witnessed another notable event in the religious literature of England—the publication of the first English edition of *The Booke of the Common Prayer and Administracion of the Sacraments, and Other Rites and Ceremonies of the Churche after the Use of the Churche of England*. The English Prayer Book (based essentially on the old use of Sarum) is as much Cranmer's legacy as the English Bible is Tyndale's. A second edition of the Prayer Book followed in 1552. Henceforth (apart from the five years of Mary Tudor's reign) the English people were to hear their church services in their own language. In the first year of Edward VI a royal injunction laid it down that the Epistle and Gospel in the Communion Service should be read in English. But now all the services for the general public were to be conducted in the common tongue, and that included all the passages of Scripture which were incorporated in them. The whole Psalter was to be gone through each month; the Great Bible version of the Psalms, first used for this purpose in 1549, was printed in the

1662 *Book of Common Prayer* and has been retained ever since. Not only so, but provision was made for the reading of a chapter from both Testaments daily at Mattins and Evensong, so that practically the whole Bible was read through publicly year by year. In 1543 an order had been given that a chapter of the New Testament in English should be read at Mattins after the *Te Deum* and at Evensong after the *Magnificat*; but the new Bible-reading provision of Cranmer and his associates, in the context of the liturgy, endeavoured to embody the ideal "of the primitive and early Church, a ministry of word and sacrament intimately conjoined Sunday by Sunday, a Communion of the Body and Blood of Christ shared by all, and side by side with it a daily office in which the scriptures read and the Psalms said or sung in unbroken course should build men up in the faith."[1]

Cheke's version

In 1550 a novel attempt at Bible translation was begun by Sir John Cheke, formerly Professor of Greek at Cambridge and tutor to Edward VI. His translation represents the opposite extreme to the ultra-latinate version which Bishop Gardiner would have preferred, for as far as possible he aimed at using words of pure English ancestry. "Proselyte", for example, appears in Cheke's translation as "freshman"; "parable" as "biword"; "resurrection" as "uprising" or even "gainrising", for he did not scruple to coin compounds to convey the sense of the old-established Greek and Latin compounds. An "apostle" is a *frosent*, "regeneration" is *gainbirth*, "superscription" is *onwriting*, "captivity" is *outpeopling*, "crucified" is *crossed*, "lunatic" is *moond*, "demon-possessed" is *devild*, "publicans" are *tollers*, "money-changers" are *tablers*, the "wise men" are *wizards*, "foreigners" are *Welschmen*, the "high priest" is *hed bishop*, a "centurion" is a *hundreder*, and so forth. Sir John was not only an original translator, but something of a spelling reformer as well. He completed only St Matthew's Gospel and the beginning of St Mark; his translation remained in manuscript until 1843, when it was published and edited by the Rev. James Goodwin. He did not eschew all words of Latin origin, as appears from his rendering of the "comfortable words" of Matt. 11 : 25–30:

[1] D. E. W. Harrison, *The Book of Common Prayer* (London, 1946), p. 61.

At that time Jesus answered and said: I must needs, O Father, acknowledge thanks unto thee, O Lord of heaven and earth, which hast hidden these things from wise and witty men, and hast disclosed the same to babes; yea and that, Father, for such was thy good pleasure herein. All things be delivered me of my Father. And no man knoweth the Son but the Father,[1] and he to whom the Son will disclose it. Come to me all that labour and be burdened and I will ease you. Take my yoke on you and learn of me, for I am mild and of a lowly heart. And ye shall find quietness for your selves. For my yoke is profitable and my burden light.

Here the words "disclosed", "pleasure", "delivered", "labour", "quietness" and "profitable" are of Latin origin, but probably Sir John regarded them as adequately naturalized in the English language.

Bishop Becke's Bible

What is sometimes called "Bishop Becke's Bible", published in 1551, consists essentially of Taverner's Old Testament and Tyndale's New Testament, compiled by John Daye and revised and edited by Edmund Becke. Becke added a translation of 3 Maccabees, and retranslated 1 Esdras, Tobit and Judith. This edition was furnished with a dedication to the young king, instructing him in the duties of his high station. If people would only devote an hour a day to reading the Bible, says the dedication, they would soon give up blasphemy, swearing, card-playing and other games of chance, together with pride, prodigality, riot, licentiousness and all kinds of dissolute living.

Becke's Bible was amply annotated, the annotations being set in the same type as the sacred text. These were felt to be objectionable, and were not reprinted; the most frequently cited note being that on 1 Peter 3 : 7, where men are exhorted to live with their wives "according to knowledge".

He dwelleth wyth his wyfe according to knowledge, that taketh her as a necessary healper, and not as a bonde servante, or a bonde slave. And yf she be not obedient and healpful unto hym,

---

[1] Note the inadvertent omission of the clause: "neither doth any man know the Father but the Son".

endeavoureth to beate the feare of God into her heade, that thereby she maye be compelled to learne her dutie, and to do it.

One wonders if the editor penned the second part of this note with his tongue in his cheek; even if he did, it is better not to indulge one's sense of humour in Bible annotations, for readers are predisposed to treat all Bible annotations seriously!

The Marian reaction

With the accession of Mary in 1553 the Reforming policy of her brother's reign was reversed. Some of the men most closely associated with the work of Bible translation, like John Rogers and Thomas Cranmer, were executed; others, like Coverdale, found safety on the Continent. But no express steps were taken against the English Bible. The injunction of 1538, ordering the setting up of the Great Bible in parish churches, was not revoked. The queen's first Parliament enacted that church services should be conducted as they had been in the last year of Henry VIII; but in the last year of Henry VIII the Great Bible was still to be seen in a large number of parish churches. And in Mary's last year, a Reformer by the name of Roger Holland appeared before Edmund Bonner, Bishop of London, with the English New Testament in his hand, and said: "You will find no fault with the translation, I think; it is of your own translation, it is according to the Great Bible." For Bonner, who occupied the see of London under Henry VIII and Edward VI (from 1539 to 1549), and again under Mary, had been foremost in having the Great Bible set up in the churches of his diocese when it appeared in 1539. And now he did not find any fault with the translation, but contented himself with arguing that Holland or anybody else could not know it to be Christ's Testament apart from the Church's authority.

There was, indeed, much burning of Bibles during Mary's reign, as Foxe's martyrologies show, but the position of the Great Bible, at any rate, does not appear to have been assailed either by act of Parliament or by royal proclamation. The queen herself, during her father's reign, had been associated with the Great Bible, when the English translation of Erasmus's paraphrase of St John's Gospel, which she prepared in collaboration with her chaplain, was bound up with the Great Bible and placed in churches along with it. "Is it possible," asks Dr J. F. Mozley, "that the queen nourished in her heart a certain tenderness for that version to whose elucidation she had contributed, and that this in part accounts for her unwillingness to condemn by proclamation the English bible?"[1]

The Great Bible at Elizabeth's accession

When Mary was succeeded by Elizabeth, one of the earliest injunctions of the new queen repeated the order of her father and brother that "one book of the whole Bible of the largest volume in English" should be procured and set up in every parish church within three months. As at the beginning of the reign of Edward VI, it was not necessary to obtain a new Bible if the old one was still available and serviceable, but there were many churches where the Bible was no longer available, or if available was too dilapidated to be of any use. Evidently the 1553 edition of the Great Bible had not been exhausted—it was printed only a short time before Mary's accession, and it would not have been a best-seller during her reign—but it had not been confiscated or destroyed, for there is good documentary evidence for the purchase of copies in the beginning of Elizabeth's reign, and it was not necessary to print a fresh folio edition until 1562. But the Great Bible had served its generation well, and thirty years after its publication in 1539 it had been superseded by a better version.

Whittingham's New Testament

While England saw no activity in the work of Bible translation during Mary's reign, there were Englishmen elsewhere who were convinced of the need for a better translation than had been attained thus far, and they gave themselves to the task of producing one. Coverdale was not the only English Reformer who found a congenial home in Geneva at this time, in the city where John Knox thought he had found "the most perfect school of Christ" since apostolic days. Here was a most favourable setting for the work of Bible study and translation. The city's most illustrious inhabitant in

[1] *Coverdale and his Bibles*, p. 296.

those years was John Calvin, the leading theologian of the Reformation, whose talents were laid out to greatest advantage in his commentaries on the books of the Bible. Another leading Reformer who had close associations with Geneva was Theodore Beza, the greatest biblical scholar of his day. He and others had contributed greatly to the better establishment and elucidation of the biblical text, and the English exiles found a group of Frenchmen in Geneva engaged on a revision of the French Bible in the light of the expert knowledge which was available there. The English exiles followed their example, under the leadership of William Whittingham, sometime Fellow of All Souls College, Oxford, who married Calvin's sister (or sister-in-law), and succeeded John Knox as pastor of the English church in Geneva. In 1557 Whittingham produced a revision of the English New Testament—substantially Matthew's edition of Tyndale, with some changes introduced from the Great Bible, and others based on Beza's Latin New Testament of 1556. Whittingham's was a small octavo edition, in roman type (except for words added to make the sense plain, which were set in a different type), and with the text divided into verses.[1] One notable feature of its wording is the use of "church" to render Greek *ekklesia*, instead of "congregation", which Tyndale and Coverdale had favoured. It contained an introductory epistle by Calvin, "declaring that Christ is the end of the law", and a preface "To the Reader", in which the principles of the revision are explained. The name of Paul does not appear in the title of the Epistle to the Hebrews, and a note points out that "seeing the Spirit of God is the author thereof, it diminishes nothing the authority, although we know not with what pen he wrote it." It is in this edition, too, that the Epistles of James, Peter, 1 John and Jude are first called the "General Epistles" (as in A.V. and R.V.) rather than "Catholic Epistles" (as in the earlier English versions, following the Vulgate).

The Geneva Bible

But Whittingham's New Testament was only an interim edition; he and his associates had something more ambitious in mind. They

[1] Whittingham took this verse-division over from the fourth edition of Robert Estienne's Greek New Testament (Geneva, 1551).

continued to work on the New Testament, and paid attention to the Old Testament as well, until the fruit of their labours appeared in 1560 in the version known as the Geneva Bible. The title-page of this new version ran thus:

The Bible and Holy Scriptures. Conteyned in the Olde and Newe Testament. Translated according to the Ebrue and Greke, and conferred with the best translations in divers languages. With most profitable annotations upon all the hard places, and other things of greate importance as may appeare in the Epistle to the Reader. "Feare not, stand stil, and beholde the salvacion of the Lord, which he wil shewe to you this day," Exod. xiv. 13. At Geneva. Printed by Rowland Hall. M.D.LX.

After a list of the books of the Old and New Testaments comes a dedicatory epistle to Queen Elizabeth.

The eyes of all that fear God in all places behold your countries as an example to all that believe, and the prayers of all the godly at all times are directed to God for the preservation of Your Majesty. For considering God's wonderful mercies toward you at all seasons, who hath pulled you out of the mouth of the lions, and how that from your youth you have been brought up in the holy scriptures, the hope of all men is so increased, that they cannot but look that God should bring to pass some wonderful work by your grace to the universal comfort of his Church. Therefore even above strength you must shew yourself strong and bold in God's matters. ... This Lord of lords and King of kings who hath ever defended his, strengthen, comfort and preserve Your Majesty, that you may be able to build up the ruins of God's house to his glory, the discharge of your conscience, and to the comfort of all them that love the coming of Christ Jesus our Lord.

For her work as a builder up of "the ruins of God's house" the queen is compared to Zerubbabel, the rebuilder of the Jerusalem temple after the Babylonian captivity. As he had his enemies, so she has hers ("whereof some are Papists ... who traitorously seek to erect idolatry"); but by faith in God and the paying of heed to His ministers she, like Zerubbabel, will have good success.

The address to the queen is followed by one to the readers, among whom all the English-speaking nations of the day are included.

> To our Beloved in the Lord, the Brethren of England, Scotland, Ireland, etc. Grace, mercy and peace, through Christ Jesus ...

The translators explain why earlier versions of the English Bible need to be revised, and continue:

> Not that we vindicate anything to ourselves above the least of our brethren (for God knoweth with what fear and trembling we have been now for the space of two years and more, day and night, occupied herein), but being earnestly desired, and by divers, whose learning and godliness we reverence, exhorted, and also encouraged by the ready wills of such whose hearts God likewise touched, not to spare any charges for the furtherance of such a benefit and favour of God toward his Church (though the time then was most dangerous and the persecution sharp and furious), we submitted ourselves at length to their godly judgments, and seeing the great opportunity and occasions which God presented unto us in this Church by reason of so many godly and learned men, and such diversities of translations in divers tongues, we undertook this great and wonderful work (with all reverence, as in the presence of God, as entreating the word of God, whereunto we think ourselves insufficient), which now God, according to his divine providence and mercy, hath directed to a most prosperous end. And this we may with good conscience protest, that we have in every point and word, according to the measure of that knowledge which it pleased Almighty God to give us, faithfully rendered the text, and in all hard places most sincerely expounded the same. For God is our witness that we have by all means endeavoured to set forth the purity of the word and right sense of the Holy Ghost, for the edifying of the brethren in faith and charity.

Evidently the Christian reader of that day was less impatient of long sentences than his modern descendant is!

While the work of translation is ascribed to "many godly and learned men" who found themselves brought together, it is highly probable that Whittingham was foremost among them. One would be interested to know what part in the work was taken by Coverdale, or even (it may be) by Knox. But of greater interest is the way in which they set about their work. In the Old Testament the Geneva Bible represents a thorough revision of the Great Bible, especially in those books which Tyndale had not translated. For these books had never been translated directly into English from Hebrew (or Aramaic). Now the existing version of the prophetical books and the poetical and wisdom literature of the Old Testament was carefully brought into line with the Hebrew text, and even with the Hebrew idiom. Indeed, the translators acknowledge their Hebraizing tendency as regards the whole Bible, New Testament as well as Old, when they say in their address to the reader:

> Now as we have chiefly observed the sense, and laboured always to restore it to all integrity, so have we most reverently kept the propriety of the words, considering that the Apostles who spake and wrote to the Gentiles in the Greek tongue, rather constrained them to the lively phrase of the Hebrew, than enterprised far by mollifying their language to speak as the Gentiles did. And for this and other causes we have in many places reserved the Hebrew phrases, notwithstanding that they may seem somewhat hard in their ears that are not well practised and also delight in the sweet sounding phrases of the holy scriptures.

For the New Testament they took as their basis Tyndale's latest edition, and revised it with the aid of Beza's Latin version and his commentary.

The books of the Apocrypha, which (as in Coverdale) appear as an appendix to the Old Testament, are described as "books which were not received by a common consent to be read and expounded publicly in the Church, neither yet served to prove any point of Christian religion save in so much as they had the consent of the other scriptures called canonical to confirm the same, or rather whereon they were grounded: but as books proceeding from godly men, were received to be read for the advancement and furtherance of knowledge of the history and for the instruction of godly manners."

The translators are careful to point out that certain actions of heroes recorded in the Apocrypha are not necessarily to be imitated. Thus the suicidal acts of Eleazar the Hasmonean (1 Macc. 6 : 43 ff.) and Razis (2 Macc. 14 : 41 ff.), it is noted, must not be followed (even although they appear to be recorded with approval) because suicide is contrary to God's commandment, and as for the commendation of prayer for the dead in 2 Macc. 12 : 44 f., "though Judas [Maccabaeus] had so done, yet this particular example is not sufficient to establish a doctrine. . . ." But they are equally ready to make it plain that certain actions by pious people in the canonical books are examples to be avoided, not imitated. Thus they point out that the Hebrew midwives of Exodus 1 : 15 ff. should not have told Pharaoh lies about their inability to strangle Hebrew boys at birth, although they were right to disobey his iniquitous orders; and against the account in 2 Chronicles 15 : 16 of King Asa's deposition of his mother for her idolatry they set the grim and often quoted comment: "Herein he shewed that he lacked zeal: for she ought to have died . . . but he gave place to foolish pity."

The notes of the Geneva Bible are famous, largely because they irritated James I so much; yet they are mild in comparison with Tyndale's. They are, to be sure, unashamedly Calvinistic in doctrine, and therefore offensive to readers who find Calvinism offensive; but for half a century the people of England and Scotland, who read the Geneva Bible in preference to any other version, learned much of their biblical exegesis from these notes. One may surmise that the Geneva Bible, translation and notes together, played no little part in making British Puritanism the strongly vertebrate movement that it was.

One might expect the notes to be outspokenly anti-Roman, and so, of course, they are, but to any marked degree only in the Revelation. The reason for this, no doubt, is that the translators were convinced that the Papacy was the persecuting power portrayed in that book, so that its exposition demanded plain and unfriendly references to Rome. Thus "the beast that cometh out of the bottomless pit" (Rev. 11 : 7) is "the Pope which hath his power out of hell and cometh thence"; and there are other comments in similar vein.

Like Whittingham's New Testament, the Geneva Bible is divided into verses (the Old Testament verses being taken over from the Hebrew Bible) and words which have no equivalent in the original text are printed in italics (the remainder being in Roman).

The expense of publishing the first edition of the Geneva Bible appears to have been borne by the English-speaking colony in Geneva, and in particular by John Bodley (father of Sir Thomas Bodley, founder of the Bodleian at Oxford). In 1561 Bodley obtained from Queen Elizabeth the exclusive right to print the Geneva Bible for a period of seven years, and in that year he printed a folio edition in Geneva (the first edition had been quarto). In all, some seventy editions of the Geneva Bible and thirty of the New Testament were published during Elizabeth's reign, most of them in England itself.[1] A revised edition of the Geneva New Testament was produced in 1576 by Lawrence Tomson, secretary to Sir Francis Walsingham (then Elizabeth's Secretary of State); this revision was often printed as the New Testament section of subsequent editions of the Geneva Bible. In 1579 a Scottish edition of the Geneva Bible was published—the first Bible ever to be printed in Scotland—"printed by Alexander Arbuthnot, Printer to the King's Majesty".

The Geneva Bible immediately won, and retained, widespread popularity. It became the household Bible of English-speaking Protestants. While its notes represented a more radical Reformed viewpoint than that favoured in the Elizabethan religious settlement, and it was never appointed to be used in the churches of England, its excellence as a translation was acknowledged even by those who disagreed with the theology of the translators. At the very time when Matthew Parker, Archbishop of Canterbury, was pressing ahead with a rival version, the Bishops' Bible, he thought so well of the Geneva Bible that he advocated a twelve years' extension of the exclusive right of printing it granted in 1561 to John Bodley. Even if he and his fellow-bishops were specially interested in the Bishops' Bible, he added, "yet should it nothing hinder but rather do much good to have diversity of translations and readings"—a remarkably enlightened opinion.

[1] None was printed in England before 1575.

In Scotland, the Geneva Bible was from the beginning the version appointed to be read in churches. The Church of Scotland was reformed in the same year as the Geneva Bible first appeared, and it was the most natural thing in the world that John Knox should prefer the version prepared by his friends and fellow-exiles at Geneva, whether or not he himself played a small part in its production. Even after the appearance of the Authorized Version in 1611, the Geneva Bible held its own for a considerable time in some parts of Scotland. In 1610 an Edinburgh printer named Andrew Hart issued an edition of the Geneva Bible, with Lawrence Tomson's revision of the New Testament, which continued to be used for fifty years. As late as 1674 it was reported that at Kintore, in Aberdeenshire, there was a Bible "for public reading in the church, but of the old translation, therefore it is recommended to cause provide one of the new translation." The "old translation" must have been the Geneva Bible, and the "new translation", of course, the A.V. And there is evidence that in the parish church of Crail, in Fife, a Geneva Bible was used even later than that.

The Geneva Bible was the Bible of Shakespeare. In the address from "The Translators to the Reader" which was prefaced to the A.V. of 1611, it is from the Geneva Bible that the Scripture quotations are taken. Nor did the publication of the A.V. bring about the immediate discontinuance of the use of the Geneva Bible in England. The *Soldier's Pocket Bible*, issued in 1643 for the use of Oliver Cromwell's army, consisted of a selection of extracts from the Geneva Bible. The following year saw the printing of the last edition of the Geneva Bible.

The Geneva Bible is popularly referred to as the "Breeches Bible", from the statement in Genesis 3 : 7 that Adam and Eve sewed fig leaves together and made themselves "breeches". This word had already been used here in the Wycliffite versions[1] and in the translation of the Pentateuch contained in Voragine's *Golden Legend*, printed by Caxton in 1483.

The Bishops' Bible

The instant success of the Geneva Bible made it impossible to go

---

[1] For its appearance in another fourteenth-century work, see p. 10.

on using the Great Bible for reading in church; its deficiencies became all too obvious in the light of the new version. The Geneva Bible might commend itself admirably for church use in Scotland, where the Reformation was profoundly influenced by Geneva, but it was unacceptable for this purpose in England, if only because the leaders in church and state, not to mention the queen herself, did not appreciate the outspoken Calvinism of its annotations.

What was to be done then? We remember how, in the reign of Henry VIII, a beginning was made with a scheme to prepare an English Bible under the direct supervision of the bishops of the Church of England. At that time the scheme came to nothing; as Cranmer put it, when he urged Thomas Cromwell to procure the royal licence for Matthew's Bible, the bishops would probably have their edition ready a day after doomsday. The scheme was now revived. In 1561 Archbishop Matthew Parker submitted to the bishops of his province a proposal for revising the Great Bible. Sections of the work were assigned to a number of bishops who were suitably qualified for it, and a few scholars who were not bishops[1] were also invited to participate, while Parker himself acted as editor-in-chief and prepared the revision for the press. He was himself a scholar with the necessary training and aptitude for work of this kind. In seven years the work was completed, and copies of the "Bishops' Bible", as this revision is called, were sent to the queen and to her chief minister, Sir William Cecil, on September 22, 1568. A list of the revisers and the sections which they had revised was enclosed; Parker had shown them this list in advance, "to make them more diligent, as answerable for their doings". Elizabeth and Cecil were both scholars in their own right, and would be capable of assessing the workmanship of the individual revisers. Indeed, Parker had invited Cecil to take some small part in the work, but that states-man declined the honour.

The directions given to the revisers were short and simple. They were to use the Great Bible as their basis, and depart from it only where it did not accurately represent the original. To check the accuracy of translations from the Hebrew they were to compare the Latin versions of the Old Testament made direct from the Hebrew

---

[1] They all became bishops in due course.

by Pagninus (1528) and Sebastian Münster (1539). (The Hebrew scholarship of the bishops and their colleagues could not compare with that of the Geneva translators.) They were to add no bitter or controversial annotations to the text; where a passage might be interpreted in the interests of one school or another, they were not to express any preference one way or the other (a timely and admirable direction). Passages containing genealogies "or other such places not edifying" were to be specially marked so that they could be left out in public reading. Expressions which, if read aloud, might be offensive to public taste were to be modified.

In 1571 the Convocation of Canterbury ordered that "every archbishop and bishop should have at his house a copy of the holy Bible of the largest volume as lately printed at London ... and that it should be placed in the hall or the large dining room, that it might be useful to their servants or to strangers", that a copy should also be procured by every cathedral and, as far as possible, by every church. To this extent it superseded the Great Bible as the authorized version of the Church of England, but it was never formally recognized by the queen, or given any preferential treatment by her. (Perhaps her scholarship was sufficiently objective to convince her that the Geneva Bible was the better translation of the two, whatever she thought of its accessories.)

Had the Geneva Bible never been produced, the Bishops' Bible would have been the best English Bible to appear thus far. But as it was, the Bishops' Bible started off with the insuperable disadvantage that there was a better version already in the field. Some nineteen editions were published between 1568 and 1606, and eleven separate editions of the New Testament—figures which, impressive as they are in comparison with those available for earlier versions, fall far short of those for the successive editions of the Geneva Bible in the same period. The second edition (1569) contains several corrections and alterations of the wording in the first; and the third edition (1572), while for the most part ignoring the corrections and alterations made in the second, contains a thorough revision of the New Testament text of the first, and it was this revised text that was reprinted in subsequent editions. In the 1572 edition the Psalter from the Great Bible was printed in parallel columns with the Psalter as translated for the Bishops' Bible, and in a number of later editions of the Bishops' Bible the Great Bible Psalter alone was printed. The Great Bible Psalter was, of course, the Psalter used in the Prayer Book services, and it would be awkward to use two different versions of the Psalms in church, one of which was so much less familiar than the other.

CHAPTER EIGHT

The King James Version

The Hampton Court Conference

WHEN ELIZABETH DIED, on March 24, 1603, the crown of England passed to James I, who had already worn the crown of Scotland for thirty-seven years as James VI. Some months after his coming to England, James summoned a conference of churchmen and theologians at Hampton Court "for the hearing, and for the determining, things pretended to be amiss in the Church". Nothing much came of the Hampton Court Conference (which was held in January 1604), except—and a notable exception it was—the resolution

> That a translation be made of the whole Bible, as consonant as can be to the original Hebrew and Greek; and this to be set out and printed, without any marginal notes, and only to be used in all Churches of England in time of divine service.

The proposal for a new translation came from Dr John Reynolds, President of Corpus Christi College, Oxford, a leader of the Puritan side in the Church of England, and one of the greatest scholars of his day. It did not meet with unanimous approval; Richard Bancroft, Bishop of London (soon to be Archbishop of Canterbury), complained that "if every man's humour were followed, there would be no end of translating." But it did meet with the approval of the man who mattered most; James seized eagerly upon the proposal. "I profess," he said, "I could never yet see a Bible well translated in English; but I think that, of all, that of Geneva is the worst. I wish some special pains were taken for an uniform translation, which should be done by the best-learned men in both Universities, then reviewed by the Bishops, presented to the Privy Council, lastly ratified by Royal authority, to be read in the whole Church, and none other."

It may be thought surprising that James, who was not deficient in scholarship, should stigmatize the Geneva version as the worst when in point of fact it was the best English translation of the Bible to have appeared thus far; but it is evident that it was not so much the translation as the accessories that he objected to. For when Bancroft urged that, if a new translation were to be undertaken, it should be without notes, James cordially agreed. He had seen, he said, among the notes annexed to the Geneva Bible some that were "very partial, untrue, seditious, and savouring too much of dangerous and traitorous conceits." He instanced two which have been mentioned above: that on Exodus 1 : 19 which suggested that the Hebrew midwives were right to disobey the Egyptian king's orders, and that on 2 Chronicles 15 : 16, which stated that King Asa's mother should have been executed, and not merely deposed, for her idolatry—it is supposed that James's suspicious mind thought that this might react unfavourably upon the memory of his own mother, Mary Queen of Scots.

In any case, the stipulation that the new version should have no such annotations was a most praiseworthy one. No one would reasonably object to notes intended to make the sense plainer, and indeed notes of this kind were provided in the new version; but notes reflecting sectional points of view in theology or church polity could only limit the usefulness of a version intended for all the English people. It was the notes in the Geneva Bible, rather than the actual text, that made it unacceptable to so many of the leaders in church and state early in Elizabeth's reign, and led to the production of the rival Bishops' Bible. If the new version was to supersede both the Geneva and Bishops' versions; if it was to be used both as the Church's Bible and as the people's Bible; if it was to commend itself to all schools of thought, then it must not include features that would gratuitously offend any one group of readers.

The Organization of the Work

King James himself took a leading part in organizing the work of translation. Six panels of translators (forty-seven men in all) had the work divided up between them; the Old Testament was entrusted to three panels, the New Testament to two, and the Apocrypha to one. Two of the panels met at Oxford, two at Cambridge, and two at Westminster. When the panels had completed their task, the draft translation of the whole Bible was reviewed by a smaller group of twelve men, two from each panel, and then the work was sent to the printer. Miles Smith, Canon of Hereford (later to be Bishop of Gloucester), and Thomas Bilson, Bishop of Winchester, saw it through the press, and Miles Smith composed the informative preface, "The Translators to the Reader".

The forty-seven men included most of the leading biblical scholars in England. They received very little in the way of financial consideration during their labours (neither King nor Parliament had much money to spare), but those who were not already incumbents of remunerative livings were not forgotten when these fell vacant.

The rules which guided them in their work were sanctioned, if they were not indeed drawn up, by James himself. The Bishops' Bible was to serve as the basis for the new translation. The names of Bible characters were to correspond as closely as possible to the forms in common use. The Geneva and Bishops' Bibles, in the Old Testament at any rate, had endeavoured to make proper names correspond closely to the Hebrew forms; thus "Isaac" appears in Geneva as *Izhák* and in the Bishops' Bible as *Isahac*. The new version reverted to common usage in this matter; but it did not attempt to maintain uniformity as between the Old Testament and the New. Thus the name which appears as Elijah in the Old Testament appears as Elias in the New, and it is particularly unhelpful to have Joshua twice referred to as "Jesus" in the New Testament (Acts 7 : 45; Hebrews 4 : 8), where some of the earlier English versions had properly put "Joshua".

It was further laid down that the old ecclesiastical words were to be kept ("church" and not "congregation", for example). Marginal notes were to be used only to explain Hebrew and Greek words, and to draw attention to parallel passages. Words necessary to complete the sense were to be printed in distinctive type. The existing chapter and verse divisions were to be retained; new headings were to be supplied for the chapters. This last provision did, of course, leave room for controversial matter, but the chapter headings actually provided were not such as to cause deep cleavages of opinion among English churchmen of that day. In most books the chapter headings are strictly factual, but in the poetical and prophetic books of the Old Testament they contain a good deal of theological exegesis. Thus, Psalm 93 is entitled "The majesty, power and holiness of Christ's kingdom"; all the mutual professions of love in the Song of Songs are declared to be exchanges between the Church and Christ; Isaiah 51 is said to contain "an exhortation after the pattern of Abraham to trust in Christ, by reason of his comfortable promises, of his righteous salvation, and man's mortality." But these were not issues that divided Bible readers in the seventeenth century.

The publication of the work

When at last the new version was published, it bore the title:

> The Holy Bible, Conteyning the Old Testament and the New: Newly Translated out of the Originall tongues, with the former Translations diligently compared and revised, by his Majesties speciall commandement. Appointed to be read in Churches. Imprinted at London by Robert Barker, Printer to the Kings most Excellent Majestie. Anno Dom. 1611.

The New Testament bore the separate title:

> The New Testament of our Lord and Savior Jesus Christ, Newly translated out of the Originall Greeke; and with the former Translations diligently compared and revised, by His Majesties speciall Commandement. Imprinted at London by Robert Barker, Printer to the Kings most Excellent Majestie. Anno Dom. 1611. cum Privilegio.

The 1611 version is commonly called the Authorized Version. If it be asked by what body its authorization was effected, the answer is best given in the words of Lord Chancellor Selborne, in the correspondence columns of *The Times* for June 3, 1881: "nothing is more probable than that this may have been done by Order in Council. If so, the authentic record of that order may be lost, because all the

Council books and registers from the year 1600 to 1613 inclusive were destroyed by a fire at Whitehall on the 12th of January, 1618 (O.S.)." The words "Appointed to be read in Churches" indicated the intention that henceforth the new version should supersede the Bishops' Bible in the services of the Church, as the Bishops' Bible had previously superseded the Great Bible.

In America the 1611 version is more commonly referred to as the "King James Version" (KJV)—a designation which is historically justified by the active part taken by King James in organizing the translation and sealing the finished product with his approval; although it is said that some people who speak of the "King James Version" imagine that he was the translator, if not indeed the original author.

Dedication to the King

The translators' dedication of their work "to the most high and mighty prince James" is well known, since it continues to be printed in the forefront of most British editions of the A.V. King James must have found the flattering terminology used towards him by his English churchmen a pleasant change from the homely language of some of his Scottish churchmen, like Andrew Melville, who plucked him by the sleeve, called him "God's silly vassal", and reminded him that although he was king in the kingdom of Scotland he was only an ordinary member in the kingdom of Christ! The translators express their pleasure at James's active interest in the translation of Holy Writ, and their hope that what they have done in this line may win his approval. No doubt, they say, they will be attacked by extremists from right and left—"traduced by Popish Persons at home or abroad, who therefore will malign us, because we are poor instruments to make God's holy Truth to be yet more and more known unto the people, whom they desire still to keep in ignorance and darkness; or ... maligned by selfconceited Brethren, who run their own ways, and give liking unto nothing, but what is framed by themselves, and hammered on their anvil." But they need not be over-concerned about such attacks, seeing they are supported by their own good conscience regarding their work and by the king's grace and favour.

The Translators to the Reader

Much more interesting is the lengthy preface, "The Translators to the Reader", which unfortunately is printed nowadays only in very few editions of the A.V. This preface begins, in a leisurely and learned fashion, by justifying the principle of Bible translation; it then goes on to declare the necessity for this new translation. No discredit, the translators insist, is intended to the memory of their predecessors, who gave the English people the Bible in their own tongue under the Tudor monarchs. Those predecessors laid a good foundation, apart from which it would not have been possible to erect such a superstructure as is now presented to the reader. To those who question the necessity of this latest work, they answer that they have obeyed the king's commandment. "And what can the King command to be done, that will bring him more true honour than this?" People ought to thank God for a ruler who takes such great interest in his people's spiritual welfare rather than cavil and criticize. To those who point out defects in their work, they answer that perfection is never attainable by man, but the word of God may be recognized in the very meanest translation of the Bible, just as the king's speech addressed to Parliament remains the king's speech when translated into other languages than that in which it was spoken, even if it be not translated word for word, and even if some of the renderings are capable of improvement. To those who complain that they have introduced so many changes in relation to the older English version, they answer by expressing surprise that revision and correction should be imputed as faults. The whole history of Bible translation in any language, they say, is a history of repeated revision and correction.

After dealing at some length with their critics, they state the principles on which they have worked.

Truly, good Christian Reader, we never thought from the beginning that we should need to make a new translation, nor yet to make of a bad one a good one; ... but to make a good one better, or out of many good ones one principal good one, not justly to be excepted against; that hath been our endeavour, that our mark. To that purpose there were many chosen, that were greater in other men's eyes than in their own, and that sought the truth rather than their own praise.[1] ... And in what sort did these assemble? In the trust of their own knowledge, or of their sharpness of wit, or decpness of judgment, as it were in an arm of flesh? At no hand. They trusted in him that hath the key of David, opening, and no man shutting; they prayed to the Lord, the Father of our Lord, to the effect that St. Augustine did: "O let thy Scriptures be my pure delight; let me not be deceived in them, neither let me deceive by them." In this confidence, and with this devotion, did they assemble together; not too many, lest one should trouble another; and yet many, lest many things haply might escape them. If you ask what they had before them, truly it was the Hebrew text of the Old Testament, the Greek of the New. ... These tongues ... we set before us to translate, being the tongues wherein God was pleased to speak to his Church by his Prophets and Apostles. Neither did we run over the work with that posting haste that the Septuagint did, if that be true which is reported of them. ... The work hath not been huddled up in seventy two days, but hath cost the workmen, as light as it seemeth, the pains of twice seven times seventy two days, and more. Matters of such weight and consequence are to be speeded with maturity: for in a business of moment a man feareth not the blame of convenient slackness. Neither did we think much to consult the translators or commentators, Chaldee, Hebrew, Syrian, Greek, or Latin; no, nor the Spanish, French, Italian, or Dutch; neither did we disdain to revise that which we had done, and to bring back to the anvil that which we had hammered: but having and using as great helps as were needful, and fearing no reproach for slowness, nor coveting praise for expedition, we have at length, through the good hand of the Lord upon us, brought the work to that pass that you see.

They mention that some readers have misgivings about the alternative renderings suggested in the margin, on the ground that they may appear to shake the authority of Scripture in deciding

[1] If the translators appear here to be guilty of unseemly self-commendation, let it be remembered that these words are actually the words of Miles Smith speaking of his colleagues.

points of controversy. This obscurantist objection has been urged against other Bible versions, of much more recent date; some people would prefer a false appearance of certainty to an honest admission of doubt. The translators do not wish to exaggerate their competence in the biblical languages.

> There be many words in the Scriptures, which be never found there but once (having neither brother nor neighbour, as the Hebrews speak), so that we cannot be holpen by conference of places. Again, there be many rare names of certain birds, beasts, and precious stones, etc., concerning which the Hebrews themselves are so divided among themselves for judgment, that they may seem to have defined this or that, rather because they would say something, than because they were sure of that which they said.

This is an important point; our understanding of the Hebrew vocabulary, especially in regard to such terms as are indicated by the A.V. translators, has been gradually increasing over the generations, and has received much welcome illumination in fairly recent times. The R.V. reflects fuller knowledge in this field than the A.V.; the R.S.V. represents an advance on the R.V.; and the New English Bible will be found to have profited greatly by recent advances in Semitic philology, but even the New English Bible makes no pretence of having attained finality. Where, then, there is doubt about the meaning of a word or phrase, is it not better to warn the reader that this is so? And what is true of uncertainties in translation applies with equal force to variant readings in the manuscripts and other authorities for the text. This too the A.V. translators point out when they criticize Pope Sixtus V for his ruling that no variant readings should be put in the margin of his edition of the Latin Vulgate. "They that are wise had rather have their judgments at liberty in differences of readings, than to be captivated to one, when it might be the other."

Another feature of their work to which the translators draw the reader's attention is their deliberate employment of a variety of English synonyms to represent the same terms in the original text.

Another thing we think good to admonish thee of, gentle Reader, that we have not tied ourselves to an uniformity of phrasing, or to an identity of words, as some peradventure would wish that we had done, because they observe, that some learned men somewhere have been as exact as they could that way. Truly, that we might not vary from the sense of that which we had translated before, if the word signified the same thing in both places (for there be some words that be not of the same sense every where), we were especially careful, and made a conscience according to our duty. But that we should express the same notion in the same particular word; as for example, if we translate the Hebrew or Greek word once by *purpose*, never to call it *intent*; if one where *journeying*, never *travelling*; if one where *think*, never *suppose*; if one where *pain*, never *ache*; if one where *joy*, never *gladness*, etc., thus to mince the matter, we thought to savour more of curiosity than wisdom, and that rather it would breed scorn in the atheist, than bring profit to the godly reader. For is the kingdom of God become words or syllables? Why should we be in bondage to them, if we may be free? use one precisely, when we may use another no less fit as commodiously? ... We might also be charged (by scoffers) with some unequal dealing towards a great number of good English words. For as it is written of a certain great Philosopher, that he should say, that those logs were happy that were made images to be worshipped; for their fellows, as good as they, lay for blocks behind the fire: so if we should say, as it were, unto certain words, Stand up higher, have a place in the Bible always; and to others of like quality, Get you hence, be banished for ever; we might be taxed peradventure with St. James's words, namely, "To be partial in ourselves, and judges of evil thoughts." Add hereunto, that niceness in words was always counted the next step to trifling; and so was to be curious about names too: also that we cannot follow a better pattern for elocution than God himself; therefore he using divers words in his holy writ, and indifferently for one thing in nature: we, if we will not be superstitious, may use the same liberty in our English versions out of Hebrew and Greek, for that copy or store that he hath given us.

An example of their procedure in this matter is provided in the opening verses of the fifth chapter of Romans. Where the A.V. says, "we ... *rejoice* in hope of the glory of God" (verse 2), "we *glory* in tribulations" (verse 3), and "we also *joy* in God" (verse 11), the italicized verbs represent one and the same Greek verb. The R.V. renders all three occurrences by "rejoice". If the aim of translation should be the production of the same effect in the reader of the translation as the original wording produced in the reader of the original text, then there is much to be said in a passage like this for translating the same original word by the same word in English; for a good part of the effect intended by the original writer was produced by his deliberate repetition of one and the same word. Certainly the translator must not be peremptorily debarred from the skilful and appropriate choice of the right synonym in the right context, but there are times when the recurrence of the same word is exactly what is required. The English language, for example, has a considerable range of words more or less synonymous with "horse"; but it is the repetition of "horse" that makes Richard III's cry so effective: "A horse! a horse! my kingdom for a horse!" Let the reader replace the second and third occurrences of "horse" by two other words with much the same meaning, and realize how inept the result is. It is probably right to say that the A.V. has gone too far in its love of variation, whereas the R.V. runs to the opposite extreme. The preface then goes on:

Lastly, we have on the one side avoided the scrupulosity of the Puritans, who leave the old Ecclesiastical words, and betake them to other, as when they put *washing* for *baptism*, and *congregation* instead of *Church*; as also on the other side we have shunned the obscurity of the Papists, in their *azymes*, *tunike*, *rational*, *holocausts*, *prepuce*, *pasche*, and a number of such like, whereof their late translation is full, and that of purpose to darken the sense, that since they must needs translate the Bible, yet by the language thereof it may be kept from being understood. But we desire that the Scripture may speak like itself, as in the language of Canaan, that it may be understood even of the very vulgar.

The reference to the Puritan preference for "non-ecclesiastical"

terms reminds us of More's criticism of Tyndale. The "late translation" of the "Papists" is the Rheims New Testament of 1582, which
we shall look at in our next chapter. Some of its vocabulary was
highly latinate, and it is on this that the preface makes such severe
comment. But of the six words which it quotes as samples, three
("tunics", "rational" and "holocausts") have passed into common
currency. The Old Testament companion to the Rheims New
Testament—the Douai Old Testament—was not published until
1609 and 1610, too late for the A.V. translators to make its acquaintance effectively.

The translators evidently worked with a proper sense of responsibility; it was no light thing in their eyes to handle the sacred scriptures as translators must. But they conclude their preface by pleading
for an equal sense of responsibility in their readers.

It is a fearful thing to fall into the hands of the living God; but
a blessed thing it is, and will bring us to everlasting blessedness in
the end, when God speaketh unto us, to hearken; when he setteth
his word before us, to read it; when he stretcheth out his hand and
calleth, to answer, Here am I, here we are to do thy will, O God.
The Lord work a care and conscience in us to know him and
serve him that we may be acknowledged of him at the appearing
of our Lord JESUS CHRIST, to whom with the Holy Ghost be all
praise and thanksgiving. Amen.

The quality of their work needs no commendation from anyone
at this time of day; three hundred and fifty years have gone by since
they completed their task, and to-day their version is still used in
preference to any other in many areas of English-speaking Protestantism. Quite apart from its formal authorization, its intrinsic
superiority over the versions that went before it soon made itself felt,
and in a very short time it established itself as the version for church
and home, for public and private use, superseding the Bishops' Bible
and the Geneva Bible alike.

Hugh Broughton on the A.V.

It would have been surprising, however, if no censorious voice
had been raised against it. The new version did not lack critics, but

none was more forthright in his root-and-branch condemnation of it than Dr Hugh Broughton, a distinguished scholar described eloquently by his fellow-scholar John Lightfoot as "the Great Albionean Divine, renowned in many Nations for Rare Skill in Salems and Athens Tongues and Familiar Acquaintance with all Rabbinical Learning". For all his erudition, Broughton was not included among the revisers; he was not cut out for collaboration with others, and would have proved an impossible colleague. Probably he resented the fact that he was not invited to serve, and when the new version appeared, he sent a critique of it to one of the king's attendants:

> The late Bible ... was sent to me to censure: which bred in me a sadness that will grieve me while I breathe, it is so ill done. Tell His Majesty that I had rather be rent in pieces with wild horses, than any such translation by my consent should be urged upon poor churches. ... The new edition crosseth me. I require it to be burnt.

Broughton had for thirty years been preparing a revision of his own, based on the Geneva Bible, which to his mind was the best existing English version. For the Bishops' Bible, on the other hand, he could find nothing good to say. "The cockles of the sea shores," he declared, "and the leaves of the forest, and the grains of the poppy, may as well be numbered as the gross errors of this Bible, disgracing the ground of our own hope"; and he thought that it "might well give place to the Alkoran, pestred with lies". He did not live long enough to publish his revision of Geneva, for he died in 1612, at the age of sixty-three, confident to the last in the supremacy of his own learning: "I will suffer no scholar in the world to cross me in Hebrew and Greek, when I am sure I have the truth."

Successive editions

The Authorized Version took no harm from his fiery outburst against it. Three editions appeared in quick succession in the year of publication. These were folio editions, measuring 16 by 10½ inches. The earliest is known as "the great HE edition" and the other two as "the great SHE editions", because the first renders the closing words of Ruth 3 : 15 "and he went into the city", whereas the others have "and she went into the city" (the Hebrew manuscripts themselves are divided between "he" and "she"). Quarto and octavo editions were published in 1612.

The heavy punctuation of the A.V. was designed to guide public readers of the Bible in church to enunciate properly and to place the emphasis in the right places. Paragraph marks (¶) indicated the beginning of each paragraph up to Acts 20 : 36, but none appear after that point. Why this should be is not at all certain. Some correspondence on the subject was published in *John o' London's Weekly* on September 28 and October 19, 1951. In the former issue John Stirling, editor of *The Bible for Today*, suggested that after Acts 20 : 36 "perhaps the printer ran out of these signs! It certainly looks, judging from the way he missed occasional references in the immediately preceding chapters, as though he were running short of them; and as there were not many more pages to set up it was, perhaps, hardly worth while making any more. Who knows?" To this suggestion the latter issue carried a reply from T. J. Tudge: "That suggestion implies that the type for the whole book was set up before printing, as is the practice to-day, but stocks of the hand-cast type then used were so small that usually only four pages were set up and printed, the type being then distributed in order to set up the next four, and so on throughout; therefore the long-suffering printer would have just as many para. marks for the end as for the start of the Bible." Perhaps no more appeared in the master copy.

There are quite a number of misprints and variations in wording and spelling in the early editions. One original misprint has been perpetuated in editions of the A.V. to the present time: "strain at a gnat" instead of "strain *out* a gnat" in Matt. 23 : 24. The first edition had, in Mark 10 : 18, "There is no man good, but one, *that is* God"; later editions have changed "no man" to the more appropriate "none". But of all the misprints that the A.V. has suffered from, none has been so scandalous as the omission of the word "not" from the Seventh Commandment in an edition of 1631, for which the King's printers were fined £300 by Archbishop Laud. The offending edition was commonly known as the "Wicked Bible". An Oxford edition of 1717 was known as the "Vinegar Bible" because the chapter-heading to Luke 20 had "Vinegar" for "Vineyard" in the title "The Parable of the Vineyard". The "Murderers' Bible" (Oxford, 1795) was so called because Mark 7 : 27 was made to read: "Let the children first be killed" ("killed" instead of "filled"). Other outstanding misprints were "he slew two lions like men" (2 Sam. 23 : 20, for "... lionlike men") and "the dogs liked (for 'licked up') his blood" (1 Kings 22 : 38). The moral of all this was pointed most effectually by the careless typesetter who made Psalm 119 : 161 read : "Printers have persecuted me without a cause"!

In the course of time the spelling of the earliest editions of the A.V. was modified and modernized; sometimes it still looks archaic (e.g. "marishes" in Ezek. 47: 11, "plaister" in Dan. 5: 5; "your's" in Luke 6: 20, "musick" in Luke 15 : 25), but a comparison with early editions will show how it has been kept up-to-date. The chapter summaries have been reduced in the course of successive editions; the marginal references have been expanded. All this has been brought about piecemeal by private enterprise. In 1701 dates were introduced into the margin, at the instance of Bishop Lloyd; these were based in the main on the calculations of Archbishop Ussher.

Prose Rhythms

The A.V. was admirably suited for public reading. A study of its prose rhythms suggests that the men responsible for it (not only King James's revisers but their predecessors as far back as Tyndale) had an instinctive feeling for good style.[1] If preachers, orators and writers would spend a little time noting the rhythms of the early English Bible, they would grow discontented with the sentences that please them now. Consider, for instance, the effect of the long row of anapaests (short short long) in Isa. 53 : 1: "Who / hath believed / our report, / and to whom / is the arm / of the Lord / revealed?" The last word, "revealed", was possibly pronounced as an amphibrach (short long short). The initial "Who" serves as an anacrusis or "striking-up" syllable. Or consider the change from iambus (short long) to anapaest in Psalm 136 : 8: "the sun / to rule / by day; / for his me/rcy endu/reth for e/ver." Another example of the use of anapaests comes in Deut. 32 : 2: "My doc/trine shall drop / as the

[1] Cf. Lane Cooper, *Certain Rhythms in the English Bible* (Cornell University Press, 1952).

rain, / my speech / shall distil / as the dew." Observe, too, the use of cretic feet (long short long) in the translation of James 1 : 19, "Swift to hear, / slow to speak, / slow to wrath," and the combination of dactyls (long short short) and spondees (long long) which occasionally produces something like the hexameter verse of Greek and Latin poetry: "Bind their / kings with / chains, and their / nobles with / fetters of / iron" (Psalm 149 : 8); "How art thou / fallen from / heaven, O / Lucifer, / son of the / morning!" (Isa. 14 : 12); "Husbands, / love your / wives, and / be not / bitter a/gainst them" (Col. 3 : 19).

Prose rhythms do not obtrude themselves on the notice of readers or hearers, but they make a powerful impression none the less. Harsh combinations of sounds or accents, on the other hand, produce a sense of distaste. "Take care of the sense, and the sounds will take care of themselves" is not such an infallible rule as the duchess in *Alice* imagined; it was to a considerable extent the failure of the men who produced the R.V. in the 1880's to consider the sounds as well as the sense that prevented their work from attaining anything like the popularity enjoyed by the A.V.

The Long Parliament

A few attempts were made later in the seventeenth century to revise the A.V. or produce a fresh translation, but nothing came of them. The Long Parliament in the reign of Charles I set up a commission to consider what might be done in the matter, but no further action was taken.

The A.V. of the Apocrypha

Like its predecessors, the A.V. included a translation of the Apocrypha. Four years later Archbishop Abbot forbade anyone to issue the Bible without the Apocrypha, on pain of one year's imprisonment. The Church of England, in accordance with Article VI, reads the books of the Apocrypha "for example of life and instruction of manners; but yet doth it not apply them to establish any doctrine." The Puritan party, however, and those who took their guidance from Geneva rather than from Canterbury, disapproved of the inclusion of the Apocrypha in the Bible at all. Some copies of the Geneva Bible published at Geneva in 1599 omitted the Apocrypha, but this omission was the binder's work; there is a gap in the page-numbering between the Testaments.[1] An Amsterdam edition of the Geneva Bible,[2] published in 1640, omitted the Apocrypha as a matter of policy, and inserted a defence of this policy between the Testaments. In 1644 the Long Parliament, in which Puritan views were very influential, decreed that only the canonical books of the Old Testament should be read in church, and three years later the *Westminster Confession of Faith* declared that "the books commonly called Apocrypha, not being of divine inspiration, are not part of the canon of the Scripture; and therefore are of no authority in the Church of God, nor to be any otherwise approved, or made use of, than other human writings."

This policy prevailed in the Church of Scotland, but was reversed in the Church of England after the Restoration. The Nonconformists, however, continued for the most part to disregard the Apocrypha except for the historical value of the books. It is not without significance that the first English Bible printed in America (1782–3) omitted the Apocrypha.[3] The fashion of printing the A.V. without the Apocrypha was reinforced by the example of the British and Foreign Bible Society (founded in 1804), which in 1826 adopted the policy of omitting the Apocrypha from its editions. It is said that, when this Society offered to provide the copy of the Bible to be presented to King Edward VII at his coronation in 1902, the offer was declined by Archbishop Frederick Temple on the ground that a "mutilated Bible" was unacceptable.

Necessity of revision

For all its merits, the A.V. could not be expected to remain unchallenged for ever. Apart from gradual changes in English usage, which have made its language seem increasingly remote and archaic

---

[1] I have a Cambridge edition of the A.V. dated 1630 which lacks the Apocrypha, but this too is a matter of binding, since the O.T. ends on p. 590 and the N.T. starts on p. 731. There is some evidence, however, that the volume has been rebound.

[2] The last edition of the Geneva Bible appeared in 1644.

[3] The first Bible printed in America was John Eliot's Algonquin version published at Cambridge, Massachusetts—the N.T. in 1661, followed by the O.T. in 1663. The first Bible printed in a European language in America was a German Bible published at Germantown, Pennsylvania, in 1743; it did include the Apocrypha.

to many people to-day who have not the literary equipment to appreciate it, the advances which have taken place during the past three and a half centuries in knowledge of the original languages and text of the Bible have made its revision imperative. Yet it is well recognized that, throughout the English-speaking world, there are hundreds of thousands of readers by whom this version is accepted as "The Word of God" in a sense in which no other version would be so accepted. Such an attitude towards what is but one among many available translations may be open to criticism, but its persistence is a tribute to the sound workmanship of the men to whom we owe the version of 1611.

NOTE. John Bois (or Boys), Fellow of St. John's College, Cambridge, served as one of the translators from 1604 to 1608 and later as a member of the committee which reviewed the whole work and delivered the one approved master copy to the printers. He was the only member of this committee to take notes, and he provided in his will for their safe keeping after his death (1643). They are now in the Library of Corpus Christi College, Oxford. An edition of them by Dr. Ward Allen, Associate Professor of English at Auburn University, Alabama, accompanied by a facsimile of the original, has recently (September 1969) been published by Vanderbilt University Press, Nashville, Tennessee.

CHAPTER NINE

The English Bible for Roman Catholics

THERE WERE, until 1965, two versions of the Bible in English approved by ecclesiastical authority for Roman Catholic readers in Britain. One of these was what we commonly refer to as the "Douai Bible" (very often the older spelling "Douay" is used); the other was the version made in our own day by the late Mgr Ronald A. Knox. For both of these the Latin Vulgate has served as the basis, rather than the Hebrew and Greek texts, although Mgr Knox's version in particular has kept the Hebrew and Greek texts in view throughout. The reason for using the Latin Vulgate as the basis for these authorized versions was that the Council of Trent in 1546 laid it down that this "ancient and vulgate version, which is approved by the long use of so many centuries in the Church herself, be held as authentic in public lectures, disputations, sermons and expository discourses, and that no one may make bold or presume to reject it on any pretext." In respect of their Latin basis, then, the Douai and Knox versions may be said to follow in the Wycliffite tradition of the English Bible, whereas the Protestant versions for the most part have followed in the tradition established by Tyndale.

The Douai Bible

When we call the older Roman Catholic version the Douai Bible, we are simplifying the situation considerably. What is usually called the Douai Bible is really a very thorough revision carried through in 1749 by Bishop Richard Challoner of a translation made a century and a half previously by one Gregory Martin, a member of the English College at Douai, in northern France.

If one group of exiles embarked on the work of Bible translation into English in Mary's reign, another group of exiles undertook a similar task in Elizabeth's reign.

William Allen, sometime Fellow of Oriel College, Oxford, refused to acquiesce in the Elizabethan religious settlement and settled in Flanders, where in 1568 he founded the English College at Douai, for the maintenance of the Roman Catholic cause. The college was moved to Rheims in 1578, where it was governed by another Oxford scholar, Richard Bristow, sometime Fellow of Exeter College. Allen later left Flanders for Rome, where he founded another English College, and in due course became a Cardinal. In 1593 the earlier college moved back from Rheims to Douai.

During the years that the college had its headquarters in Rheims one of its most distinguished professors, Gregory Martin (formerly Scholar of St John's College, Oxford), translated the Bible from the Latin Vulgate into English for the benefit of English-speaking adherents of the old religion. He translated the Old Testament first and then the New; his New Testament translation, however, was published first, in 1582, while the College was still at Rheims (whence it is properly known as the Rheims New Testament), but his Old Testament translation was not published until 1609–10, after the return of the College to Douai (whence it is properly called the Douai Old Testament). He is said to have carried through his work of translation systematically, at the rate of two chapters a day, and as each section was completed it was revised by his colleagues Allen and Bristow.

Principles of Translation

The preface to the Rheims New Testament asserts that this work has been rendered necessary by the circulation of many "false translations" by Protestants, who have corrupted the truth of Holy Writ, "adding, detracting, altering, transposing, pointing, and all other guileful means: specially where it serveth for the advantage of their private opinions." The use of the Latin version rather than the Greek original as the base of the new translation is defended and so is the retention of Latin or latinate terms in the English text. The translator and his colleagues explain their practice thus:

In this our translation, because we wish it to be most sincere, as becometh a Catholic translation, and have endeavoured so to make it: we are very precise and religious in following our copy, the old vulgar approved Latin: not only in sense, which we hope we always do, but sometimes in the very words also and phrases, which may seem to the vulgar reader and to common English ears not yet acquainted therewith, rudeness or ignorance. ... Moreover we presume not in hard places to mollify the speeches or phrases, but religiously keep them word for word, and point for point, for fear of missing, or restraining the sense of the Holy Ghost to our fantasy, as Eph. vi. 12, "Against the spirituals of wickedness in the celestials" ... We add the Latin word sometimes in the margin, when either we cannot fully express it, or when the reader might think it cannot be as we translate.

And they conclude:

Thus we have endeavoured by all means, to satisfy the indifferent reader, and to help his understanding every way, both in the text, and by annotations: and withal to deal most sincerely before God and man, in translating and expounding the most sacred text of the holy Testament.

The statement that they do not presume "in hard places to mollify the speeches or phrases, but religiously keep them word for word", may be illustrated by a few simple examples. In Heb. 13 : 4 the A.V. reads "Marriage *is* honourable in all", whereas the R.V. reads "*Let* marriage *be* had in honour among all". The verb "to be" must be supplied, as its presence is not required either in the Greek original or in the Latin Vulgate. But the supplying even of such a simple verb as this calls for a measure of interpretation. Should the verb be supplied in the indicative or in the imperative mood? Is the writer stating a fact or laying down the law? The A.V. prefers the former alternative, the R.V. the latter. Gregory Martin refuses to be impaled on either horn of this dilemma: "Mariage honorable in all", he says, translating the Latin literally, and if it be objected that his rendering is not English, so much the worse for the English!

Again, in the story of the changing of the water into wine, A.V. and R.V. make our Lord say to His Mother, "Woman, what have I to do with thee?" whereas R.S.V. renders His words: "O woman, what have you to do with me?" (John 2 : 4). These are two possible alternative renderings of the original idiomatic wording, found in Greek and Latin alike, of which a literal translation would be "What to me and to thee, woman?" This, incidentally, is the precise wording of the Wycliffite version. Gregory Martin compromises here to the extent of supplying the verb "to be"; his version reads: "What is to me and thee woman?"—which, whatever it is, is not English. In the eighteenth century, when Bishop Challoner revised the Douai-Rheims version, he saw that Martin's rendering would not stand here, so he changed it to "Woman, what is it to me and to thee?"—which is good English, but unfortunately is just not what our Lord said. What He did say is admirably expressed in R. A. Knox's version: "Nay, woman, why dost thou trouble me with that?"

The Old Testament

In the Old Testament the opening words of Isaiah's vineyard song are strangely unintelligible: "A vineyard was made to my beloved in horn, the son of oil" (Isa. 5 : 1)—but that is because Jerome translated a Hebrew idiom over-literally into Latin, and his Latin was followed over-faithfully by Gregory Martin. "Horn" is a metaphorical term for "hill", and "son of oil" means "fertile" or "abundant"; hence the A.V. gives the true sense when it says: "My wellbeloved hath a vineyard in a very fruitful hill."

In all the Douai Old Testament it is the Psalter that contains the highest proportion of unintelligible expressions, but that is because the Latin edition of the Psalter which Martin translated was not Jerome's version from the Hebrew, but one of the versions which he made from the Greek Septuagint—the Gallican Psalter, which was the version chiefly used in the services of the Church. The Douai Psalter is thus a translation of a translation of a translation. In Psalm 68 : 12 (67 : 13 in the Vulgate and Douai numbering) the Hebrew text is reasonably well represented by the A.V., "Kings of armies did flee apace: and she that tarried at home divided the spoil". But the Douai rendering is not only widely divergent from this, but is meaningless as it stands: "The king of hoastes the beloved of the beloved; and to the beauty of the house, to divide the spoils". The error, however, is primarily due to the Septuagint translators; that is how they misrendered the Hebrew, and their misrendering was reproduced in the Gallican Psalter and thence in the Douai Old Testament. Challoner's revision of the Douai rendering could make but little improvement here: "The king of powers is of the beloved, of the beloved; and the beauty of the house shall divide spoils"—for he was still tied to the Gallican Psalter. When Mgr Knox, in his turn, had to see what he could make of the Gallican Psalter here, he produced, as might be expected, something that was good English, but something which inevitably bore little relation to the Psalmist's meaning and not very much to the construction of the Gallican Psalter. He tied the verse in question closely to the preceding one, and rendered the two as follows: "Here are bringers of good news, with a message the Lord has given them, from the army he leads; a king, leading the armies of a beloved people; a people how well beloved! He bids the favourites of his court divide the spoil between them." But in addition to his version of the Gallican Psalter, Knox appended to the first edition of his Old Testament translation a version of a new Latin Psalter based directly on the Hebrew,[1] and in this version the verse is rendered: "Routed the kings, routed their armies; they have left their spoils for housewives to carry away"— which gives much the same sense as the A.V.

Latinisms in the Douai Bible

Another feature of the Douai-Rheims version to which the editors draw attention is its preference for the traditional ecclesiastical terms, derived from Latin, over alternative renderings which, even if they were homely English expressions, had not the same religious associations in the sixteenth century as some of them have subsequently acquired. Where no theological associations were involved, Martin's English could be as "racy of the soil" as Tyndale's, and occasionally more so; thus in the story of Peter's escape from prison, when he arrives at the house of Mary, the Rheims version goes on: "And when he knocked at the doore of the gate, there came

[1] This new Latin Psalter, prepared by members of the Pontifical Biblical Institute, was published in 1945 and approved by Pope Pius XII for liturgical use as an alternative to the Gallican Psalter.

forth a wenche to see, named Rhodè" (here Tyndale and the Protestant versions generally, following Wycliffe, call Rhoda a "damozel"
or "damsel"). But in general the vocabulary of the Douai-Rheims
version is highly latinate (although not so latinate as Stephen
Gardiner's draft of 1542). Here, for example, is the Lord's Prayer
according to Matt. 6 : 9–13:

> OVR FATHER which art in heauen, sanctified be thy name. Let
> thy Kingdom come. Thy wil be done, as in heauen, in earth also.
> Giue vs to day our supersubstantial bread. And forgiue vs our
> dettes, as we also forgiue our detters. And leade vs not into tenta-
> tion. But deliuer vs from euil. Amen.

Here we note that Rheims uses "sanctified" where English-speaking
Protestants use the native English "hallowed"; but it is a matter of
no importance which of these synonyms is used. But what is the
"supersubstantial" bread for which God is asked? The word goes
back to Jerome, who used (and possibly coined) the Latin *super-
substantialis* to represent the Greek *epiousios*, because of what appears
to have been a mistaken idea of the etymology of the Greek word.
In the light of papyrus evidence, Jesus should be understood as
teaching His disciples to pray for (and to be content with) a day's
ration of bread at a time; but "supersubstantial" bread can only be
supernatural bread, that is to say Christ Himself, as the bread of life.
It is indeed a good thing to pray to be satisfied with the living bread,
but this was probably not the intention of this petition in the Lord's
Prayer.

The parable of the Good Samaritan is told thus in the Rheims
version:

> A certaine man went downe from Hierusalem into Iericho, and
> fel among theeues, who also spoiled him, and giuing him woundes
> went away leauing him halfe-dead. And it chaunced that a
> certaine Priest went downe the same way: and seeing him, passed
> by. In like maner also a Leuite, when he was neere the place, and
> saw him, passed by. But a certaine Samaritane going his iourney,
> came neere him: and seeing him, was moued with mercie. And
> going vnto him, bound his woundes, powring in oile and wine:

and setting him vpon his owne beaste, brought him into an inne, and tooke care of him. And the next day he tooke forth two pence, and gaue to the host, and said, Haue care of him: and whatsoeuer thou shalt supererogate, I at my returne will repay thee. Which of these three in thy opinion was neighbour to him that fel among theeues? But he said, He that did mercie vpon him. And Iesvs said to him, Go, and doe thou in like maner.

Here the story is told straightforwardly in plain English, until we come to the Samaritan's request to the innkeeper: "whatsoever thou shalt supererogate". This is simply a question of taking Jerome's Latin verb over into English. To many English readers it would mean nothing; to some it would convey a meaning different from that originally intended, for they would think of it in the light of the doctrine of supererogation,[1] whereas the proper sense is conveyed exactly by the A.V., "whatsoever thou spendest more."

It is when we come to the Epistles, however, that the latinate vocabulary of Rheims becomes most impressive. One frequently quoted passage should not be regarded as typical, as its proportion of Latinisms is well above average; but it is worth reproducing (Eph. 3 : 8–13):

> To me the least of al the sainctes is giuen this grace, among the Gentils to euangelize the vnsearcheable riches of Christ, and to illuminate al men what is the dispensation of the sacrament hidden from worldes in God, who created al things, that the manifold wisedom of God may be notified to the Princes and Potestats in the celestials by the Church, according to the prefinition of worldes, which he made in Christ Iesvs our Lord. In whom we haue affiance and accesse in confidence, by the faith of him. For the which cause I desire that you faint not in my tribulations for you, which is your glorie.

The opening paragraph of Hebrews runs as follows in Rheims:

> Diversely and many waies in times past God speaking to the fathers in the prophets: last of al in these daies hath spoken to vs

---

[1] Works of supererogation, in Roman Catholic teaching, are works done over and above what the law of God requires.

in his Sonne, whom he hath appointed heire of al, by whom he made also the worldes. Who being the brightnesse of his glorie and the figure of his substance, and carying all things by the word of his power, making purgation of sinnes, sitteth on the right hand of the Maiestie in the high places: being made so much better then Angels, as he hath inherited a more excellent name aboue them.

This is no more latinate than the A.V. Rheims says "figure of his substance" where Tyndale had "very ymage of his substance" (A.V., "express image of his person") because the phrase in the Vulgate is *figura substantiae eius.* The most important point of difference in the Rheims version of this paragraph is its use of the present participle "making purgation for sins", as though this were something which the Son of God is still doing during His heavenly session. Tyndale and the versions dependent on him make it clear that the "making purgation for sins" is something which precedes the Son's taking His seat at the Father's right hand. An important theological issue is involved here, but the divergence between the Rheims version and the Protestant versions is due to nothing more than the unfortunate fact that most Latin verbs do not have a perfect participle in the active voice. The Greek says plainly, "having made purification for sins he sat down", but there is no participial form in Latin that means "having made", so the Latin translators used the present participle instead, and have naturally been followed in this regard by most versions based on the Vulgate, from the earlier Wycliffite version ("he makith purgacioun of synnes") to Knox ("making atonement for our sins").

The more latinate passages in Douai-Rheims sound strangely in English ears, as the editors knew they would. We must remember, indeed, that the Douai-Rheims version represents the losing side in the English Reformation conflict, and that even among Roman Catholics it has never been the household work that the A.V. has been among Protestants. Mgr Knox argues[1] that, if the rôles had been reversed, the Douai-Rheims language would have become what we know as "Bible English" and the A.V. idiom would have

[1] *On Englishing the Bible* (London, 1949), p. 47.

sounded barbarous and exotic. It is true that much of the A.V. idiom is as essentially Hebrew as much of the Douai-Rheims idiom is essentially Latin;[1] and whereas many originally Hebraic turns of phrase found in the A.V. have become naturalized in English, others (for all their familiarity) have never made their way into ordinary speech. For example, the Hebrew idiom "and it came to pass that...", so common in the A.V. and R.V., has never been accepted as normal English, and so it has been dropped from the R.S.V. and other recent English versions. In the A.V., however, if the idiom is often Hebraic, the vocabulary is not; whereas in Douai-Rheims the vocabulary as well as the idiom is strongly influenced by the Latin of the Vulgate. Would all these latinate terms have become part and parcel of our ordinary speech if Douai-Rheims, instead of the A.V., had become the Bible of the English-speaking peoples as a whole? Where the might-have-been's of history are concerned, it is easier to ask interesting questions than to return confident answers. The Rheims editors had sufficient consideration for their readers to provide a glossary at the end of their work which gave the meanings of fifty-eight unusual words used in the version. Quite a number of these have now become familiar English words (such as "acquisition", "adulterate", "advent", "allegory", "cooperate", "prescience", "resuscitate", "victim"), some have never become generally current (such as "prefinition" in Eph. 3 : 11), while others are now employed in a different sense from that which they were given by the Rheims editors (such as "evacuate" in "you are evacuated from Christ" in Gal. 5 : 4).

The Rheims editors also adhered to their policy of retaining the old ecclesiastical words and phrases, even where lapse of time had given these a different sense from that which they originally had: thus John the Baptist and Jesus alike call upon their hearers to "*doe penance*, for the kingdom of heaven is at hand" (Matt. 3 : 2; 4 : 17). When Peter was imprisoned by Herod, "it was the daies of the *Azymes*" and Herod's intention was "after the *Pasche* to bring him forth to the people" (Acts 12 : 3 f.). Not only is the cup of the Holy Communion called the "chalice" (Matt. 26 : 27, etc.), but Jesus in

---

[1] But there are many instances in Douai-Rheims of Hebrew idioms which Jerome had taken over into the Vulgate.

Gethsemane prays that "this *chalice*" may pass from Him (Matt. 26 : 39, etc.). Paul and Barnabas ordain "*Priests* in euery Church" in southern Asia Minor (Acts 14 : 23); although "priests" is a reduced form of "presbyters" (the word used here in Greek and Latin), it had acquired a specialized sense (those who officiate at sacrifices) in the course of centuries, and so Tyndale and his successors rendered the term more accurately by "elders". In other places, indeed, the Rheims version itself recognizes the true meaning of the word: thus, 1 Peter 5 : 1 reads, following the Vulgate: "The seniors therfore that are among you I beseche, my self a fellow senior with them" (A.V., "The elders ... I exhort, who am also an elder").

The Rheims New Testament was consulted by the men who gave us the A.V., and in a number of instances its Latinisms appear to have influenced the A.V. vocabulary. (The Douai Old Testament was not published in time for it to be of much use to the A.V. translators.) Bishop Westcott[1] has listed from one epistle alone (the Epistle to the Romans) an impressive number of words of Latin origin which, in his opinion, the A.V. took over from Rheims. But these words do not strike us as unusual words—perhaps for the simple fact that they occur in the A.V.!

Another point which Bishop Westcott draws attention to[2] is particularly noteworthy. The Hebrew and Greek languages possess the definite article; Latin does not. Where the definite article occurs in the original texts of the Old and New Testaments, there is for the most part no equivalent in the Latin Bible. We might therefore expect that a translation made from the Latin Bible would be less accurate in its treatment of the definite article than one made from the Hebrew and Greek. But because the Latin text failed them here, Gregory Martin and his colleagues had recourse to the original text and (so far, at least, as their New Testament work is concerned) their treatment of the definite article is not only more satisfactory than the treatment given to it by earlier English translators, but even more accurate than in the A.V. It occasionally omits the article

---

[1] B. F. Westcott, *History of the English Bible* (London, 1905), p. 253. His list must be scrutinized carefully; some of the words he lists appear in earlier English versions. Thus "concupiscence" (Rom. 7 : 8), which he says was taken over by A.V. from Rheims, is found in Tyndale and Whittingham.

[2] *Op. cit.*, p. 254.

where the A.V. and earlier versions wrongly insert it, and even more frequently inserts it where the A.V. and earlier versions wrongly omit it.

The Apocrypha

In the Douai Old Testament the books of the Apocrypha are not gathered together in an appendix, as they are in the Protestant versions from Coverdale onwards; they appear in the positions which they have in the Vulgate. The Third and Fourth Books of Esdras, however (which correspond respectively to First and Second Esdras of the English Protestant editions of the Apocrypha),[1] are not included among the canonical books of the Old Testament, but printed separately at the end of the Old Testament, along with the Prayer of Manasseh.

Annotations

The Douai-Rheims Bible was equipped with a very full apparatus of annotations. Some of these were intended to clear up difficulties of a non-theological character, but the main purpose of the annotations was to interpret the sacred text in conformity with the faith as the editors understood it, more particularly in conformity with the pronouncements of the Council of Trent, and to rebut the arguments of the Reformers. They are as controversial and outspoken as Tyndale and Geneva at their raciest, and taken together they constitute, as Father Hugh Pope puts it, "a veritable catechism of Christian doctrine such as must have proved invaluable at a time when the Catholic body was for the most part deprived of pastors, and which to this day is most useful for those seeking a detailed knowledge of their religion."[2] They were apparently not the work of Gregory Martin himself, but of William Allen and some others. The last annotation, on the words "Come, Lord Jesus" in the second-last verse of the New Testament, strikes a sympathetic chord in the heart of any Christian reader:

And now, O Lord Jesus Christ, most just and merciful, we thy

[1] First and Second Esdras in Douai (as in the Vulgate) are our Ezra and Nehemiah respectively.
[2] H. Pope, *English Versions of the Bible* (St. Louis and London, 1952), p. 301.

poor creatures that are so afflicted for confession and defence of the holy Catholic and Apostolic truth, contained in this thy sacred book, and in the infallible doctrine of thy dearest spouse our mother the Church, we cry also unto thy Majesty with tenderness of our hearts unspeakable: COME LORD JESUS QUICKLY, and judge betwixt us and our adversaries, and in the mean time give patience, comfort, and constancy to all that suffer for thy name, and trust in thee. O Lord God, our only helper and protector, tarry not long. Amen.

One could well imagine the Marian exiles who prepared the Geneva Bible praying the same prayer, with but little modification of the language. Even if Christ is preached in contention, said Paul, it matters little, so long as He is preached;[1] even if the Bible be translated in contention, we may say, it matters little, so long as it is translated.

Bishop Challoner's revision

From time to time after 1610 the Douai-Rheims Bible received some slight revision, but the radical revision which has left its mark on all subsequent editions is the work of Bishop Richard Challoner (1691–1781), Vicar Apostolic of the London District. By the middle of the eighteenth century the language of Douai-Rheims was largely unintelligible to the rank and file of English-speaking Roman Catholics, and Challoner's aim was to revise it in such a way that they could read and understand it with ease. The fifth edition of the Rheims New Testament (1738) was probably issued under his editorship, but he saw that it was not simply editing, but revising, that the version demanded if it were to serve its proper purpose. Accordingly he published five successive revisions of the New Testament, between 1749 and 1772, and two of the Old Testament, in 1750 and 1763.

Challoner was a convert from Protestantism, as was also Francis Blyth, Vicar Provincial of the English Carmelites, who collaborated with him in his work of revision. Both men were familiar from their earliest days with the language of the A.V., and it is therefore not

---

[1] Philippians 1 : 15-18.

surprising that the language of the A.V. exercised a profound influence on their revision of Douai-Rheims. The ecclesiastical terms have been retained: our Lord and His forerunner still call upon their hearers to "do penance" and Christians are still exhorted to pray for their "supersubstantial" bread; "the parasceve of the pasch" (John 19 : 14) has not yet become Passover Eve. But Christ is now said to have "emptied himself" in Phil. 2 : 7 instead of "exinanited himself"; the "azymes" remain in Acts 12 : 3 but are changed into "unleavened bread" in Mark 14 : 12 and Luke 22 : 1; the "scenopegia" of John 7 : 2 becomes intelligible as the "feast of tabernacles". Rhoda is no longer a wench, but a damsel. It is, however, even more in the cadences of the language than in the vocabulary that the influence of the A.V. is most clearly to be recognized, by anyone who will take the trouble to compare the old Douai-Rheims Bible with Challoner's revision.

We have already quoted the opening paragraph of Hebrews in the Rheims version; it follows the word-order of the Latin (and, through Latin, of the Greek) as it begins: "Diversely and in many waies ...". But here is the same paragraph in Challoner's revision:

> God, who at sundry times and in divers manners spoke in times past to the fathers by the prophets, last of all, in these days hath spoken to us by his Son, whom he hath appointed heir of all things, by whom also he made the world. Who being the brightness of his glory, and the figure of his substance, and upholding all things by the word of his power, making purgation of sins, sitteth on the right hand of the majesty on high, being made so much better than the Angels, as he hath inherited a more excellent name than they.

No need to ask what influence has brought about so marked a change from the Rheims wording!

Here is how Challoner deals with the excessively latinate passage quoted above from the Rheims version of Eph. 3 : 8-13:

> To me, the least of all the saints, is given this grace, to preach among the gentiles the unsearchable riches of Christ, and to enlighten all men, that they may see what is the dispensation of the

mystery which hath been hidden from eternity in God who created all things: that the manifold wisdom of God may be made known to the principalities and powers in the heavenly *places* through the church, according to the eternal purpose, which he made in Christ JESUS our Lord, in whom we have boldness and access with confidence by the faith of him. Wherefore I pray you not to faint at my tribulations for you, which is your glory.

The Douai-Rheims-Challoner Bible was authorized for use by the English-speaking Roman Catholics of America in 1810.

In Challoner's revision the ample annotations of the old Douai-Rheims Bible were severely pruned; readers who examine the footnotes in an ordinary edition of Douai-Rheims-Challoner to-day see but a shadow of the original. "The glory," says Knox, "has departed."[1] Even so, some of the notes that were included in editions early in the nineteenth century were sufficiently forthright in their anti-Protestant vigour to cause considerable embarrassment to the Roman Catholic bishops of Ireland during the Catholic Emancipation campaign.

Three private ventures in Bible translation from the Hebrew or Greek by Roman Catholic scholars deserve to be mentioned. In 1792 Alexander Geddes, a critic of exceptionally liberal mind for his day, issued the first volume (Genesis–Joshua) of *The Holy Bible... translated from corrected texts of the originals*, followed in 1797 by Judges–2 Chronicles and Prayer of Manasseh and in 1807 posthumously by the Psalter. About a century later F. A. Spencer published *The Four Gospels*, a new translation from the Greek direct with reference to the Vulgate and the ancient Syriac (New York, 1898), which was followed by the posthumously published version of *The New Testament* (New York, 1937). *The New Testament rendered from the Original Greek with Explanatory Notes*, by J. A. Kleist and J. L. Lilly, was issued at Milwaukee in 1954. But the story of Roman Catholic Bible translation in our own generation remains to be told in Chapter XV.

[1] R. A. Knox, *On Englishing the Bible*, p. 47.

CHAPTER TEN

After King James

The Revised Text

THE PRINCIPAL DEFECT of the A.V. is one for which the translators cannot be held responsible. In the New Testament especially, the text which they used was an inferior one. The earliest printed editions of the Greek New Testament were based on later manuscripts—manuscripts which exhibit what textual critics know as the "Byzantine" type of Greek text. This Byzantine text-type represents a revision of the New Testament text made in the fourth century A.D. and later; it is farther removed from the text of the first century than certain earlier text-types which have been distinguished in more recent times. But throughout centuries of copying and recopying even the Byzantine text-type was no longer represented in its purity by the later manuscripts which were so largely drawn upon by the editors of the earliest printed texts. Erasmus did, indeed, ask a friend in Rome to consult on one particular point[1] the greatest biblical treasure of the Vatican Library—the Vatican Codex of the fourth century A.D.—although it was not until centuries later that the great value of this manuscript was appreciated.

The edition of the Greek Testament which became standard in England was one issued in 1550 by the Paris printer Estienne (Stephanus). The printing house of Elzevir in Leyden took this edition as the basis for two editions which they issued in 1624 and 1633. Their 1633 edition is noteworthy because the Latin preface assures the reader that here he has "the text which is now received by all" without either alteration or corruption. It is from this piece of "publisher's blurb" that the designation "The Received Text" (*Textus Receptus*) has been applied more generally to the text of the

[1] The particular point was the passage about the three heavenly witnesses (1 John 5 : 7, A.V.), which appears in no Greek manuscript apart from a few very late ones, of the fifteenth and sixteenth centuries. See pp. 141 f.

earliest printed editions of the Greek Testament, and in particular to the Greek text underlying the A.V. in the New Testament. Sometimes ignorance of the original circumstances of the designation leads people to appeal to the words "The Received Text" as though the very word *received* carried a certain weight of authority with it.

Better Manuscripts

Sixteen years after the publication of the A.V., King Charles I was presented by Cyril Lucar, Patriarch of Alexandria, with a Greek manuscript of the Bible (the Old Testament part being in the Septuagint translation) which was older than any biblical manuscript previously available in the west. This fifth-century manuscript is known as the Alexandrine Codex, and is housed in the British Museum. Although nowadays its value is overshadowed by that of other biblical manuscripts, both earlier and better, it represented in those days a considerably more accurate text than that with which the A.V. translators had operated. Unfortunately it did not come to England in time for them to make use of it.

During the eighteenth and nineteenth centuries much important work was done on the study of the New Testament text, and further manuscripts were either discovered (like the fourth-century Sinaitic Codex, discovered by Tischendorf in 1844) or made generally available (like the Vatican Codex, already referred to). It became increasingly clear that the A.V. required to be revised in order to be brought into closer conformity with the Greek text of the New Testament, as established by more intensive textual study on the basis of more reliable evidence than had been accessible in 1611.

Whitby, Wells, Mace, Whiston

Throughout the eighteenth and nineteenth centuries several private ventures in Bible translation attempted to incorporate the results of the newer knowledge. Some of these were in the main revisions of the A.V.; others were more independent.

In 1703 Daniel Whitby's *Paraphrase and Commentary on the New Testament* included an explanatory expansion of the A.V. Whitby's chief claim to fame is his pioneering advocacy of the post-millennial interpretation of the biblical doctrine of the Second Advent of Christ.

Edward Wells produced a revised text of the A.V. in *The Common Translation Corrected* (1718–24); Daniel Mace in 1729 published anonymously a critical Greek text of the New Testament with the A.V. alongside it, corrected so as to be brought into line both with the accompanying Greek text and with current English usage. The vigour of his version may be illustrated by the following sample (James 3 : 5 f.):

> The tongue is but a small part of the body, yet how grand are its pretensions! a spark of fire! what quantities of timber will it blow into a flame! The tongue is a brand that sets the world in a combustion: it is but one of the numerous organs of the body, yet it can blast whole assemblies: tipped with infernal sulphur it sets the whole train of life in a blaze.

William Whiston, Sir Isaac Newton's successor at Cambridge and best known nowadays for his translation of Josephus, published his *Primitive New Testament* in 1745, when he was seventy-eight years old. This edition follows the A.V., except where it requires to be brought into line with those manuscripts which Whiston regarded as the most authentic—mainly manuscripts exhibiting what is now called the "Western Text" of the New Testament. For the Gospels and Acts he followed the Codex of Beza in the University Library at Cambridge—a bilingual manuscript (Greek and Latin) of the fifth or sixth century, to which he ascribed an impossible antiquity, dating it "within thirty years of the death of John the Apostle". Because he followed this codex, he added to Luke 6 : 5 in his version the peculiar Bezan incident:

> On the same day seeing one working on the sabbath, he said unto him, Man, if thou knowest what thou doest, thou art blessed: but if thou dost not know thou art cursed, and art a transgressor of the law.

Wesley's New Testament

In 1768 John Wesley issued a revised edition of the A.V., with notes "for plain, unlettered men who understand only their Mother Tongue". This revision was based on careful study of the Greek original; there were some 12,000 alterations in all, but none of them, the reader is assured, for altering's sake. The English text is divided into sense-paragraphs, "a little circumstance which makes many passages more intelligible to the Reader".

A literary curio

A literary curio is Edward Harwood's *Liberal Translation of the New Testament: Being an Attempt to translate the Sacred Writings with the same Freedom, Spirit, and Elegance, with which other English Translations from the Greek Classics have lately been executed* (1768). Harwood was a classical and biblical scholar, whose *Introduction to the New Testament* procured him the D.D. degree from Edinburgh University. But his rendering of the New Testament into the idiom of Hume and Johnson was bound to have a very temporary and limited appeal. The opening words of the Lord's Prayer ("Our Father which art in heaven: Hallowed be thy name") appear as follows in his version:

> O Thou great governour and parent of universal nature—who manifestest thy glory to the blessed inhabitants of heaven—may all thy rational creatures in all the parts of thy boundless dominion be happy in the knowledge of thy existence and providence, and celebrate thy perfections in a manner most worthy thy nature and perfective of their own!

Septuagint translations

An English translation of the Old Testament from the Greek Septuagint was produced in 1808 by Charles Thomson, one of the founding fathers of the United States of America. It was republished in 1954 by the Falcon's Wing Press of Indian Hills, Colorado. Another translation of the Septuagint, by Sir Lancelot C. L. Brenton, Bart., which appeared in 1844, is printed by Messrs Bagster of London alongside their edition of the Septuagint text itself.

Samuel Sharpe

Samuel Sharpe, a Unitarian scholar, issued in 1840 his *New Testament, translated from the Greek of J. J. Griesbach*; this was essentially a revision of the A.V. in the light of Griesbach's critical Greek text. Sharpe's *Hebrew Scriptures Translated*—a revision of the A.V. of the Old Testament—followed in 1865.

Jewish Versions

Two Jewish translations of the Hebrew Bible call for honourable mention at this point: Isaac Leeser's *The Law of God* (i.e. the Pentateuch, Philadelphia, 1845–46), followed by *The Twenty-Four Books of the Holy Scriptures* (Philadelphia, 1854; revised edition, London, 1865); and A. Benisch's *Jewish School and Family Bible* (London, 1861).

Dean Alford's New Testament

Henry Alford, Dean of Canterbury, who is chiefly memorable for his magnificent edition of the Greek New Testament with a copious commentary, issued a revision of the A.V. of the New Testament in 1869. This scholarly work was intended merely as an "interim report" pending the appearance of an authoritative revision. "It is impossible, to say nothing more, that *one man's work* can ever fulfil the requisites for an accepted Version of the Scriptures." Alford expressed the hope that his work might speedily be rendered useless by the setting up of a Royal Commission to revise the A.V. His prayer was answered in 1870—not, indeed, by the setting up of a Royal Commission, but by the action of Convocation of Canterbury. In his preface he showed himself a true prophet by warning the reader of some criticisms of his version which were sure to be made; they were destined to be made even more vociferously against the Revised Version of 1881 and 1885, and later against the Revised Standard Version of 1946 and 1952. Many of these criticisms, said Alford, would arise from failure to consider that changes were made "simply as an act of honest obedience to truth of testimony, or truth of rendering." It had never dawned on those who made such criticisms "that a translator of Holy Scripture must be absolutely colourless; ready to sacrifice the choicest text, and the plainest proof of doctrine, if the words are not those of what he is constrained in his conscience to receive as God's testimony."

J. N. Darby

Another private version which embodies the results of the new textual knowledge available in the second half of the nineteenth century is John Nelson Darby's *New Translation* (New Testament, second and revised edition, 1871; Old Testament, 1890). Darby, one of the leaders of the Brethren movement, translated the Bible into German (the Elberfeld version) and French (the Pau version) before his English version appeared; indeed, his English version was left incomplete when he died in 1882 and was completed on the basis of his German and French versions. In the New Testament especially it is based on a sound critical appraisal of the evidence, and was consulted by the company which prepared the Revised New Testament of 1881. The version was equipped with a full critical apparatus at the foot of each column of the New Testament which set forth in detail the evidence on which particular readings and renderings were adopted. The version, however, falls short in regard to English style —which would surprise no one acquainted with Darby's voluminous prose writings. (He also produced an Italian version of the New Testament.)

Young's Literal Translation

Some versions and editions of the Bible which appeared in the nineteenth century were designed to put the English reader as far as possible on a level with the reader of the Hebrew and Greek texts. Such a work was Robert Young's *Literal Translation of the Bible* (1862). Young, best known for his valuable *Analytical Concordance to the Bible,* was an Edinburgh bookseller with an insatiable appetite for the mastery of eastern languages, ancient and modern (among his minor works is a translation of the books of Chronicles into Gujarati). His *Literal Translation* is practically a word-for-word rendering of the original texts into English, but in the Old Testament it is largely vitiated by an eccentric theory about the tenses of the Hebrew verb. The impression one gets from Young's translation with regard to Naaman the Syrian's compromising behaviour in the house of Rimmon is quite different from that given by other versions:

> For this thing Jehovah be propitious to thy servant, in the coming in of my lord into the house of Rimmon to bow himself

there, and he was supported by my hand, and I bowed myself *in* the house of Rimmon; for my bowing myself in the house of Rimmon Jehovah be propitious, I pray thee, to thy servant in this thing (2 Kings 5 : 18).

Here Naaman is made to beg pardon for his previous idolatrous conduct, instead of his "going through the motions" of Rimmon-worship in the future when he accompanies his royal master to the temple of Rimmon in his capacity as national commander-in-chief.

Rotherham's Emphasized Version

Then there is *The Emphasized Bible* by Joseph Bryant Rotherham, of which the New Testament part first appeared in 1872 and the Old Testament in 1897-1902. This is a fairly literal translation by a man who knew his Hebrew and Greek texts thoroughly. The first two editions of the New Testament were based on Tregelles's text, the third on Westcott and Hort's. Rotherham's English text is set out and supplied with various signs in such a way as to convey the most detailed shades of emphasis in the original; hence the title of his version. To say that "Rotherham's interest was rather that of an elocutionist than that of a translator"[1] is scarcely accurate; both interests are simultaneously evident. His version is one of the first to render the ineffable name of the God of Israel throughout the Old Testament by "Yahweh".

The Newberry Bible

The Englishman's Bible, edited by Thomas Newberry (New Testament, 1870; complete Bible, 1884, and several later editions), is not a new version but the text of the A.V., arranged by means of distinctive type and a whole battery of dots, dashes, marginal notes and so forth, so as to give the English reader information about the tenses of the Hebrew and Greek verbs, the divine names, and many other grammatical and linguistic details. The New Testament is equipped with a critical apparatus exhibiting variant readings. Newberry had no axe to grind. He was a careful and completely unpretentious student of the Hebrew and Greek texts, whose

[1] H. Pope, *English Versions of the Bible* (St. Louis and London, 1952), p. 546.

one aim was to make the fruit of his study available as far as possible to Bible students whose only language was English. His procedure tended to make the biblical text self-explanatory as far as possible; he had no thought of imposing on it an interpretative scheme of his own.

Other Nineteenth-Century Versions

In 1885 there appeared *A Translation of the Old Testament Scriptures from the Original Hebrew*, by Helen Spurrell, based on an unpointed text. Other nineteenth-century translations of parts of the Bible were included in commentaries on biblical books and similar works. One of the best-known examples may be found in the version of Paul's epistles included in *The Life and Epistles of St. Paul*, by W. J. Conybeare and J. S. Howson (1864). It must be borne in mind that much excellent Bible translation is to be found, down to the present day, embedded in commentaries on various books of the Bible. For example, the new series of New Testament commentaries which is being published by A. and C. Black in London and by Harper and Brothers in New York presents fresh translations of the books as well as commentaries on them.

CHAPTER ELEVEN

The Revised Version

The Genesis of the Revision

THE HISTORY of the Revised Version of the English Bible begins properly on February 10, 1870, when Dr Wilberforce, Bishop of Winchester, submitted the following motion to the Upper House of Convocation of the Province of Canterbury:

> That a Committee of both Houses be appointed, with power to confer with any Committee that may be appointed by the Convocation of the Northern Province, to report upon the desirableness of a revision of the Authorized Version of the New Testament, whether by marginal notes or otherwise, in all those passages where plain and clear errors, whether in the Hebrew or Greek text originally adopted by the translators, or in the translation made from the same, shall, on due investigation, be found to exist.

It was odd that a motion which restricted its scope to the New Testament should make reference to the correction of errors "in the Hebrew or Greek text"; however, the situation was speedily regularized when Dr Ollivant, Bishop of Llandaff, moved that the words "the New Testament" be amplified to "the Old and New Testaments". The Upper House agreed to the motion as amended, and communicated its decision to the Lower House. Both Houses set up a joint committee to frame the desired report. The Convocation of the Province of York, while it approved of the correction of errors, did not accept the invitation to set up a committee to confer with the southern committee.

The Canterbury committee therefore set to work on its own, and on May 3, 1870, it presented its report, which took the form of five resolutions:

1. That it is desirable that a revision of the Authorized Version of the Holy Scriptures be undertaken.

2. That the revision be so conducted as to comprise both marginal renderings and such emendations as it may be found necessary to insert in the text of the Authorized Version.

3. That in the above resolutions we do not contemplate any new translation of the Bible, or any alteration of the language, except when in the judgment of the most competent scholars such change is necessary.

4. That in such necessary changes, the style of the language employed in the existing version be closely followed.

5. That it is desirable that Convocation should nominate a body of its own members to undertake the work of revision, who shall be at liberty to invite the co-operation of any eminent for scholarship, to whatever nation or religious body they may belong.

This report was adopted by both Houses of Convocation, and another joint committee was set up to consider and report on a scheme of revision in accordance with the resolutions of the report now adopted. The second committee decided to separate itself into two companies, one to be responsible for the Old Testament and one for the New. The former company was to tackle the Pentateuch first, the latter was to tackle the Synoptic Gospels first. A number of well-known scholars were nominated to be invited to join one company or the other: the Church of Scotland and the English and Scottish Free Churches were well represented among them. The catholicity of the committee's outlook may be illustrated by the inclusion among those invited to join the New Testament company of John Henry Newman, the most eminent Roman Catholic theologian in the English-speaking world, and (at the other end of the scale) a distinguished Unitarian scholar, Dr G. Vance Smith. Newman was unable to accept the invitation. Dr Vance Smith did accept, and his presence among the revisers caused considerable misgivings among the orthodox public, which were not allayed when he joined with his fellow-revisers in the inaugural celebration of Holy Communion in Westminster Abbey on June 22, 1870.

The Principles of the Revision

The general principles on which both companies of revisers were instructed to proceed were these:

1. To introduce as few alterations as possible into the Text of the Authorized Version consistently with faithfulness.

2. To limit, as far as possible, the expression of such alterations to the language of the Authorized and earlier English versions.

3. Each Company to go twice over the portion to be revised, once provisionally, the second time finally, and on principles of voting as hereinafter is provided.

4. That the Text to be adopted be that for which the evidence is decidedly preponderating; and that when the Text so adopted differs from that from which the Authorized Version was made, the alteration be indicated in the margin.

5. To make or retain no change in the Text on the second final revision by each Company, except *two-thirds* of those present approve of the same, but on the first revision to decide by simple majorities.

6. In every case of proposed alteration that may have given rise to discussion, to defer the voting thereupon till the next Meeting, whensoever the same shall be required by one-third of those present at the Meeting, such intended vote to be announced in the notice for the next Meeting.

7. To revise the headings of chapters, pages, paragraphs, italics, and punctuation.

8. To refer, on the part of each Company, when considered desirable, to Divines, Scholars, and Literary Men, whether at home or abroad, for their opinions.

The Oxford and Cambridge University Presses undertook to defray the bare expenses incurred in the work of revision in return for the copyright. The revisers gave their time and labour without charge.

The Course of the Revision

Later in 1870 negotiations were opened with leading biblical scholars in the United States, and in that country two parallel companies were formed (one for the Old Testament, one for the New) to co-operate with their opposite numbers in Britain and help them with suggestions and criticisms. It was hoped that one agreed revision might be adopted on both sides of the Atlantic, but this did not prove possible. The American revisers, while they took a very conservative view of their responsibilities, did not feel able to confine themselves to the excessively strict terms of reference by which their British colleagues were bound. The British revisers published the New Testament part of their work in May 1881, the Old Testament part in May 1885. They included appendices listing the points on which the judgment of the American revisers diverged from their own. The American companies remained in being for several years more, until the fruit of their labours was issued in 1901, the American Standard Version.

When the two Testaments were published in Britain, some of the revisers, divided into four committees, set to work on the revision of the Apocrypha, and the Revised Version of these books appeared in 1895. The American companies did not include the Apocrypha in their revision.

The character of the two Testaments in the Revised Version presents such disparity in many ways that they must be considered separately.

The Revised New Testament

The appearance of the Revised New Testament caused tremendous excitement. The text was telegraphed to Chicago, and appeared as a special supplement to a well-known daily newspaper there. The sales of the revision were enormous, and it immediately became the subject of animated and, at times, acrimonious discussion.

The Underlying Text

When we try to assess the quality of the Revised New Testament, we must draw a clear distinction between its worth as a representative of the Greek text, and its worth as a translation. With regard to the former point, it represents a great advance on the A.V. The most distinguished textual critics in the country were invited to join the

New Testament company, including F. H. A. Scrivener, S. P. Tregelles, B. F. Westcott and F. J. A. Hort. Dr Tregelles was prevented by ill health from taking any part in the revision, but the other three were active throughout the duration of the work. While Dr Scrivener took a generally conservative position, leaning to the support of the Byzantine text (substantially the same as the "Received Text"), Westcott and Hort, both occupants of professorial chairs at Cambridge, ardently espoused the claims of the two great uncial manuscripts, the Vatican and Sinaitic codices, to reproduce the original text in as pure a state as could well be attained. While other groups of manuscripts and early versions represented deviations from the original text in one direction or another, the text of the two great codices did not seem to them to stray from what they believed to be the norm, and they dignified it with the title of the "Neutral Text". While the work of revision was going on, Westcott and Hort were engaged simultaneously on their epoch-making edition of the Greek Testament, which appeared five days before the Revised New Testament. They placed their critical work at the disposal of their colleagues on the revision company, and to a very large degree their findings on the text were approved by the majority—Dr Scrivener, it is said, being repeatedly outvoted by two-thirds of those present. While Westcott and Hort's devotion to the text of the Vatican and Sinaitic codices was excessive (as may be seen more clearly in the light of further textual study), yet at that time they did establish the Greek text of the New Testament as accurately as it could well be established on the evidence then available.

Those who were interested in such questions were already well aware of the prevalent tendencies in the textual criticism of the New Testament; many of the results had already been made accessible to a wider public in some private translations of the New Testament in whole or in part. But now they were incorporated in a version which was designed in due course to replace the Authorized Version and thrust upon the attention of the general Bible-reading public. It was felt by some cautious theologians that it was a tactical mistake to draw attention so frequently as the margin of the R.V. does to variations in the wording of the ancient witnesses to the text: "the effect which these ever-recurring announcements produce on the

devout reader of Scripture", said the redoubtable Dean Burgon, "is
the reverse of edifying: is never helpful: is always bewildering."[1]
But this is simply a theological way of saying that "where ignorance
is bliss, 'tis folly to be wise." Scripture deserves to have intelligent
readers, and intelligent readers will not have their faith shaken by
being reminded that the men who copied the sacred text throughout
the early Christian centuries could occasionally fail to copy exactly
what lay before them in the master-copy. Even the marginal note
at Luke 23 : 34, to the effect that "some ancient authorities omit 'And
Jesus said, Father, forgive them; for they know not what they do' "[2]
need not shake anyone who knows the proneness of copyists to omit
material sections of what they are copying—although this note
stirred Burgon to one of his fiercest onslaughts (directed primarily
against Westcott and Hort's Greek text rather than against the R.V.):

These twelve precious words ... Drs. Westcott and Hort enclose
within double brackets in token of the "moral certainty" they
entertain that the words are spurious. And yet these words are
found in *every known uncial* and in *every known cursive Copy*, except
four; besides being found *in every ancient Version*:[3] and, *what,—*
(we ask the question with sincere simplicity),—*what* amount of
evidence is calculated to inspire undoubting confidence in any
existing Reading, if not such a concurrence of Authorities as this?
... We forbear to insist upon the probabilities of the case. The
Divine power and sweetness of the incident shall not be enlarged
upon. We introduce no considerations resulting from Internal
Evidence. True, that "few verses of the Gospels bear in themselves
a surer witness to the Truth of what they record, than this." (It is
the admission of the very man[4] who has nevertheless dared to
brand it with suspicion.) But we reject his loathsome patronage
with indignation. "Internal Evidence,"—"Transcriptional Probability",—and all such "chaff and draff," with which he fills his

[1] J. W. Burgon, *The Revision Revised* (London, 1883), p. 5.
[2] In this case, however, the omission may have been due to the reflection that the destruc-
tion of Jerusalem in A.D. 70 showed that Jesus' Jewish enemies had not been forgiven (it being
assumed that the prayer was for them and not, as is probable, for the Roman soldiers); it was
then argued that if the prayer had not been answered, Jesus could never have uttered it.
[3] The words actually appear to be absent from the earliest known forms of the Latin,
Syriac and Coptic versions.
[4] Dr Hort.

pages *ad nauseam*, and mystifies nobody but himself,—shall be allowed no place in the present discussion (*op. cit.*, pp. 82 f.).

He then goes on to cite forty passages from the writings of the Fathers where the familiar words are referred to as part of the Gospel text.

Ordinary readers might not pay much attention to marginal notes on variant readings or anything else. But in quite a number of places well-known words and verses which the A.V. contained were absent from the R.V. The passage about the angel troubling the water of the pool of Bethesda (John 5 : 3 f.) was relegated to the margin. So was Acts 8 : 37, where Philip stipulates that the Ethiopian eunuch must believe with all his heart before his request to be baptized can be granted, and the Ethiopian responds with a confession of faith in Jesus Christ as the Son of God. But a special omission was 1 John 5 : 7, as it appears in the A.V.—"For there are three that bear record in heaven, the Father, the Word, and the Holy Ghost: and these three are one." In the R.V. these words are not found; what does appear there as verse 7 of 1 John 5 is the sentence which the A.V. gives as the second part of verse 6: "And it is the Spirit that beareth witness, because the Spirit is truth" (R.V., "the truth"). Then the R.V. goes on with verse 8: "For there are three who bear witness, the Spirit, and the water, and the blood: and the three agree in one." The words omitted in the R.V. were no part of the original Greek text, nor yet of the Latin Vulgate in its earliest form. They first appear in the writings of a Spanish Christian leader named Priscillian, who was executed for heresy in A.D. 385. Later they made their way into copies of the Latin text of the Bible. When Erasmus prepared his printed edition of the Greek Testament, he rightly left those words out, but was attacked for this by people who felt that the passage was a valuable proof-text for the doctrine of the Trinity. He replied (rather incautiously) that if he could be shown any Greek manuscript which contained the words, he would include them in his next edition. Unfortunately, a Greek manuscript not more than some twenty years old was produced in which the words appeared: they had been translated into Greek from Latin. Of course, the fact that the only Greek manuscript exhibiting the words belonged to the sixteenth century was in itself an argument against their authenticity, but Erasmus had given his promise, and so in his 1522 edition he included the passage. (To-day one or two other very late Greek manuscripts are known to contain the passage; all others omit it.)

The omission of the "three heavenly Witnesses" alarmed many Christian readers of the R.V., who felt that the doctrine of the Trinity was being undermined by the removal of the text. But they need not have worried: for one thing, the Christian faith is not well served when attempts are made to defend it by weak arguments, and in any case the doctrine of the Trinity is much more securely based throughout the New Testament than on one text of more than doubtful genuineness.

The Translation

With regard to the work of *translating* the New Testament the R.V. does lay itself more open to criticism. It has often been called a schoolmasters' translation, and there is much truth in this. Not that this was a defect in itself; the almost pedantic accuracy and precision which the revisers aimed at makes their work an admirable version for the student, but to a large extent accounts for the failure of the R.V. to replace the A.V. in public worship and private devotion.

Dr C. J. Cadoux points out that there are two ideals in translation, associated respectively with the Universities of Oxford and Cambridge. While the Oxford method aims at conveying the sense in free and idiomatic English without much regard for the exact wording of the original, the Cambridge method aims at translating the words and nuances of the original as literally as possible, provided that no actual violence is done to English usage. "For good or ill," he adds, "the Cambridge genius presided over the English Revision."[1]

The revisers had been directed "to introduce as few alterations as possible, consistently with faithfulness". In their Preface to the New Testament they give an account of their stewardship in this matter. They list five kinds of alteration: (1) alterations due to the adoption of a different text from that underlying the A.V., (2) alterations in places where the A.V. rendering seemed to be wrong, (3) alterations

---

[1] *The Bible in its Ancient and English Versions* (ed. H. W. Robinson), p. 251.

in places where the A.V. was ambiguous, (4) alterations where the A.V. was inconsistent with itself in the rendering of two or more passages confessedly alike or parallel, and (5) alterations rendered necessary by consequence of changes already made, although not in themselves required by the general rule of faithfulness.

The fourth class of alteration is specially important. The A.V. translators, as we have seen, aimed at variety in the English wording, even where the original text exhibited the same word in the same sense. Up to a point, this policy might be justified on stylistic grounds; but it was carried too far. For example, St Mark's narrative is characterized by the repeated use of the Greek adverb *euthys*, which means "immediately". In his first chapter he uses it ten or eleven times. The A.V. translated it most often by "straightway", but three times by "immediately", twice by "forthwith", and once by "anon". The R.V., on the ground that a better idea of Mark's style is conveyed if the adverb is translated by one English word throughout, uses "straightway" each time.

Again, where parallel passages in two or more books show the same wording in the original, it is desirable to preserve identity of wording in the translation. This is especially so in the three Synoptic Gospels, where it is useful for someone who can read them only in translation to see how far the Evangelists agree in vocabulary and phraseology, and how far they diverge.

Sometimes, however, the changes in translation which the revisers introduced (where no question of text was involved) have not commended themselves as changes for the better. For example, in 2 Peter 1 : 5-7 the A.V. wording "add to your faith virtue; and to virtue knowledge ..." might well have been left as it was instead of being changed to "in your faith supply virtue, and in *your* virtue knowledge ..." Dr Rendel Harris tells how he once took Dr Philip Schaff of New York (a member of the American revision team) to call on Dr Westcott, because Dr Schaff was anxious to have certain barbarisms removed from the new version. One of the barbarisms mentioned was this very passage in 2 Peter, and Westcott angrily replied "that he would sooner cut off his right hand than alter that translation."[1] Evidently Schaff's fellow-revisers in America did not agree

---

[1] J. R. Harris, *Sidelights on New Testament Research* (London, 1908), p. 11.

with him, because the American Standard Version has the same awkward wording as the R.V. here.

It is natural that the work of Bible translation should be carried out by scholars, but their work (when the translation is intended for wide use by the general public) should be checked by intelligent readers who are not necessarily expert in biblical philology or exegesis, but who do have a sense of the impression that language will make on the ordinary reader.[1] For example, the revisers, being scholarly men, knew exactly what they meant when they used the expression "if thy right eye causeth thee to stumble ... if thy right hand causeth thee to stumble" in Matt. 5 : 29 f. But did they stop and think what sort of impression these words would make on the ordinary English reader, who could not be expected to know the special sense which "stumble" has in moral theology? To be sure, the A.V. "if thy right eye offend thee ... if thy right hand offend thee ..." requires to be changed, because "offend" there does not have its present-day meaning, but it would have been better not to replace it by the ludicrous picture of a man's right hand tripping him up. "If your right eye leads you into sin ... if your right hand leads you into sin ..."—that is what our Lord meant, and it would have been better to express His meaning in terms that were immediately intelligible.

The Revised Old Testament

As regards the Old Testament in the R.V., this was from all points of view an excellent achievement. The revisers did not operate with a newly constructed text; they used as their basis the Massoretic Hebrew text which had served the 1611 revisers before them. They were extremely conservative in the use that they made of the ancient versions (*e.g.* the Septuagint). But they understood their Hebrew text better than their seventeenth-century predecessors had done, and in the poetical and prophetic books especially they helped English readers to understand the Old Testament as they had previously been unable to do.

[1] I once allowed myself to use the expression "pneumatic body" in a manuscript (referring to the Greek of 1 Cor. 15 : 44). My intelligent publisher served the reading public well by sending the sheet back to me with the marginal note: "Shades of Dunlop!"

Let one example do duty for many. The first eleven verses of
Job 28 run as follows in the A.V.:

> Surely there is a vein for the silver, and a place for gold *where*
> they fine *it*. Iron is taken out of the earth, and brass *is* molten *out*
> *of* the stone. He setteth an end to darkness, and searcheth out all
> perfection: the stones of darkness, and the shadow of death. The
> flood breaketh out from the inhabitant; *even the waters* forgotten of
> the foot: they are dried up, they are gone away from men. *As for*
> the earth, out of it cometh bread: and under it is turned up as it
> were fire. The stones of it *are* the place of sapphires: and it hath
> dust of gold. *There is* a path which no fowl knoweth, and which
> the vulture's eye hath not seen: the lion's whelps have not trodden
> it, nor the fierce lion passed by it. He putteth forth his hand upon
> the rock; he overturneth the mountains by the roots. He cutteth
> out rivers among the rocks; and his eye seeth every precious thing.
> He bindeth the floods from overflowing; and *the thing that is* hid
> bringeth he forth to light.

It sounds magnificent, but what does it mean? How many of those
who read it, or hear it read, realize that it is a description of mining
operations? See now how the sense is clarified in the R.V.:

> Surely there is a mine for silver,
> And a place for gold which they refine.
> Iron is taken out of the earth,
> And brass is molten out of the stone.
> *Man* setteth an end to darkness,
> And searcheth out to the furthest bound
> The stones of thick darkness and of the shadow of death.
> He breaketh open a shaft away from where men sojourn;
> They are forgotten of the foot *that passeth by;*
> They hang afar from men, they swing to and fro.
> As for the earth, out of it cometh bread:
> And underneath it is turned up as it were by fire.
> The stones thereof are the place of sapphires,
> And it hath dust of gold.
> That path no bird of prey knoweth,
> Neither hath the falcon's eye seen it:

> The proud beasts have not trodden it,
> Nor hath the fierce lion passed thereby.
> He putteth forth his hand upon the flinty rock;
> He overturneth the mountains by the roots.
> He cutteth out channels among the rocks;
> And his eye seeth every precious thing.
> He bindeth the streams that they trickle not;
> And the thing that is hid bringeth he forth to light.

The Hebrew of the Book of Job is none of the easiest, and even the R.V. did not say the last word about its meaning. The R.S.V. of 1952 marks an advance on the R.V., and some people have found that in the New English Bible Job reads like a new book, thanks to the abundance of new light on Semitic languages which the last few years have brought us.

Occasionally in the R.V. of the Old Testament we come across a rendering which is no improvement on the A.V., but not often. In Eccles. 12 : 5, in the course of the well-known poetical description of old age, the statement that "the caper-berry shall fail" conveys no meaning to English readers unacquainted with the properties ascribed to the caper-berry; it would have been better to retain the A.V. "desire shall fail", instead of moving it into the margin. On the other hand, instead of retaining the A.V. "he hath set the world in their heart" in Eccles. 3 : 11 the revisers would have been better advised to set in the text the rendering which they have noted as an alternative in the margin: "he hath set eternity in their heart".

From the quotation given above from Job 28 : 1–11 it will be seen that the R.V. prints poetical passages in the O.T. as poetry. At least it does so in the poetical books and in poems which are quoted as such in the other books, and this is a great help to the reader; but it would have been better had the same procedure been followed with the poetical oracles of the prophetical books, and in the New Testament with those sayings of our Lord which exhibit the same poetical structures as the oracles of the Old Testament prophets.

Paragraphs and Margins

The R.V. departs from the practice of its predecessors which printed every verse as a separate paragraph. This practice, for all its practical convenience, tended to atomize the text by breaking it up into sections which were not natural sense-units; and it may to some extent have encouraged the practice, still surviving here and there, of quoting "verses" of Scripture out of their context. The R.V. retains the verse-numbers for ease in reference, but prints sense-paragraphs as paragraphs.

The revisers were instructed to "revise the headings of chapters, pages, paragraphs, italics, and punctuation". They dealt, as we have just said, with the paragraphing; they brought more consistency into the use of italics to distinguish words not occurring in the original texts; they revised the punctuation, retaining the heavier system suitable for guidance in public reading; but, they say, "the revision of the headings of chapters and pages would have involved so much of indirect, and indeed frequently of direct interpretation, that we judged it best to omit them altogether."

The margins were used for notes on alternative renderings and variant readings. Usually where a reading different from that underlying the A.V. was preferred, the A.V. reading is mentioned in the margin. There are several places, however, where the text agrees with the A.V. and the variant reading or alternative rendering in the margin was relegated there because it did not gain the necessary two-thirds majority of votes in the final revision; in most of these places the margin is to be preferred to the text.

The University Presses of Cambridge and Oxford decided in 1895 that the public demand for an apparatus of cross-references to accompany the R.V. should be met, and a committee was appointed to deal with this. In 1898 an edition of the R.V. with marginal references was published; in this edition the revisers' marginal notes are printed as footnotes. The marginal references comprise exact verbal parallels and direct quotations, passages where there is similarity of idea or expression, passages adduced by way of explanation or illustration, and passages illustrating differences of reference between the A.V. and R.V. The compilation of these references was carried through with admirable care and sound judgment by the scholars to whom it was entrusted, and the R.V. with these marginal references is still the most useful edition of the Bible for the careful student who knows no language but English.

The Revised Apocrypha

The revision of the Apocrypha for the R.V. seems to have been carried out with less concentrated care than the Old and New Testaments; it has been suggested that the R.V. of the Apocrypha shows signs of being the work of tired men. It was ready, however, in time for the committee which compiled the marginal references to include it in their work.

Dean Burgon and the R.V.

Since most of the leading textual scholars in the United Kingdom had some part in the revision, and most of those in the United States were similarly involved in the American Standard Version, reviews, if they were to be the work of uncommitted reviewers, must for the most part be entrusted to men less competent in the relevant fields of study than the revisers themselves. But this could not be said of the most distinguished and remorseless reviewer of the R.V.—Dr John William Burgon, Dean of Chichester from 1876 till his death in 1888. Burgon was an able textual scholar in his own right, and was actually ahead of his time in his appreciation of the importance for textual criticism of biblical citations in early Christian writers and of early Christian lectionaries. In both these areas of study he did much valuable pioneer work. Temperamentally, however, he was so conservative as to be the ideal Oxonian defender of lost causes,[1] and his old-fashioned high-church outlook disposed him to pay much more deference to the "voice of catholic antiquity" with regard to the biblical text than the canons of textual criticism could countenance. He was completely out of sympathy with the prevalent trends of nineteenth-century textual study of the New Testament, as shown in the work of Lachmann, Tregelles, Tischendorf, and Westcott and Hort. He disapproved of the high regard shown by Westcott and Hort in particular for the authority of the Vatican and Sinaitic codices; their antiquity was to him no index to their value, for he suggested that they had survived because they were so bad that no one would use them. In reading Burgon, at times one might be

---

[1] Compare the title of a sermon preached by him before the University of Oxford in 1884: "To educate young women like young men, and with young men,—a thing both inexpedient and immodest."

forgiven for supposing that in his judgment the older a manuscript, the worse it was. He reviewed the R.V. of the New Testament in a series of articles in the *Quarterly Review* for 1881 and 1882, which were published in 1883 in volume form under the title *The Revision Revised*. As a sample of good old-fashioned theological and academic polemic, with no holds barred and no quarter given, Burgon's attack on the R.V. is hard to beat. He had been whetting his blade for this engagement ever since the R.V. was launched in 1870. In 1871 he published his treatise on *The Last Twelve Verses of the Gospel according to S. Mark*, a work which may fairly be regarded as having said the last word in defence of the authenticity of these verses.[1] If even Burgon's advocacy could not prevent the Markan authorship of Mark 16 : 9-20 from being generally abandoned, it is unlikely that any less competent advocacy will succeed, the more so since further textual discoveries made since his day have supplied further evidence against their originally forming part of the Gospel.

We have already given a sample of Burgon's style from *The Revision Revised*. Here is a further one, in which he defends his view that the oldest manuscripts are not necessarily the purest in text:

I request that the clock of history may be put back seventeen hundred years. This is A.D. 183, if you please; and—(indulge me in the supposition!)—you and I are walking in Alexandria. We have reached the house of one Clemens,—a learned Athenian, who has long been a resident here. Let us step into his library,— he is from home. What a queer place! See, he has been reading his Bible, which is open at S. Mark x. Is it not a well-used copy? It must be at least 50 or 60 years old. Well, but suppose only 30 or 40. It was executed therefore *within fifty years of the death of S. John the Evangelist*. Come, let us transcribe two of the columns ... as faithfully as we possibly can, and be off. ... We are back in England again, and the clock has been put right. Now let us sit down and examine our curiosity at leisure. ... It proves on inspection to be

[1] The R.V. prints these verses as an appendix to Mark, mentioning in the margin that "the two oldest Greek manuscripts, and some other authorities, omit from ver. 9 to the end. Some other authorities have a different ending to the Gospel." Burgon's volume on them was reprinted in U.S.A. in 1959, with a preface by Dr E. F. Hills, who maintains that "for an orthodox Christian Burgon's view is the only reasonable one". It all depends what is meant by "orthodox"!

a transcript of the 15 verses (ver. 17 to ver. 31) which relate to the coming of the rich young Ruler to our LORD.

We make a surprising discovery. ... *It is impossible to produce a fouler exhibition of S. Mark x. 17–31 than is contained in a document full two centuries older than either B or Aleph[1],—itself the property of one of the most famous of the ante-Nicene Fathers.* ... The foulness of a Text which must have been penned within 70 or 80 years of the death of the last of the Evangelists, is a matter of fact—which must be loyally accepted, and made the best of (*op. cit.*, pp. 326 ff.).

We know what Clement of Alexandria's text of these verses of Mark 10 was like, because he quotes the passage in his treatise *Who is the Rich Man that shall be saved?* But he may have quoted from memory, and not always *verbatim*. For the rest, however, most textual critics would say that since the text used by Clement of Alexandria is so ancient a text, it is for that very reason entitled to respect. Clement's text-type is one found mainly in western citations and manuscripts, and it is therefore commonly known as the Western Text; Burgon's estimate of its "foulness" is due to its considerable divergence from the traditional (substantially the Byzantine) text.

Burgon could find nothing good to say about the R.V. As a translation, it was weighed in his balances and found wanting—and on that score such an accomplished stylist as he was could speak with some authority.

How it happened that, with so many splendid Scholars sitting round their table, they should have produced a Translation which, for the most part, reads like a first-rate school-boy's *crib*,—tasteless, unlovely, harsh, unidiomatic;—servile without being really faithful,—pedantic without being really learned;—an unreadable Translation, in short; the result of a vast amount of labour indeed, but of wondrous little skill:—how all this has come about it were utterly useless at this time of day to enquire (*op. cit.*, p. 238).

As usual, he exaggerates, but one can appreciate his criticism.

Theologically, he found it unsatisfactory; but he expected nothing better from a company of revisers which included Dr Vance Smith. The alternative punctuations suggested in the margin of Romans 9 : 5

---

[1] B and Aleph are the Vatican and Sinaitic codices respectively.

—particularly that which makes "God blessed for ever" an independent doxology ("God be blessed for ever") instead of a phrase in apposition to "Christ"—he denounced as *a Socinian gloss gratuitously thrust into the margin of every Englishman's N.T."* (p. 214). The revision was in his eyes *"the most astonishing, as well as the most calamitous literary blunder of the age"* (p. xi), and the Revisers, who had given their time and labour ungrudgingly for eleven years to providing the English-speaking world with as faithful a rendering of the New Testament as they could produce, ought to receive from the Church, he declared, "nothing short of stern and well-merited rebuke" (p. 2).

But his fiercest attack was reserved for the underlying text, and for Westcott and Hort's edition of the Greek Testament, which had so profoundly influenced the revisers. *"The systematic depravation of the underlying Greek,"* he affirmed, " … is nothing else but a poisoning of the River of Life at its sacred source. Our Revisers, (with the best and purest intentions, no doubt,) stand convicted of having deliberately rejected the words of Inspiration in every page" (pp. vi f.). This was, of course, a begging of the question; the revisers' position was that the excluded words were excluded precisely because they had no claim to be regarded as "the words of Inspiration".

The Verdict of Succeeding Days

Some scholars did attempt to reply to Burgon—competently, like Professor William Sanday of Oxford in the *Contemporary Review* for December 1881, and less competently, like Bishop Ellicott, chairman of the revisers, who was no match for Burgon in textual criticism, or like Dean Farrar, whose characteristically rhetorical defence of the revision in the *Contemporary Review* of March 1882 was dismissed by Burgon as a "vulgar effusion" (*op. cit.*, p. xv). The one scholar who could have answered Burgon conclusively—Dr Hort—chose to say nothing; perhaps he was content to submit the issue to the verdict of succeeding days, to which Burgon himself confidently appealed. The verdict of succeeding days, if it has not entirely vindicated Hort's confidence in the near-finality of the text which he and Westcott established, has at least recognized that text as a highly important stage on the right road to the recovery of the original New Testament text, while it has been almost unanimously adverse to Burgon's position. The underlying text of the R.V., in fact, is its most valuable feature.

The R.V. To-day

Although the R.V. has been widely used in schools, colleges and universities, as well as by private students who realize its superiority in accuracy over the A.V., it never began to replace the A.V. in popular esteem. There is real substance in the point of view reflected in that splendid satire of F. Brittain and B. Manning, *Babylon Bruis'd & Mount Moriah Mended*,[1] where the members of a twentieth-century Dowsing Society, in the course of a purgatorial visitation of the churches and colleges of Cambridge, record that:

> In yᵉ chapel at *Ridley Hall* we turned yᵉ lecterne straight. We tooke awaye therefrom .i. superstitiouse booke called yᵉ *Revised Version* & did put yᵉ Bible in place thereof.

In the years following the publication of the R.V., knowledge of the biblical text and languages made rapid advances. Further ancient manuscripts and versions continued to come to light; the vernacular papyri from the Egyptian sands made a great contribution to the understanding of biblical Greek; the decipherment of texts in ancient Semitic languages illuminated the vocabulary as well as the history of the Old Testament. Inevitably in due course the question of a further revision of the R.V. was broached. A revision was actually undertaken and completed in the United States, thanks to which we have the Revised Standard Version of the English Bible. In England, when the copyright of the R.V. was running out in the 1930's, the Oxford University Press approached two scholars, Professor G. R. Driver of Oxford and Professor J. M. Creed of Cambridge, and invited them to revise and submit specimen passages from the R.V. of the Old and New Testaments respectively. Specimens were prepared and submitted, but with the outbreak of war in 1939 and Professor Creed's death in 1940 the scheme came to nothing. The plan was probably to bring the R.V. abreast of contemporary textual and linguistic knowledge. But after the war a plan of a much more radical character was initiated and carried through.

[1] Published by Heffer, Cambridge (1940).

CHAPTER TWELVE

Early Twentieth Century Versions

The Twentieth Century New Testament

THE PRESENT CENTURY had not well begun when there appeared, on both sides of the Atlantic, a volume bearing the appropriate title *The Twentieth Century New Testament: A Translation into Modern English Made from the Original Greek (Westcott & Hort's Text)*. This work, published in 1902,[1] was the first of a series of "modern English" versions of which we have not seen the end yet (may their number go on increasing!). That it was the work of about twenty persons was revealed by the preface, in which the translators gave some account of the principles which guided them, but the identity of the translators was not revealed until more than fifty years later.

In 1891 W. T. Stead, editor of *The Review of Reviews*, received two letters from writers who had no idea of each other's existence. One was the wife of a Congregational minister in Oldham, Mrs Mary Higgs; the other was a signal and telegraph engineer of Hull, Ernest de Mérindol Malan, grandson of an eminent Swiss divine, César Malan. Both these writers were concerned about the inadequacy of the existing versions (even the R.V.) to make the meaning of the Bible plain to young people, and both wanted to do something to repair this deficiency. Stead introduced them to each other, and they began to collaborate on the translation of St Mark's Gospel. As their work advanced, they got into touch with other likeminded people—mainly Christians of a radical outlook in social and religious matters—until at last over thirty of them were associated with the enterprise, although several of these were unable to take any active part in it. Some were ministers of various churches, others were lay people, but none of them belonged to the class of linguistic and textual experts who had produced the R.V. They did on occasion

---

[1] It appeared first in three parts in 1898, 1900 and 1901, and in one volume (revised) in 1904.

consult experts; but the real work was done by themselves. They drew up rules for their guidance, which guarded against private excesses in interpretation and wording, but in fact for a "non-professional group, whose translating was motivated by social causes and by the desire to mediate the Word of God in a plainer English idiom",[1] they seem to have had very little in the way of private axes to grind or private whims to indulge. How they succeeded in producing such an excellent version is difficult to understand. In later years several scholars have been glad to avail themselves of interpretations and renderings suggested by this non-specialist effort. "Somewhere along the line, some transforming miracle seems to have occurred. We are forced to conclude that the devotion to their task has made of them better scholars than they were at first."[2]

In 1933 the last survivor of the group of translators (so far as is known) deposited the secretary's records of the work in the John Rylands Library, Manchester. There, twenty years later, they were studied by an American scholar, Dr Kenneth W. Clark, whose fascinating account of "The Making of the Twentieth Century New Testament" appears in the *Bulletin of the John Rylands Library* for September 1955.

They divided the work into a number of sections: (1) The Four Gospels and the Acts (in which Mark is placed first); (2) St Paul's Letters to the Churches (arranged in what was believed to be their chronological order); (3) Pastoral, Personal and General Letters (the Epistles to Timothy and Titus, Philemon, 2 and 3 John, Hebrews, James, 1 John, 1 and 2 Peter, Jude); (4) The Revelation.

The Matthaean form of the Lord's Prayer is rendered thus:

> Our heavenly Father,
> May thy Name be held holy,
> thy Kingdom come,
> and thy will be done—
> on earth, as in Heaven.
> Give us to-day
> our bread for the day before us;

---

[1] *Rylands Library Bulletin*, Sept. 1955, p. 66.   [2] *Ibid.*, p. 81.

And forgive us our debts,
    as we, too, have forgiven our debtors;
And do not take us into temptation,
    but rescue us from Evil.

The parable of the Good Samaritan is rendered thus:

"A man was once going down from Jerusalem to Jericho when he fell into the hands of robbers, who stripped him of everything, and beat him, and then went off leaving him half dead. It so happened that a priest chanced to be going down by that road. He saw the man, but passed by on the opposite side. In the same way a Levite, too, came up to the spot, but when he saw him, passed by on the opposite side. But a Samaritan, travelling that way, came up to the man, and when he saw him, his heart melted at the sight. He went to him and bound up his wounds, dressing them with oil and wine, and then put him on his own animal, and led him to an inn, where he took care of him. The next day he took out four shillings, and gave them to the inn-keeper. 'Take care of him,' he said, 'and whatever more you spend I will myself repay on my way back.' Now which, do you think, of these three men," asked Jesus, "proved himself a neighbour to the man who fell into the robbers' hands?"

"The one that took pity on him," was the answer; on which Jesus said:

"Go and do the same yourself."

And here is the opening passage of the Epistle to the Hebrews:

God, who in the old days spoke to our ancestors, through the Prophets, at many different times and in many different ways, has in these latter days spoken to us through the Son, whom he had appointed heir to everything, and through whom he had made the universe. He is the reflection of God's Glory and the embodiment of the divine nature, and upholds all creation by the power of his word. He made an expiation for the sins of men, and then *took his seat at the right hand* of God's Majesty on high, having shown himself as much greater than the angels as the Name that he has inherited surpasses theirs.

The italicized words in the last passage are words quoted from the Old Testament; in this regard the translators imitated the practice of Westcott and Hort, in whose Greek New Testament distinctive type marks quotations from the Old Testament.

Weymouth's New Testament

One of the scholars who were consulted from time to time by the translators of the *Twentieth Century New Testament* was Dr Richard Francis Weymouth, Fellow of University College, London, and at one time Headmaster of Mill Hill School. Dr Weymouth, a distinguished classical scholar, published an edition of the Greek New Testament entitled *The Resultant Greek Testament*, which exhibited the text representing the greatest measure of agreement among the leading nineteenth-century editors, with a critical apparatus at the foot of each page indicating where the Received Text or more recent editions deviated from the text which he himself had established on the basis of a majority consensus. This work was published with an introductory note by Dr J. J. S. Perowne, Bishop of Worcester; it was printed several times, and is a useful edition of the Greek Testament.

When this text had been published, Dr Weymouth turned his mind to translating it into modern English, and produced *The New Testament in Modern Speech*. He died before it could be published, and it was edited and seen through the press by E. Hampden-Cook, a Congregational minister who was himself one of the translators of the *Twentieth Century New Testament*. He equipped the translation with notes, some of which reflected opinions of his own which were regarded in that day as falling short of orthodoxy. Dr Weymouth himself deviated from traditional orthodoxy in his views of the state of the dead and the future life. While he was a good classical scholar, he did not appreciate the Semitic idiom underlying the New Testament phrases translated "eternal life" and so forth, and used expressions like "the life of the ages" which do not convey their meaning immediately to English readers. What the expression actually meant was "the life of the age to come"—which, according to St John's writings in particular, Christ makes available here and now to those who believe in Him.

But the translator had no other object in view than the rendering of the New Testament into dignified modern English, with no theological or ecclesiastical bias. It was published in 1903, and was frequently reprinted. In 1924 it was thoroughly revised by Professor James Alexander Robertson of Aberdeen; in this revision "the life of the ages" disappeared in favour of the older and more intelligible rendering "eternal life".

As a classical scholar and headmaster, Weymouth might be expected to pay careful attention to points of grammatical accuracy; his treatment of Greek tenses, for example, marks an improvement over the R.V. His "modern speech" is not ultra-modern; he had no objection to using archaic words provided that they were still understood at the beginning of the twentieth century. "Without at least a tinge of antiquity, it is scarcely possible that there should be that dignity of style that befits the sacred themes." He had no wish that his version should supplant the A.V. and R.V., or that it should be used for public reading in church; he envisaged it rather as "a succinct and compressed running commentary (not doctrinal) to be used side by side with its elder compeers." Yet he hoped that his version might point the way one day to a new English translation of the Bible which would replace both A.V. and R.V.

The flow of the narrative or the argument is made easier for the reader in this version by the provision of indented sub-headings which summarize the successive sections. Thus, on one page which lies open before me, comprising Matt. 6 : 1–18, the following sub-headings appear: *"Do not parade your Good Deeds"* (v. 1), *"Avoid Display in Charity"* (vv. 2–4), *"Avoid Display in Prayer"* (vv. 5–6), *"Do not use needless Repetitions"* (vv. 7–8), *"The Lord's Prayer"* (vv. 9–15), *"Avoid Display in Fasting"* (vv. 16–18).

This is his rendering of the Lord's Prayer (Matt. 6 : 9–13):

Our Father in heaven, may Thy name be kept holy; let Thy Kingdom come; let Thy will be done, as in heaven so on earth; give us to-day our bread for the day; and forgive our shortcomings, as we also have forgiven those who have failed in their duty towards us; and bring us not into temptation, but rescue us from the Evil one.

Debts and trespasses alike have disappeared, but the prayer for forgiveness becomes more relevant to the ordinary concerns of life in which shortcomings and failures in duty play a much larger part than positive injuries.

And here is the parable of the Good Samaritan:

"A man was once on his way down from Jerusalem to Jericho when he fell among robbers, who after both stripping and beating him went away, leaving him half dead. Now a priest happened to be going along that road, and on seeing him passed by on the other side. In like manner a Levite also came to the place, and seeing him passed by on the other side. But a certain Samaritan, being on a journey, came where he lay, and seeing him was moved with pity. He went to him, and dressed his wounds with oil and wine and bound them up. Then placing him on his own mule he brought him to an inn, and took care of him. The next day he took out two shillings and gave them to the innkeeper.

" 'Take care of him,' he said, 'and whatever further expenses you are put to, I will repay you at my next visit.'

"Which of those three seems to you to have acted like a neighbour to him who fell among the robbers?"

"The one who showed him pity," he replied.

"Go," said Jesus, "and act in the same way."

We can trace here some echoes both of the older versions and of the *Twentieth Century New Testament*. It is interesting that, while Weymouth was content to translate a *denarius* by a shilling (like the American Standard Version), the *Twentieth Century* translators, more mindful, perhaps, of the buying power of shillings around the year 1900, turned the Samaritan's two *denarii* into *four* shillings.

In the epistles of Paul, Weymouth helps the reader to grasp the apostle's meaning by cutting his long sentences into sentences of more manageable size. Take, for example, the A.V. rendering of Eph. 1 : 7–12:

In whom we have redemption through his blood, the forgiveness of sins, according to the riches of his grace; wherein he hath abounded toward us in all wisdom and prudence; having made known unto us the mystery of his will, according to his good pleasure which he hath purposed in himself: that in the dispensation of the fulness of times he might gather together in one all things in Christ, both which are in heaven, and which are on earth; *even* in him: in whom also we have obtained an inheritance, being predestinated according to the purpose of him who worketh all things after the counsel of his own will: that we should be to the praise of his glory, who first trusted in Christ.

It calls for no little skill to read a sentence like that aloud so that the congregation can understand the drift of it. But now compare Weymouth's rendering of the same passage:

It is in Him, and through the shedding of His blood, that we have our deliverance—the forgiveness of our offences—so abundant was God's grace, the grace which He, the possessor of all wisdom and understanding, lavished upon us, when He made known to us the secret of His will. And this is in harmony with God's merciful purpose for the government of the world when the times are ripe for it—the purpose which He has cherished in His own mind of restoring the whole creation to find its one Head in Christ; yes, things in heaven and things on earth, to find their one Head in Him.

In Him too we have been made heirs, having been chosen beforehand in accordance with the intention of Him whose might carries out in everything the design of His own will, so that we should be devoted to the extolling of His glorious attributes—we who were the first to fix our hopes on Christ.

Instead of one sentence we have three—still longish ones by the standards of the 1970's, but sentences whose structure and meaning can be readily grasped. And as for the language, God's purpose "that in the dispensation of the fulness of times he might gather together in one all things in Christ" (words which the Revisers of 1881 did not render much more intelligible) becomes luminous when it is seen to be His "merciful purpose for the government of the world when the times are ripe for it."

One further sample of Weymouth's version may be given—the first four verses of Hebrews:

God, who of old spoke to our forefathers in many fragments and by various methods through the Prophets, has at the end of these days spoken to us through a Son, who is the predestined Lord of the universe, and through whom He made the world. He brightly reflects God's glory and is the exact representation of His being, and upholds the universe by His all-powerful word. After securing man's purification from sin He took His seat at the right hand of the Majesty on high, having become as far superior to the angels as the Name He possesses by inheritance is more excellent than theirs.

The phrase "at the end of these days" (taken over from the R.V.) is a literal translation of the Greek, but the Greek phrase is really the rendering of an Old Testament phrase meaning "in the latter days" or "in these latter days". The prophets had pointed forward to the consummation of God's redeeming purpose "in the latter days"; the point in Heb. 1 : 2 and similar places in the New Testament is that with the coming of Christ the "latter days" have arrived, so that they can be referred to as "these latter days".

It is difficult to decide whether the *Twentieth Century New Testament* or Weymouth's *New Testament in Modern Speech* is the better rendering; Weymouth would naturally be preferable in several places on the score of accuracy, but on the whole they should be bracketed very high up in the order of merit. It was a good omen that the first years of this century should see two such admirable versions of the New Testament in good twentieth-century English.

Ferrar Fenton's version

The Holy Bible in Modern English, containing the complete sacred scriptures of the Old and New Testaments, translated into English direct from the original Hebrew, Chaldee and Greek, by Ferrar Fenton, M.R.A.S., M.C.A.A., with introductions and critical notes, is an impressive piece of work, especially when one considers that it is the single-handed achievement of a man whose special training did not lie in the field of biblical languages. Ferrar Fenton was a business man, who believed that his commercial experience was a divine preparation to fit him to be a competent translator of the Bible. The spirit in which he tackled and accomplished his self-imposed task may be gathered from the dedication of his work:

> I dedicate this complete translation of the Holy Scriptures of the Hebrew and Christian faith to all those nations who have sprung from the race of the British Isles, and to whom the English language, in its developed power, is the mother tongue; and with them to all the inhabitants of the world to whom English has become, or may become, the language of thought, in hope that a clear presentment of the laws of creation and human existence will restore them from the mental distress of atheistic doubt, to a firm reliance upon God, their Creator, and the practice of His revealed laws of life, bodily and spiritual.

Ferrar Fenton began the publication of his translation with the Epistle to the Romans, which appeared in 1882. Two years later he had finished translating the epistles, the complete New Testament was published in 1895, and the whole Bible in 1903. It was frequently reprinted; the demand for it was so great that even during the Second World War two new impressions appeared—in 1941 and 1944. Just why it should have proved so popular is difficult to determine; perhaps it was the fact that it was the work of an amateur (in the best sense of that word), for in biblical and theological studies even more than in others there is a widespread feeling that to be an "expert" positively disqualifies a man from the right to a serious hearing on the subject.

Any initial good will with which one approaches this version is rudely shaken by the first verse of Genesis: "By Periods GOD created that which produced the Solar Systems; then that which produced the Earth." Leaving aside the curious circumlocution which replaces the far more expressive "heaven and earth", one may wonder how the phrase so commonly translated "in the beginning" should be rendered "by periods". The translator anticipates his reader's wonder, and gives an explanation in a footnote: "Literally 'By Headships'. It is curious that all translators from the Septuagint have rendered this word ... into the singular, although it is plural in the Hebrew. So I render it accurately.—F.F." It is curious, rather, that a man who set out to translate the Old Testament should have been guilty of such an elementary blunder in Hebrew. The noun in question is *reshith*, which is a noun in the singular number; and not the most self-confident assertion can make it plural.

Fortunately, the translation as a whole is not so completely off beam as the first verse of Genesis is, but the footnote illustrates the translator's main defect—an undue depreciation of the work of his predecessors, and an undue regard for his own opinion. The preface to the 1910 edition of his translation ends with the paragraph:

> As every effort has been made to attain it, I believe this fifth edition of my work is the most accurate rendering into any European language, ancient or modern, ever made, not only in words, but in editing, spirit, and sense. I contend that I am the only man who has ever applied real mental and literary criticism to the Sacred Scriptures. I specially refer to my rediscovery of the Hebrew laws of Syllabic verse.

On this the best comment is perhaps that of Proverbs 27 : 2, in Ferrar Fenton's own translation:

> Let a stranger praise you, not your mouth,
> Another, and not your own lips.

His claim to have rediscovered "the Hebrew laws of Syllabic verse" relates, as he tells us elsewhere, to his realization that Hebrew and Persian poetry were characterized by a similarity in cadence, as well as in imagery and thought. He was also greatly impressed one day when a lady asked him to let her hear how the Hebrew language sounded, and he read aloud a passage from one of the poetical books of the Old Testament. "Why," she exclaimed, "that is poetry! it is verse!" "Yes," he replied, "so it is"—having evidently only half-realized it before. Ferrar Fenton does, to his credit, print the poetry of the Old Testament as poetry, and translates it into rhythmical English which goes with a vigorous swing, as may be seen from his version of the hundredth Psalm:

> Hurrah to the LORD all the Earth;
> Serve the LORD with delight;

Come into His Presence with cheering,
Acknowledge the LORD as the GOD,
Who made us, and not we, ourselves,
His People, and sheep of His fold.
Come enter His Gates, then, with thanks,
Extol Him with praise in His Courts,
    By blessing His Name.
For THE LIFE is eternally kind,—
His mercy will last for all time,
    And for ages His Truth.

"THE LIFE" is one of the ways in which he translates the divine name Yahweh. At other times he renders it "The EVER-LIVING", most frequently in the law and in the historical books; in the poetical and prophetical books it appears more often as "the LORD".

He has transliterated proper names in the Old Testament according to a principle of his own; thus Jezebel (in Hebrew *Izebel*) appears as "Aisebal", Elisha as "Alisha", Gehazi as "Ghikhazi", and the names which in our common Bibles have Jeho- as their first element appear in such forms as Jhoshafat, Jhoash, Jhoakhaz, and so forth.

In the Old Testament the order of the books is that found in the Hebrew Bible; in the New Testament the common order is followed, with a couple of remarkable exceptions: John's Gospel and First Epistle, instead of coming in their usual positions, appear first and second respectively among the New Testament books. John's Gospel is placed first for two reasons: (1) it "is specially the Doctrinal Record of our Lord's life"; (2) "There is ample reason for believing that the Gospel of John was written at an earlier date than those of the other three Evangelists". The second of these reasons is surprising indeed, for it is generally held that there is "ample reason" for believing this Gospel to be the latest of the canonical four. Evidently, however, it is not to the Greek Gospel that Ferrar Fenton ascribes this early date, but to an older Hebrew edition, which the Evangelist in his old age translated into Greek for the benefit of the Greek-speaking churches. He supposes further that the Evangelist, when translating his original draft into Greek, added a number of comments on his narrative; these are placed between square brackets. Several of these appear in the first chapter; they consist for the most part of the interpretations given of Hebrew or Aramaic terms, such as Rabbi (verse 38), Messiah (verse 41), Cephas (verse 42); but verse 15 (an insertion in the Prologue to the Gospel, anticipating the Baptist's words about Jesus in verse 30) is also marked in this way.

The First Epistle of John is placed immediately after John's Gospel because "it is evidently the concluding section of the same", added to the Greek translations of the Gospel which the Evangelist is supposed to have made about A.D. 90. To call the Epistle the concluding section of the Gospel is going farther than the view that it was designed as a covering letter accompanying the Gospel as it was sent to various churches, and summarizing its main themes. However, there is no doubt a certain advantage in bringing together two documents which undoubtedly are closely associated, although the two shorter Johannine letters might as well have been placed after 1 John instead of being left between 2 Peter and Jude. For the two shorter Epistles of John are closely associated with 1 John and may also have a connection with the Gospel; it would then have been possible to present 2 Peter and Jude in juxtaposition, most appropriately in view of the close connection between these two documents.

An incidental consequence of the transposition of John's Gospel to first place is that Luke's Gospel is followed immediately by Acts, which, of course, was originally designed as the sequel to Luke. Acts is said in a footnote to be the work of Luke, who was not only Paul's physician but also his cousin—no doubt because he is identified with Paul's kinsman Lucius in Romans 16 : 21 (translated by Fenton: "My assistant, Timothy, and my cousins, Luke and Jason, and Sosipater, send you regards").

In the Epistle to the Romans, which was the first part of Fenton's work to see the light, supposed objections to statements made by Paul in the course of his argument are indicated by captions as follows:

(Jewish Opponent.) "Then what advantage has the Jew? or what is the benefit of the circumcision?"

(Paul.) "Great in all respects; for first, indeed, they were entrusted with the intentions of God."

(Jew.) "What for? If some were unfaithful, would not their unfaithfulness destroy God's trust?"

(Paul.) "It would not ..." (Rom. 3 : 1 ff.).

The same device is followed occasionally in the other Epistles, as (for example) in 1 Cor. 6 : 12 f.:

(Sophist.) "Everything is allowable to me."

(Paul.) "But everything does not benefit."

(Sophist.) "Everything is permissible to me."

(Paul.) "But I will not be deluded by any."

(Sophist.) "The foods for the stomach, and the stomach for the foods."

(Paul.) "But God can abolish both it and them ..."

A good example of the translator's appreciation of the sacred writings which he dealt with is given in his appended note to 2 Corinthians:

The two Epistles to the Corinthians present St Paul to us as a Statesman and Social Organizer of the highest ability, and of the clearest common sense. He would seem to have been accused of teaching a Code of Morality too high for practical life, but in reply he calmly enacts Laws for the conduct of Christians, that, while easy to obey, do not make obedience a slavery, or a struggle against the natural necessities of mankind, but instead will make existence pleasant, healthful, virtuous, and consequently happy. They have no asceticism, or prohibition of any innocent pleasure, but encourage bodily and mental comfort in every way, and enforce the principles of Duty, Justice and Mercy, and the equality in moral accountability to God of rich and poor alike, and the mutual duties of every class of Society to each other, and that without any revolution—any assault upon existing social systems and legal rights, but showing how the worst conditions of the hideously corrupt morality and laws of his day could be reformed without any resort to political violence, and to the especial benefit of the followers of Christ. I am not aware that St Paul has been ever before studied in this position of a Legislator, but as such his influence has re-organized the Civilized World.

His translation, for all its limitations, has probably commanded much popularity among serious-minded people because they found themselves so heartily in accord with his forcefully expressed sentiments.

In 1911 the tercentenary of the A.V. was celebrated by the publication of *The 1911 Tercentenary Commemoration Bible*, an evangelical enterprise issued by the Oxford University Press, in which the text of the A.V. was reproduced with light corrections and improvements carried through by biblical scholars in North America. It was, for example, a great improvement to have the unwanted "not" removed before the words "increased the joy" in Isa. 9 : 3. A similar revision of the A.V., by E. E. Cunnington, was published three years later by G. Routledge and Sons, London.

In 1923 William G. Ballantine produced a version of the New Testament in modern English, based on the Nestle Greek text of 1901, under the title *The Riverside New Testament* (revised edition, 1934). The completion of the first hundred years of the work of the American Baptist Publication Society was marked in 1924 by the publication of the *Centenary Translation of the New Testament*, another modern speech version by Helen Barrett Montgomery.

CHAPTER THIRTEEN

Moffatt, Goodspeed and Others

The Moffatt Version

OF INDIVIDUAL TRANSLATORS in the twentieth century none is better known than James Moffatt. So well known was he in this capacity that once, when he visited a certain town in the United States to deliver a public lecture, he found himself billed on the public hoardings: "Author of Bible to Lecture To-night".

Moffatt was a brilliant Scottish scholar, whose first essay in Bible translation, *The Historical New Testament*, which appeared in 1901, secured for him the honorary degree of doctor of divinity from the University of St Andrews, at the early age of thirty-one. This work was an original translation of the New Testament documents, arranged in their chronological order, and edited with prolegomena, historical tables, critical notes, and an appendix—an outstanding contribution to New Testament scholarship.

But the translation by which Moffatt made his name was quite a different one from that. *The New Testament: A New Translation* appeared in 1913, when Moffatt was Yates Professor of New Testament in Mansfield College, Oxford. This was followed in 1924 by *The Old Testament: A New Translation;* by this time Moffatt was Professor of Church History in the United Free Church College, Glasgow. Some years later he was appointed to the Washbourne Chair of Church History in Union Theological Seminary, New York.

A one-volume edition of his version appeared in 1928, *A New Translation of the Bible.*

Moffatt's translation is characterized by the freedom and vigour of his idiom. His idiom, to be sure, at times seemed to justify those who called his work the translation of the Bible into Scots; for expressions like "You may wash yourself with lye and plenty soap" (Jer. 2 : 22) and the parable of the dishonest "factor" (Luke 16 : 1 ff.) sound a little exotic in English ears.[1] But if a translator's business is to produce on his readers the same effect as the original text produced on those who read and heard it, Moffatt succeeded wonderfully; and this is part of the secret of the popularity of his version. He did not intend to replace the A.V., and much of the criticism that was levelled against his work was due to the fact that it sounded so different from the A.V.; it had none of the characteristics of "Bible English". We have all heard of the modern young minister in Scotland who visited an aged member of his flock and read to her a chapter from Moffatt's version. "Well," said she, "that was very nice; but now, won't you just read a bittie of the Word of God before you go?"

To some people, however, "very nice" was no description of Moffatt's version. Perhaps in no book of the Old Testament did Moffatt make for the goal of equivalent effect so ruthlessly as in the Song of Songs. Several readers, however, did not like the equivalent effect, and felt he had completely secularized the book by saying "The girls are all in love with you" where the A.V. had the statelier wording "therefore do the virgins love thee" (1 : 3), or "come, dear, come away, my beauty!" instead of the A.V., "Arise, my love, my fair one, and come away" (2 : 13). Perhaps they felt that the language of the A.V. was sufficiently removed here from that of daily life to be allegorized in the traditional way; but Moffatt's renderings were too realistic and up-to-date to be easily allegorized. Whatever else may be said, they were too prosaic in such a book as this. Similarly, "Train a child for his proper trade" (Prov. 22 : 6) lacked the religious and moral overtones of the A.V., "Train up a child in the way he should go"; one could base an exhortation at a baptismal or dedication service on the A.V. text, but hardly on Moffatt's rendering.

For all the breadth of his scholarship, Moffatt was more of an expert in the New Testament than in the Old, and this is evident in his translation. His New Testament version was based on the Greek text which had been edited and published not long before by Hermann von Soden. This was a pity; the more von Soden's text was examined by textual critics, the more defects was it seen to contain.

[1] So, at least, I am told; as a Scot, I am conscious of no exotic flavour in such locutions.

But Moffatt was quite ready to accept conjectural emendations of the text; thus, in 1 Peter 3 : 19 he introduces a new character into the vexed passage about the spirits in prison by saying that "Enoch also went and preached to the imprisoned spirits."[1] Enoch is not mentioned in any of our authorities for the text, but William Bowyer (1772) anticipated a number of more recent scholars in suggesting that his name had fallen out by accident. Again, in 1 Tim. 5 : 23 Paul's injunction to Timothy to give up drinking water and take a little wine for his health's sake is expelled from the text and reproduced in a footnote: "The words, 'Give up being a total abstainer; take a little wine for the sake of your stomach and your frequent attacks of illness,' which follow, are either a marginal gloss or misplaced."

In the supper-room discourses of John 13–16 there is major rearrangement of the order; the fifteenth and sixteenth chapters are placed immediately after the words "When he had gone out, Jesus said," in John 13 : 31. Some weighty arguments can be put forward for this rearrangement, which in several respects makes the flow of thought run on more smoothly; but we should not be too sure that the Evangelist had the same ideas about logical sequence as we have.

The title "The Word" in the opening paragraph of St John's Gospel has been a thorn in the flesh of many translators; there is, in fact, no one English word that represents its meaning adequately. Moffatt did not attempt to translate it, but retained the Greek term "Logos". " 'Logos'," he says, "is at any rate less misleading than 'Word' would be to a modern reader." So he renders the first verse of the Gospel:

> The Logos existed in the very beginning,
> the Logos was with God,
> the Logos was divine.

In that last clause he falls short of the ideal of equivalent effect; considering the wide use of the adjective "divine" in modern English, we must observe that "the Logos was divine" says something rather less than the Evangelist himself says.

Moffatt's version of the Old Testament begins with the words, "This is the story of how the universe was formed." Then he goes

---

[1] So also Goodspeed's version.

on with the familiar first two verses of Genesis: "When God began to form the universe, the world was void and vacant ..." The words which he puts at the beginning of the book actually appear in the original text as the first half of Gen. 2 : 4, and there they form the colophon, or tail-piece, of the creation narrative Gen. 1 : 1—2 : 3. Whether such a summary appeared as an initial title or as a colophon was a matter of small moment in ancient documents, but Moffatt might have left the original order as it was. His rearrangement of the text here called forth a fierce attack from a veteran Scottish minister, W. L. Baxter,[1] in a pamphlet entitled *The Bible's First Verse: Moses or Moffatt?*

Throughout the first five books of the Old Testament Moffatt endeavoured by the use of alternating roman and italic type and other means to indicate the various sources which, according to the regnant documentary hypothesis, were brought together to form our Pentateuch. This was a less elaborate means to that end than the means adopted by the *Polychrome Bible*, which used different colours to distinguish the sources. But, apart from the merits or otherwise of that particular documentary hypothesis, it is not really part of a translator's business to incorporate source-critical theories into his work, especially when his version is intended for the general public.

An example of Moffatt's proneness to conjectural emendation in the Old Testament may be found in 1 Sam. 14 : 11, in the story of Jonathan's attack on the Philistine garrison at Michmash. According to Moffatt, when Jonathan and his armour-bearer showed themselves to the Philistine garrison, "the Philistines said, 'Look at the mice creeping out of their hiding-holes!'" The original text does not say "mice", but "Hebrews". But in the Hebrew consonantal text the letter *k* is all that is needed to change "Hebrews" into "mice", and some editors and commentators had conjectured—baselessly—that "mice" was the original reading.

The name of the God of Israel is regularly rendered by "The Eternal", except in such compound titles as "The Lord of hosts". Moffatt tells us that it was with some reluctance that he decided, almost at the last moment, not to use the form "Yahweh" (which he

---

[1] Many years before Dr Baxter had won a secure place in the literature of Biblical criticism with his work *Sanctuary and Sacrifice—A Reply to Wellhausen* (London, 1895).

would have used in a version intended for scholars). "The Eternal" (*L'Éternel*) is commonly used for Yahweh by Frenchmen, and it was also preferred by Matthew Arnold, although for rather different reasons from Moffatt's. In such a book as the Psalter "The Eternal" is quite an effective equivalent for Yahweh.

In spite of many criticisms that can quite justly be urged against Moffatt's version, by scholar and layman alike, it is but fair to say that to read through an Old Testament prophetical book or a New Testament epistle in his version is one of the best ways to get a grasp of the general argument. And people who have been brought up to know and love the A.V. from infancy should consider that much of it sounds foreign to those who have not been brought up to appreciate its wording. To such people Moffatt undoubtedly has made the Bible message intelligible, in spite of the detailed imperfections that may be found in his translation.

At times, too, Moffatt can rise to the heights. His version of Paul's hymn in praise of heavenly love in 1 Cor. 13 is moving by its very simplicity:

> Love is very patient, very kind. Love knows no jealousy; love makes no parade, gives itself no airs, is never rude, never selfish, never irritated, *never resentful*; love is never glad when others go wrong, love is gladdened by goodness, always slow to expose, always eager to believe the best, always hopeful, always patient. Love never disappears.

The man who gave us that translation knew what he was talking about; it is no wonder that one of his great works is entitled *Love in the New Testament*.

Moffatt's work as a Bible translator did not come to an end with his last revision of his own version. In his closing years he served as executive secretary of the committee which was given the responsibility of producing the Revised Standard Version. By the time of his death in 1944 the New Testament section of this revision was practically complete. Dr Luther A. Weigle, chairman of the revisers, tells how a proposed rendering was turned down in committee one day. The man who had proposed it turned to Moffatt and said: "Do you know where I got that phrase which you just now rejected?" "No," said Moffatt. "In Moffatt's translation of the New Testament!" said the other. "Well," said Moffatt, "that phrase was right for my translation, but it will not do for this."

The Goodspeed Version

What may be regarded as the American counterpart of Moffatt is *The Complete Bible: An American Translation* (1927, revised 1935). The first instalment of this version was Dr Edgar J. Goodspeed's *The New Testament: An American Translation*, which appeared in 1923. Dr Goodspeed pointed out that "for American readers ... who have had to depend so long upon versions made in Great Britain, there is room for a New Testament free from expressions which, however familiar in England or Scotland, are strange in American ears." The production of a companion version of the Old Testament was entrusted to the editorship of Dr J. M. Powis Smith, who secured the collaboration of three other scholars. One of these, who was entrusted with the translation of Proverbs and the Major Prophets, was a Scot, resident in Canada, the late Alexander R. Gordon; but one does not detect in his work the Scotticisms which were a feature of Moffatt's work. The revised edition of the Old Testament was supervised throughout by Dr Theophile J. Meek, who in the first edition had been responsible for the first eight books and also the Song of Songs and Lamentations.

In 1938 Dr Goodspeed, who had launched the enterprise with his New Testament, completed it with a translation of the Apocrypha.

Even if this version is an "American translation", it has a dignity which commends itself to readers on this side of the Atlantic as much as to Americans. Some years ago, when I had reviewed a new edition of the New Testament part of the work in a British periodical, I received a letter from an unknown correspondent. In it he said:

> I have just read your review of Dr Goodspeed's translation of the New Testament and thought you would be interested in my views and experience with this translation.
>
> I first came into contact with it through the generosity of a G.I. friend in Calcutta during the war. He gave me the combined volume—Smith and Goodspeed's translation of the Old and New

Testaments together with the Apocrypha. Ever since I have blessed my G.I. brother's munificence. He himself used it for Bible study and he told me that it was a favourite with his fellow G.I. Christians.

I have found the translation free from harsh Americanisms, and apart from spelling variations find the poise, turn of speech and rhythmic flow of the language more "English" than some of our more prominent home translations.

Some of Dr Goodspeed's renderings are singularly fortunate and I have found quite a stream of new light upon passages which are, in the Authorized Version, dulled over by the archaic turn of speech. ... Compared with Moffatt by and large I find Goodspeed far more real, more readable and, more important still, more satisfying.

As regards Dr Smith's translations in the Old Testament as well as that of Dr Theophile Meek, here again I would far rather advise a beginner in Bible study to use these than I would Moffatt's. ...

P.S. I have read through the entire O.T. and N.T. of Smith and Goodspeed twice. Now on my third run. It grows upon one!

I regard such an assessment, from an articulate but non-specialist representative of the class of reader (albeit an Englishman) for which the translation was designed, as more valuable in its way than any critical review by a scholar.

Wade's Version

The Documents of the New Testament, by G. W. Wade (1934), may be described as an attempt to do, on a less elaborate scale, what Moffatt's *Historical New Testament* had done over thirty years before. It is a fresh translation of the New Testament documents, arranged in what the translator believed to be their chronological order, with historical and critical introductions and notes. The translation is expanded in order to make the sense plainer, the expansions being usually distinguished by italicization. Thus the clause which the A.V. renders "If ye then be risen with Christ" (Col. 3 : 1) appears as: "If, then, *after being immersed in the waters of Baptism, you emerged from them and were thereby symbolically* raised with the Christ."

The Book of Books

The United Society for Christian Literature celebrated the four hundredth anniversary of the placing of a copy of the English Bible in every parish church in England (1538) and the centenary of the publication of the *Annotated Paragraph Bible* by the Religious Tract Society (1838) by sponsoring a translation of the New Testament entitled *The Book of Books* (Lutterworth Press, 1938), in which the language of the older versions was modernized and the text arranged according to the latest standards of book production.

St Mark for the Children

By contrast with such scholarly productions, we may look briefly at the work of Edward Vernon, who maintained that it should be possible for the Synoptic Gospels at least to be read without explanatory notes. "The ideal would be a version in which no word would be employed which could not be readily understood by the average intelligent child of twelve years old and upwards." To show what he meant, he produced a most engaging edition of *The Gospel of St Mark: A New Translation in simple English* (1951). The Gadarene demoniac "turned away and went off; and all over Ten-Town-Land he spread the story of what Jesus had done for him. What a sensation it caused!" (Mark 5 : 20). When Jairus's daughter was raised up, "her father and mother were almost crazy with wonder and joy" (Mark 5 : 42). And—best of all, if a trifle macabre—Herodias's daughter ran up to Herod and said: "Please, I'd like the head of John the Baptizer on a plate; and please can I have it now?" (Mark 6 : 25).

The Basic English Bible

It might have been thought that such a work as *The Bible in Basic English* laboured under so heavy an initial handicap in the severe limitation of its vocabulary that its value as a Bible version was very small. Actually, it is much more valuable than might have been expected.

Basic English is a simple form of the English language, produced by Mr C. K. Ogden, of the Orthological Institute, which claims to be able with a vocabulary of 850 words to give the sense of anything that may be said in English. Its value for enabling those whose native language is not English to express themselves in English is obvious. But if such people begin to read English literature, their basic vocabulary will soon increase rapidly. Therefore, it might be argued, if they are to read the Bible, why should they not read one of the better-known versions? On the other hand, if people are trying to make themselves proficient in Basic English, a Basic English version of the Bible might well be a very useful aid to this end.

At any rate, shortly before the outbreak of the Second World War, the Orthological Institute arranged for Professor S. H. Hooke to undertake the production of a Basic English version of the Bible; the New Testament was published in 1940 and the whole Bible in 1949. By the addition of fifty special "Bible" words, together with a further hundred words listed as giving most help in the reading of English verse, the available vocabulary was raised from 850 to 1,000.

Inevitably it proved impossible, even with this increased vocabulary, to convey the more delicate shades of meaning in the original. But the very limitations of the vocabulary compelled the translators to pay the most careful attention to the sense of the original and to their selection of the best "Basic" words to convey that sense. And it is but right to say that much of the success attending the Basic English Bible is due to the genius of Professor Hooke, a scholar who combined an accurate mastery of biblical philology and religion with qualities of spiritual insight not always found in scholars. He, with Mrs Hooke as his sole collaborator, did not turn any existing version of the English Bible into Basic English, but produced an independent translation from the original languages.

Basic English is remarkably deficient in verbs; but mark how this handicap is overcome in the rendering of John 21 : 15–17:

Then when they had taken food, Jesus said to Simon Peter, Simon, son of John, is your love for me greater than the love of these others? He said to him, Yes, Lord; you have knowledge that you are dear to me. He said to him, Then give my lambs food. Again, a second time, he said to him, Simon, son of John, have you any love for me? Yes, Lord, he said, you have knowledge that you are dear to me. Then take care of my sheep, said Jesus. He said to him a third time, Simon, son of John, am I dear to you? Now Peter was troubled in his heart because he put the question a third time, Am I dear to you? And he said to him, Lord, you have knowledge of all things: you see that you are dear to me. Jesus said to him, Then give my sheep food.

The only real awkwardness here is "you have knowledge" for "you know". Apart from that, Professor and Mrs Hooke have been able, by the skilful use of the words at their disposal, to make some things clear which are ambiguous in the A.V. and R.V. Thus it is plain in the Basic version that, when Jesus said to Peter, "lovest thou me more than these?", He meant "more than these other disciples do" (not "more than you love these other disciples", and even more emphatically not "more than you love these fish"—or "this fishing business"). The reference is certainly to the occasion, a week or two earlier, when Peter had loudly protested that even if all the other disciples denied their Lord, he at least would be faithful to the end. Again, the reader of the A.V. does not realize that two different Greek verbs are used for "love" in the recurring question "Lovest thou me?" and two for "feed" in the command "Feed my sheep". But the distinction between the two is preserved in each case by the Basic version. (Whether in fact there is such a significant difference between the two words for "love" as some expositors and preachers maintain is another question.)

Here is another example of the telling simplicity of the Basic version (Matt. 6 : 28–34):

And why are you troubled about clothing? See the flowers of the field, how they come up; they do no work, they make no thread: but I say to you that even Solomon in all his glory was not clothed like one of these. But if God gives such clothing to the grass of the field, which is here today and tomorrow is put into the oven, will he not much more give you clothing, O you of little faith? Then do not be full of care, saying, What are we to have for food or drink? or, With what may we be clothed? because the Gentiles go in search of all these things: for your Father in heaven has knowledge that you have need of all these things: but let your first care be for his kingdom and his righteousness; and all these other things will be given to you in addition. Then have no care for tomorrow: tomorrow will take care of itself. Take the trouble of the day as it comes.

The capacity of Basic English to reproduce biblical poetry may be illustrated by the twenty-third psalm:

The Lord takes care of me as his sheep; I will not be without any good thing. He makes a resting-place for me in the green fields: he is my guide by the quiet waters. He gives new life to my soul: he is my guide in the ways of righteousness because of his name. Yes, though I go through the valley of deep shade, I will have no fear of evil; for you are with me, your rod and your support are my comfort. You make ready a table for me in front of my haters: you put oil on my head; my cup is overflowing. Truly, blessing and mercy will be with me all the days of my life; and I will have a place in the house of the Lord all my days.

A few years ago, a newly-married couple in the north of England decided to put above the mantelpiece in their living-room the words of 2 Corinthians 3 : 17 which appear in the A.V. as "where the Spirit of the Lord is, there is liberty." They regarded the A.V. rendering as too ambiguous, and consulted a number of other versions in order to find what they believed to be the true sense of the words. At last they were successful, when they turned up the Basic English version and found the rendering: "where the Spirit of the Lord is, there the heart is free." These are the words which hang in their living-room as the motto of their home. It is not every modern English version of the Bible that could be used for such a purpose.

The "Plain English" New Testament

Another simplified form of the English language is what is called "Plain English". "Plain English" is based on a list of 1,500 "fundamental and common words that make up ordinary English speech", drawn up as part of the *Interim Report on Vocabulary Selection* (London, 1936). *The New Testament: A New Translation in Plain English*, published in 1952, was the work of Charles Kingsley Williams, Assistant Vice-Principal of Achimota College, Ghana, and formerly Vice-Principal of Wesley College, Madras. Mr Williams had considerable experience in teaching people whose native tongue was not English, but who had to learn English as their medium of higher education and of communication with the wider world; and his version of the New Testament has people of that kind specially in mind. He does not indeed restrict himself to the 1,500 words which make up "Plain English"; he makes use of 160 or 170 words not found in that list, but these are explained in a glossary at the end of the volume, thus: "DOCTRINE. That which is taught as true in a particular department of knowledge, especially religion."

This version naturally provokes comparison with the Basic English version. It has an obvious advantage in being able to draw on a larger vocabulary—a vocabulary, moreover, which is much better provided with verbs than Basic English. Thus Peter is able to say to Jesus "you know that I love you" as against the Basic rendering, "you have knowledge that you are dear to me" (John 21 : 15–17.)

The Greek text underlying this version is Souter's (in other words, the text presumed to underlie the R.V. of 1881), although Mr Williams deviates from it occasionally when it seems better to do so. The Lord's Prayer in Plain English (Matt. 6 : 9–13) runs thus:

> Our Father in heaven, thy name be kept holy,
> Thy Kingdom come,
> Thy will be done, on earth as it is in heaven;
> Give us this day our daily bread,
> And forgive us our debts,
> As we forgive them that are in debt to us;
> And lead us not into temptation,
> But deliver us from the evil one.

And here is the opening paragraph of Hebrews in this version:

In old times God spoke to our fathers by the prophets in many different ways; in these last days he has spoken to us by a Son; he appointed him the heir of all the world; he created the world through him; he is the reflection of God's glory and the living image of his being; he holds up the world by his word of power; when he had made purification from sin, he took his seat at the right hand of the majesty on high; and so is seen to be as much better than the angels, as the name which he has come to possess is a better name than theirs.

With this we may compare the Basic rendering:

In times past the word of God came to our fathers through the prophets, in different parts and in different ways; but now, at the end of these days, it has come to us through his Son, to whom he has given all things for a heritage, and through whom he made the order of the generations; who, being the outshining of his glory, the true image of his substance, supporting all things by the word of his power, having given himself as an offering making clean from sins, took his seat at the right hand of God in heaven; having become by so much better than the angels, as the name which is his heritage is more noble than theirs.

The Basic version here preserves the periodic structure of the original better than the Plain English rendering, which, by its multiplication of principal clauses, gives a somewhat staccato effect.

The Language of the People?

Charles Kingsley Williams' version in Plain English must not be confused with *The New Testament in the Language of the People*, by Charles B. Williams, first published in America in 1937. The translator was a Greek scholar who aimed as far as possible at conveying the exact shade of meaning of the Greek tenses in the New Testament. His efforts to do this are specially apparent in his renderings of the distinction between the present and aorist tenses of the imperative and infinitive. The chief difficulty here is that delicate Greek variations, if they are to be made explicit in English, must be expressed by the use of auxiliaries and the like to a point where the effect is prosaic and flat-footed. This is specially so in a succession of imperatives. Thus the injunctions of Eph. 4 : 25–31 are rendered:

So you must lay aside falsehood and each of you practice telling the truth to his neighbor, for we are parts of one another. If you do get angry, you must stop sinning in your anger. Do not ever let the sun go down on your anger; stop giving the devil a chance.

The man who used to steal must now stop stealing; rather he must keep on working and toiling with his own hands at some honest vocation, so as to have something to contribute to the needy. You must stop letting any bad word pass your lips, but only words that are good for building up as the occasion demands, so that they will result in spiritual blessing to the hearer. You must stop offending the Holy Spirit of God by whom you have been stamped for the day of redemption. You must remove all bitterness, rage, anger, loud threats, and insults, with all malice.

There is no doubt about the scholarly care with which linear and punctiliar action are distinguished in these verses; but the language is hardly "the language of the people". "Keep on running from sexual immorality" (1 Cor. 6 : 18) is no improvement on the A.V., "Flee fornication"; nor is "Stop forming intimate and inconsistent relations with unbelievers" (2 Cor. 6 : 14) an improvement on "Be ye not unequally yoked together with unbelievers." Where the "aspect" of the verbal action may be readily inferred from the context, it is not really necessary to weight the sentence by making it explicit in English.

Some reviewers of this version have singled out for special commendation a tense-rendering which is almost certainly wrong. The words of our Lord to Peter in Matt. 16 : 19 are here rendered: "whatever you forbid on earth must be what is already forbidden in heaven, and whatever you permit on earth must be what is already permitted in heaven." The similar words addressed to all the disciples in Matt. 18 : 18 are rendered in the same way. This gives the opposite sense to that of the common versions, of which we may take the A.V. as the best known example: "whatsoever thou shalt bind on earth shall be bound in heaven: and whatsoever thou shalt loose on earth shall be loosed in heaven." Charles B. Williams has treated the Greek future-perfect as if it had the same force as the English future-perfect, whereas the Greek future-perfect commonly has the force of a specially emphatic future, denoting the immediate performance of a future action, or the permanence of its results. In fact, if our Lord had wished to make the statement of the A.V. and the versions which agree with it as solemnly and emphatically as possible, He could not have done so more explicitly than in the words of our Greek text here. Those reviewers who have rejoiced in Charles B. Williams' rendering may have felt that it was a good thing to get rid of a rendering which seemed to place too much power in the hands of church officials; but it is no part of a translator's business to soften down our Lord's "hard sayings". When our Lord used solemn phraseology such as we find in Matt. 16 : 19 and 18 : 18, it was not in order to voice impressive platitudes. The comparable passage in John 20 : 23 (A.V., "whose soever sins ye remit, they are remitted unto them, *and* whose soever *sins* ye retain, they are retained") is curiously translated: "If you get forgiveness for people's sins, they are forgiven them; if you let people's sins fasten upon them, they will remain fastened upon them." A footnote justifies this rendering by stating that in these words Jesus "is emphasizing their winning others"; this is no doubt true, but there is an impartation of apostolic authority in His words which this rendering dilutes almost to the point of disappearance.

But there are passages of real power in this translation; we may take the words of Paul in 2 Cor. 4 : 7–11:

> But I am keeping this jewel in an earthen jar, to prove that its surpassing power is God's, not mine. On every side I am ever hard-pressed, but never hemmed in; always perplexed, but never to the point of despair; always being persecuted, but not deserted; always getting a knock-down, but never a knock-out; always being exposed to death as Jesus was, so that in my body the life of Jesus may be clearly shown. For all the time I continue to live I am being given up to death for Jesus' sake, so that in my mortal lower nature the life of Jesus may be clearly shown.

The phrase "always getting a knock-down, but never a knock-out" is a happy one; J. B. Phillips has almost the same rendering in *Letters to Young Churches*: "we may be knocked down but we are never knocked out."

Wuest's Expanded Translation

Kenneth S. Wuest, in his three-volume *Expanded Translation of the New Testament* (1956–59), does for all the parts of speech what

Charles B. Williams does for the verb; he endeavours, however, to bring out theological as well as philological nuances. Here is his rendering of John 1 : 14:

> And the Word, entering a new mode of existence, became flesh, and lived in a tent [His physical body] among us. And we gazed with attentive and careful regard and spiritual perception at His glory, a glory such as that of a uniquely-begotten Son from the Father, full of grace and truth.

And here is his rendering of 2 Cor. 4 : 7–12, which may be compared with Charles B. Williams' rendering reproduced above:

> But we have this treasure [the reflection of the light of the knowledge of the glory of God in the face of Jesus Christ] in earthenware containers, in order that the superexcellence of the power might be from God as a source and not from us. We are being hard pressed from every side, but we are not hemmed in. We are bewildered, not knowing which way to turn, but not utterly destitute of possible measures or resources. We are being persecuted, but not left in the lurch, not abandoned, not let down. We are being knocked down, but not destroyed, always bearing about in our body the dying of the Lord Jesus in order that the life of Jesus might be clearly and openly shown in our body, for, as for us, we who are living are perpetually being delivered over to death for Jesus' sake in order that the life of Jesus might be clearly and openly shown in our mortal body. So that death is operative in us but the life is operative in you.

Stylistically this falls below Charles B. Williams' standard; but such an expanded translation as this cannot be judged by stylistic criteria; it is intended for the study, in order that the Greekless student of the New Testament may be made acquainted with all the shades of meaning in the original. Sometimes, indeed, one may wonder whether some of the shades of meaning have not to be read into the Greek in order to be read out of it, as when the injunction which the A.V. renders "Husbands, love your wives" (Eph. 5 : 25) appears in

Wuest's version as: "The husbands, be loving your wives with a love self-sacrificial in its nature."

The Amplified Bible

Another "expanded" version is *The Amplified Bible*, published between 1958 and 1965. This version, based on Westcott and Hort's Greek text in the New Testament and the Massoretic text in the Old, was produced by a committee of twelve editors, working on behalf of the Lockman Foundation of La Habra, California. It is "amplified" in the sense that alternative renderings or additional words designed to bring out the full sense are incorporated in the text instead of appearing in the margin or as footnotes. Thus Luke 18 : 18 reads as follows:

> And a certain ruler asked Him, Teacher (You who are essentially and perfectly morally) good, what shall I do to inherit eternal life [that is, to partake of eternal salvation in the Messiah's kingdom]?

Or, to take a longer example, Romans 12 : 1–2 runs thus:

> I appeal to you therefore, brethren, *and* beg of you in view of [all] the mercies of God, to make a decisive dedication of your bodies—presenting all your members and faculties—as a living sacrifice, holy (devoted, consecrated) and well pleasing to God, which is your reasonable (rational, intelligent) service *and* spiritual worship. Do not be conformed to this world—this age, fashioned after and adapted to its external, superficial customs. But be transformed (changed) by the [entire] renewal of your mind—by its new ideals and its new attitude—so that you may prove [for yourselves] what is the good and acceptable and perfect will of God, *even* the thing which is good and acceptable and perfect [in His sight for you].

Thus, by the skilful use of curved and square brackets, dashes and italics, the various shades of thought and meaning are given as full expression as possible. The work includes several of the features of a commentary as well as a translation. Like Wuest's *Expanded Translation*, this is a work for the study rather than the pulpit.

The Concordant Version

None of these "expanded" versions aims at the production of equivalent effect. Neither does the *Concordant Version of the Sacred Scriptures* (1926 and following years), a version which is based on the principle that "every word in the original should have its own English equivalent." But—and this is particularly relevant in translation from an ancient language into a modern one—it happens very rarely that one word in Language A is the exact equivalent of a corresponding word in Language B. In the New Testament part of the version the aorist indicative in Greek (which should mostly be rendered by our past historic, and sometimes by our perfect) is regularly rendered by the present tense. The Old Testament part of the work (not yet complete) proceeds on the assumption that Hebrew was the language which God and Adam spoke in Eden, and that the Hebrew of the Scriptures has retained its pristine paradisaic purity, whereas otherwise it has become corrupted. When a Hebraist compares (say) the Hebrew of the Song of Deborah (Judges 5) with the Hebrew of Ecclesiastes, he finds evidence of a long period of linguistic change, stretching over the best part of a millennium; but no place can be allowed for this evidence if the idiom used throughout the Old Testament continued to be that which God used in Eden.

In passing these strictures we should not withhold a generous tribute to the translator's labour of love, prolonged over many years, and the devotion to the Word of God which characterizes his work.

The New World Translation

The *New World Translation of the Christian Greek Scriptures* (1950), followed by the *New World Translation of the Hebrew Scriptures* (1953-1960), is a publication of the Watchtower Bible and Tract Society, Inc., and some of its distinctive renderings reflect the biblical interpretations which we have come to associate with Jehovah's Witnesses (e.g., "the Word was a god" in John 1 : 1). Sometimes it renders the text with an un-English literalness (e.g., "Let continue yours what is yours" in Gen. 33 : 9); at other times we find such colloquial phraseology as "Excuse me, Jehovah" (Ex. 4 : 10) and "the Nile river will fairly stink" (Ex. 7 : 18). Some of the renderings which are free from a theological tendency strike one as quite good; thus "a jealous God" is "a God exacting exclusive devotion", and the Hebrew phrase which the A.V. variously renders as "on this side Jordan" and "on the other side of Jordan" according to the context appears as "in the region of the Jordan".

Jewish Versions

In 1917 the Jewish Publication Society of America published *The Holy Scriptures according to the Masoretic Text*, a rendering of the Hebrew Bible bearing a close affinity to the idiom of the A.V. A departure from such "Bible English" was heralded in 1963 with the publication by the same Society of *The Torah: The Five Books of Moses*, the first section of *A New Translation of the Holy Scriptures according to the Masoretic Text*, the work of a committee of American Jewish scholars under the chairmanship of Professor H. M. Orlinsky; the idiom here is that of the twentieth century. Further sections of this new translation have since been published, and include *The Book of Isaiah*, *The Book of Jeremiah* and *The Book of Psalms*.

CHAPTER FOURTEEN

The Revised Standard Version

THE AMERICAN Standard Version of 1901 was copyrighted in order to protect the text against unauthorized changes. In 1928 the copyright was acquired by the International Council of Religious Education, a council in which forty major denominations of the United States and Canada were associated through their boards of education and publication. The Council appointed a committee of scholars to take charge of the text of the A.S.V. and consider the question of further revision. This committee, after two years of deliberation, recommended a thorough-going revision of the A.S.V., but a revision which nevertheless should remain recognizably within the tradition established by Tyndale.

The New Revision

The Council adopted the committee's recommendation, and authorized the work of revision in 1937. The resultant version was to "embody the best results of modern scholarship as to the meaning of the Scriptures, and express this meaning in English diction which is designed for use in public and private worship and preserves those qualities which have given to the King James Version a supreme place in English literature."

A committee of thirty-two scholars was set up to make the revision. It worked in two sections, dealing respectively with the Old Testament and the New. The Revised Standard Version of the New Testament was first published in 1946. The revision of the whole Bible appeared on September 30, 1952; the opportunity was taken of making some changes in the text of the New Testament revision which had originally appeared six years previously. A smaller committee was then appointed to prepare a revision of the English Apocrypha—this, of course, could not be a revision of the

A.S.V., but of the versions published in England in 1611 and 1895. The Revised Standard Version is copyrighted by the Division of Christian Education of the National Council of the Churches of Christ in the U.S.A.

While the R.S.V. is the work of American scholars, British readers have for the most part given it a warm welcome; they have not found their appreciation of it prejudiced by Americanisms. The idiom used is that which is accepted as good literary English on both sides of the Atlantic. Professor T. W. Manson spoke for many of his fellow-countrymen when he said in a broadcast review: "I like the Revised Standard Version; and I like it because it is reliable and because it speaks directly to the man in the pew in language he can reasonably be expected to understand."

Modernization of Language

One obvious concession to modern English is the replacement of the final *th* by *s* in the ending of the third person singular of the present tense of verbs: thus *saith* becomes *says* and *sendeth* becomes *sends*. The constant repetition of the conjunction "And" in narrative passages has been greatly reduced, although it is not quite clear on what principle it is sometimes retained and sometimes omitted. The Semitic idiom "And it came to pass" has disappeared, and thus the R.S.V. dispenses with one of the most distinctive features of what English-speaking people have come to regard as "Bible language". "And it came to pass after these things, that God did tempt Abraham", says the A.V. of Gen. 22 : 1, introducing the story of the offering up of Isaac; R.V. and A.S.V. do likewise, except that they say "prove" instead of "tempt"; but R.S.V. begins the story in the more direct form, "After these things God tested Abraham."

"Thou" and "You"

The pronoun of the second person singular (thou, thee, thy, thine) has been dropped "except in language addressed to God"; otherwise "you" (your, yours) has been used indiscriminately whether one person or more be addressed, in accordance with modern English usage. The retention of the singular pronoun for addressing God also accords with much modern usage (although in

more informal devotions "you" is now increasingly used in addressing Him, especially by younger people). But a delicate question is
raised when it has to be decided whether Christ in the Gospels
should be addressed as "thou" or "you". In the R.S.V. He is
addressed as "you" during His life on earth, for plainly those who
spoke to Him then did not use a different form of address from that
which they used in speaking to other people. But after His ascension
He is generally addressed as "thou". Some critics of the R.S.V. have
used this changing use of pronouns to charge the revisers with deny-
ing the deity of Christ, at least during His earthly life; but in fact the
inconsistency, as it may appear to some, is not due to any theological
judgment one way or another, but to English usage in regard to the
pronouns of the second person, which differs from the usage of
other modern European languages.

Even after the ascension of Christ, however, the R.S.V. represents Paul as saying to Him on the Damascus road, "Who are
you, Lord?" (Acts 9 : 5; 22 : 8; 26 : 15), and not "Who art thou,
Lord?" The reason for this is that, until the risen Christ replied "I
am Jesus," Paul did not know whom he was addressing. Indeed,
"Who are you, sir?" might have been an even better rendering here
than that of R.S.V. But when Christ appeared to Paul on a later
occasion, Paul knew at once who was speaking to him, and so he
says (according to R.S.V.): "Lord, they themselves know that in
every synagogue I imprisoned and beat those who believed in thee"
(Acts 22 : 19).

Again, it may happen that "you" appears in an Old Testament
passage, but "thou" in the same passage when it is quoted in the New
Testament. Thus in Psalm 45 : 6 f. the king whose marriage is being
celebrated is addressed thus:

> Your divine throne endures for ever and ever.
>   Your royal sceptre is a sceptre of equity;
>   you love righteousness and hate wickedness.
>   Therefore God, your God, has anointed you
>   with the oil of gladness above your fellows.

But these words are quoted in Heb. 1 : 8 f. in the following form:

Thy throne, O God, is for ever and ever,
the righteous sceptre is the sceptre of thy kingdom.
Thou hast loved righteousness and hated lawlessness;
therefore God, thy God, has anointed thee
with the oil of gladness beyond thy comrades.

The reason for the variation in the pronouns as between the Old
Testament passage and its New Testament reproduction is clear: the
writer to the Hebrews expressly takes the words of the psalm as
addressed to Christ, the Son of God, whereas the revisers have
judged that in the psalmist's original intention they were addressed
to one of the old kings of Israel. Here again some theological objections have been raised to the procedure of the R.S.V., and in any
case it is so difficult to be entirely consistent that there is much to be
said in favour of retaining "thou" throughout where one person is
being addressed (as Knox does), or else using "you" indiscriminately
for the second person, both singular and plural, no matter who is
being spoken to. One translator[1] has adopted the typographical
device of spacing the letters of the pronoun—"y o u"—when it is
used in the plural. Without some such device the reader is unable at
times to recognize a distinction between the singular and plural
which is plain when "thou" is used for the singular. For example,
when R.S.V. renders Luke 22 : 31 f. "Simon, Simon, behold, Satan
demanded to have you, that he might sift you like wheat, but I have
prayed for you that your faith may not fail; and when you have
turned again, strengthen your brethren", it is necessary to add a footnote pointing out that the first two occurrences of "you" are plural,
while the others are singular. Similarly, in John 1 : 50 Jesus says to
Nathanael, "Because I said to you, I saw you under the fig tree, do
you believe? You shall see greater things than these." There "you"
is singular, referring to Nathanael alone. But when Jesus goes on to
say to him (verse 51), "Truly, truly, I say to you, you will see heaven
opened", there is nothing in the English version to show that "you"
is now plural, referring to Nathanael's companions as well as himself; and here there is not even a footnote in R.S.V. to indicate the
change of number.

[1] Dr William Hendriksen, in his *New Testament Commentary* (Grand Rapids, Michigan).

Quotation Marks

Throughout R.S.V. direct speech is regularly indicated by the use of quotation marks. This involves a measure of interpretation (as indeed all punctuation marks must do to some extent). For example, in St John's Gospel it is often difficult to decide where the dividing line must be drawn between the words of Jesus and the Evangelist's meditation on His words. In the narrative of Jesus' conversation with Nicodemus in John 3, Jesus' words to Nicodemus are indicated as coming to an end with verse 15; verses 16 to 21 are then the Evangelist's comment on the conversation. But some expositors would make Jesus' words to Nicodemus end earlier, and others would prolong them beyond verse 15. A version which does not use quotation marks does not need to commit itself on a question like this.

Poetical Passages

In R.S.V. the practice of printing the poetical parts of the Bible as poetry has been carried further than in R.V. and A.S.V. The construction of the prophetic oracles in the Old Testament now stands out more clearly than in the older versions. The practice might, indeed, have been carried further still; there are in the sayings of Jesus quite a number of passages which exhibit the same poetical forms as the prophetic oracles of the Old Testament do, but they have been printed as prose.

Variation in Renderings

The R.S.V. is much less pedantic than the R.V. and A.S.V.; for example, it does not adhere as rigidly to the policy of using the same English word as far as possible to render one Greek or Hebrew word in its various occurrences. It reverts in this regard to the A.V. policy of using a variety of synonyms.

The Greek adjective *psychikos*, which appears in a number of places in the New Testament, is a particularly difficult word to translate. A.V. and R.V. render it "natural" in its Pauline occurrences (1 Cor. 2 : 14; 15 : 44, 46) and "sensual" elsewhere (Jas. 3 : 15; Jude 19). But R.S.V. has "unspiritual" in 1 Cor. 2 : 14 (so also

Moffatt) and in Jas. 3 : 15, "physical" in 1 Cor. 15, and "worldly" in Jude 19. Of these the least adequate is "physical" (it is even less adequate than its synonym "natural", used in A.V. and R.V.); if Paul had meant "physical", he would have used another word. Paul uses the adjective *psychikos* in 1 Cor. 15 to denote a body animated by the *psyche* (shall we say by the senses?) in contrast to the resurrection body, animated by the spirit, the God-conscious factor in man, if not indeed by the very Spirit of God. But while it is easy to point out the inadequacy of existing renderings, and possible to express Paul's intention by means of a sentence, is there one word which will convey his precise meaning in intelligible English? Perhaps there is none.

In the 1946 edition of the New Testament, R.S.V. generally replaced the older term "sanctify" by "consecrate" as the translation of the Greek verb *hagiazo*. In the 1952 edition "sanctify" was restored, partly for the sake of consistency with the Old Testament, where "sanctify" was retained, and partly because the use of "consecrate" gave rise to "mistaken inferences", as the preface to the 1952 edition states. In John 17 : 19, however, Jesus is still made to say "for their sake I consecrate myself, that they also may be consecrated in truth", in spite of the fact that "consecrate" has been changed back to "sanctify" in verse 17 : "Sanctify them in the truth; thy word is truth."

But not all the second thoughts which the committee had about the New Testament renderings were happy. In the 1946 edition of Luke 24 : 28, in the story of Jesus' appearance to the two disciples on the Emmaus road, the rendering "he made as though he would go further" was quite right; in the 1952 edition it was replaced by the more insipid "He appeared to be going further", which is not what the Greek text says.

The relative freedom which the revisers permitted themselves has at times led to inaccurate renderings. While the common reader may think it matters little whether Jesus said to Peter, "If I wash thee not, thou hast no part with me" (John 13 : 8, R.V.) or "If I do not wash you, you have no part in me" (R.S.V.), there is in fact a difference between having no part *with* Christ and having no part *in* Him, and what He really said was "no part *with* me."

The Divine Name

One striking difference between A.S.V. and R.S.V. so far as the Old Testament is concerned is in the rendering of the personal name of the God of Israel. While A.S.V. regularly uses "Jehovah", R.S.V. follows A.V. and R.V. and normally renders it by "the LORD".

Emendations

In general, R.S.V. has followed the traditional Hebrew text of the Old Testament, deviating from it only where there is general agreement among Hebrew scholars that it is defective. Most of the R.S.V. departures from the traditional Hebrew text have the support of ancient versions. Two which have not this support are found in Psalm 2 : 11 ("Serve the LORD with fear, with trembling kiss his feet"), involving a change in the order of the Hebrew consonants, and Amos 6 : 12 ("Does one plow the sea with oxen?"), where there is no change in the consonants, but only in the word-division and vowel-points.

Among emendations which have the support of ancient versions a few may be mentioned. Gen. 4 : 8 is improved by the restoration of the words actually spoken to Abel by Cain: "Cain said to Abel his brother, 'Let us go out to the field'." (This restoration is supported by the Greek Septuagint and by the Samaritan Bible.) In Deut. 32 : 8 we read that God "fixed the bounds of the peoples according to the number of the sons of God" and not (as our older English versions said, following the Hebrew text) "according to the number of the children of Israel". The R.S.V. footnote to this reading cites the Greek version in its support; since then a fragmentary Hebrew manuscript has been found among the Qumran texts which exhibits this reading. In 1 Sam. 14 : 41 the prayer of King Saul is given in its full form, which enables us to learn something about the operation of the sacred lot called "Urim and Thummim": "If this guilt is in me or in Jonathan my son, O LORD, God of Israel, give Urim; but if this guilt is in thy people Israel, give Thummim." Some words have dropped out of the Hebrew text here, but the Septuagint and Latin Vulgate preserve the fuller reading, which R.S.V. adopts. It is surprising, however, that verse 18 of the same chapter has not also been emended in accordance with the Septuagint, which reads "And Saul said to Ahijah, 'Bring hither the ephod'. For it was he who carried the ephod at that time before Israel." R.S.V., like its predecessors, follows the Hebrew text in referring here to the ark of God and not the ephod; but in fact the ark of God at this time was in seclusion at Kiriath-jearim, whereas the ephod was the priestly vestment to which the Urim and Thummim were attached. Another restoration appears in Solomon's quotation of a divine oracle at the dedication of the temple (1 Kings 8 : 12): where the older versions reproduce the defective Hebrew text ("The LORD said that he would dwell in the thick darkness"), R.S.V. follows the Septuagint and reads:

"The LORD has set the sun in the heavens,
      but has said that he would dwell in thick darkness."

But here again R.S.V., to our surprise, does not go on to add at the end of verse 13, "See, is it not written in the book of Jashar?" for which there is also Septuagint authority. Solomon's profitable exploitation of the trade in horses and chariots between Egypt and Cilicia is made more intelligible by the correct translation of 1 Kings 10 : 28 f. (to which the Septuagint and Vulgate supply the clue), although the reader who is told that "Solomon's import of horses was from Egypt and Kue" may well wonder where Kue was; it might have been better to replace this ancient place-name by the commoner Cilicia.

We have mentioned one place where the Qumran texts have supported a reading preferred by R.S.V. The first of the Qumran texts to be studied—the complete scroll of Isaiah from the first cave—was available just in time for some of its readings to be recorded in R.S.V. Thirteen readings of this scroll were adopted by the revisers, but Dr Millar Burrows, one of the revisers, who is also a leading authority on the Qumran texts, doubts on further reflection whether some of these are so certainly right as was thought at the time. One of its readings which the revisers did not adopt is that found in Isa. 53 : 11, "after the travail of his soul he shall see light". This reading, which many scholars had already conjectured to be original on the basis of the Septuagint, was found in both the Hebrew scrolls of Isaiah discovered in the first cave at Qumran, and has now a very strong claim to be regarded as the true text.

One reading from the complete Isaiah scroll which R.S.V. has been thoroughly justified in adopting comes in Isa. 21 : 8. Here the traditional Hebrew text is represented by A.V. "And he cried, A lion" or R.V. "And he cried as a lion"; but the intrusion of the lion into this context is odd. What appears to have happened is that two letters have been accidentally transposed in the course of copying; instead of "a lion" we should read "he who saw", and so R.S.V., following the complete Isaiah scroll from Qumran, reads the entirely intelligible "Then he who saw cried"—"he who saw" being the watchman of verse 6, who is waiting for the approach of a messenger from the east over the Syrian desert.

A Brief Assessment

When the R.V. appeared, many people thought that the Old Testament part of the work was better than the New. The same judgment might be passed on R.S.V., though for different reasons. If the revisers of 1881 went too far in the direction of grammatical pedantry in their work on the New Testament, their successors of 1946 and 1952 have perhaps gone too far in the other direction, and blurred some of the finer distinctions in New Testament wording which, while they are of little importance to the general reader, have some significance for those who are concerned with the more accurate interpretation of the text. To a large extent, the revisers have succeeded in satisfying the requirements of those mid-twentieth century readers who look for an English Bible which will do for to-day and to-morrow what the A.V. did for the seventeenth and following centuries.

The Voice of Criticism

The R.S.V. was launched with a publicity campaign such as few, if any, of its predecessors enjoyed; but that did not protect it against adverse criticism when it appeared. Some of the criticism came from people who did not care for its deviations from the wording of the A.V.; that was probably inevitable, but the same criticism would be the lot of any new English version. Some criticism, on the other hand, came from people who thought it to be unnecessarily conservative and not to deviate far enough from the A.V.; but then it was not intended to be a completely new translation but "the version set forth A.D. 1611, revised A.D. 1881–1885 and A.D. 1901, compared with the most ancient authorities and revised A.D. 1952." Since the copyright of the new revision was owned by the Division of Christian Education of the National Council of the Churches of Christ in the U.S.A., a good deal of criticism came, as in private duty bound, from supporters of rival church groupings and other people who disapproved of the National Council and all its works.

The criticism of the New Testament part of the work, when it was first published in 1946, was more restrained than that which greeted the whole Bible six years later, but it was sharp enough. Sometimes the new revisers were condemned for preferring readings which had already been accepted and established by R.V. and A.S.V., and the preference of these readings was ascribed to theological unsoundness. Thus, to give two examples in one, a leaflet entitled *The Eye Opener*, which claims to be "an unbiased, non-sectarian examination of the Revised Standard Version Bible", says: "Any version of the Bible which omits Acts 8 : 37, or 'through his blood' in Col. 1 : 14, evidently has for its foundation a corrupted manuscript." Then it goes on to make Origen of Alexandria (A.D. 185–254), the greatest textual scholar of the Early Church, responsible for the corruption. Acts 8 : 37 in A.V., following the "Received Text", represents the following conversation between Philip the evangelist and the Ethiopian chamberlain when the latter asked for baptism: "And Philip said, If thou believest with all thine heart, thou mayest. And he answered and said, I believe that Jesus Christ is the Son of God." This represents an attempt to bring the Ethiopian's baptism into line with what soon became regular church procedure, and it may well be that something of the kind was said on that occasion, but the conversation is absent from the best early texts of Acts, and therefore Acts 8 : 37 is absent from the text of R.V. and A.S.V., not to mention the majority of latter-day versions. But its absence from the text of R.S.V. was explained as due to a desire to suppress a passage testifying to the deity of Christ. Similarly the R.S.V. reading of Col. 1 : 14, "in whom we have redemption" (cf. R.V. and A.S.V. "in whom we have our redemption"), where A.V. has "in whom we have redemption through his blood", was attacked as an attempt to weaken the biblical doctrine of the atonement. But if the critics had looked up Eph. 1 : 7 in the R.S.V., they would have found the familiar language there in full, "In him we have redemption through his blood"; and in fact it was through the influence of the Ephesians passage that the shorter and original reading of the Colossians passage was expanded in later Greek copies.

Some criticisms, as we might expect, were perfectly fair and reasonable, and such as any translators or revisers might welcome, since they were constructive and not captious. And indeed the 1952 edition of the New Testament was amended here and there in the light of criticisms that had been passed on certain features of the 1946 edition, and the 1962 editions of both Testaments profited by criticisms that had been expressed since 1952.

But when the whole Bible was published in 1952, the criticism which greeted it from some quarters was remarkably reminiscent of criticism voiced in earlier days against the Greek Septuagint and the Latin Vulgate, against the versions of Luther and Tyndale, against the A.V. and R.V. One American preacher was reported to have burned a copy of the R.S.V. with a blowlamp in his pulpit, remarking that it was like the devil because it was hard to burn. Anything more certainly calculated to make every family in the congregation acquire a copy for itself is hard to imagine; one could almost believe that the whole incident was an ingenious publicity stunt engineered by the sponsors of the new version! Pamphlets appeared bearing such titles as *The Bible of Antichrist* (an echo, unwitting no doubt, of More's description of Tyndale's New Testament), *The New Blasphemous Bible*, and *Whose Unclean Fingers Have Been Tampering With The Holy Bible, God's Pure, Infallible, Verbally Inspired Word?* (The last-named opens with the sentence: "Every informed and intelligent person knows that our government is crawling with communists, or those who sanction and encourage communism"—which indicates another line along which the version was attacked.)

It is most desirable that ordinary Christians should want to be assured about the trustworthiness of a Bible version which they are invited to accept as a standard version for home, school and church. The Bible was not given especially to scholars, and although we are dependent on scholars for accurate Bible versions, we need to be sure that the versions which they provide present the essential message of the Bible as clearly as possible. But, while R.S.V. was no more immune from critical scrutiny than any other work of fallible men, the very exuberance of the language in which some of its detractors attacked it had the opposite effect from that which was intended; it was so manifestly exaggerated that it was widely discounted. And even where the attacks were more restrained, they were sometimes launched at the least vulnerable features of the version. Here, for example, is another unfavourable pamphlet (*The New Bible ... Why Christians Should Not Accept It*) which, in addition to criticizing R.S.V. on theological grounds, finds fault with it for printing certain sections of the Old Testament as poetry, so that "when one looks at the book, he thinks he is reading English verse since it is so similar to what he studied in high school." The same author says: "How are God's people going to like the Ten Commandments as they are now to be learned? '*You shall not take the name of the Lord your God in vain.*' The older King James Version says: '*Thou shalt not take the name of the Lord thy God in vain*'." This might be a stylistic criticism, but one gets the impression that it is a religious criticism too—but why should it be so?

The theological record of the members of the revising committee was examined, and some of the shortcomings of the version were confidently traced back to the unorthodoxy of some of them, although in fact one gets the impression that for the most part they leaned over backwards so as not to let their varying theological opinions colour it. But some people specially deprecated the presence on the committee of a Jewish scholar, Dr Harry M. Orlinsky, a distinguished authority on the Septuagint version. Here again history tended to repeat itself; critics of Jerome's Latin rendering of the Old Testament from the Hebrew original suspected that it had been influenced in an antichristian direction by his Jewish mentor Bar Hanina.

One of the principal complaints was that many of the traditional "messianic" passages in the Old Testament had been rendered in such a way as to blunt the point of their Christian application. Thus the royal bridegroom of Psalm 45 is told "Your divine throne endures for ever and ever" (verse 6), while a footnote gives two alternative renderings: "your throne is a throne of God" or "your throne, O God." But the New Testament application of this passage to our Lord (Heb. 1 : 8) runs: "Thy throne, O God, is for ever and ever" (with the improbable footnote alternative "God is thy throne"). Here it must be said that, although a case of sorts could be made out for the R.S.V. rendering "Your divine throne", the rendering of the older versions, "Thy throne, O God", is a much more straightforward translation of the Hebrew text.

Again, the oracle of Isa. 7 : 14, where the translation "Behold, a (or the) virgin shall conceive ..." goes back to the Septuagint, appears in R.S.V. in the form "Behold, a young woman shall conceive ..." (with the alternative "virgin" relegated to the footnote). But in Matt. 1 : 23 (where the Evangelist reproduces the Septuagint rendering) R.S.V. preserves the traditional wording, "Behold, a virgin shall conceive ..." The Hebrew word 'almah, used in Isa. 7 : 14, may mean "virgin", but does not have the explicit and exclusive sense of "virgin" borne by the Greek word parthenos, which is used in the Septuagint here and also in Matt. 1 : 23. This variation between the Old Testament passage and its New Testament quotation may remind us that Isaiah's oracle may well have had a more immediate as well as a more remote fulfilment, and the R.S.V. wording covers both; in Matt. 1 : 23, on the other hand, only the more remote fulfilment (the conception and birth of Christ) is in view, and hence the word "virgin" alone is appropriate there. It might be added, however, that Isaiah was probably echoing an ancient annunciation oracle which is referred to also in Micah 5 : 3 ("when she who is in travail has brought forth"), and which did imply a miraculous sign; some tradition of this sense of Isa. 7 : 14 may have moved the Septuagint translators to render 'almah by parthenos. In any case, it is hardly fair to charge the R.S.V. committee, as some have done, with trying to obscure the biblical testimony to our Lord's virginal conception; for this is stated as plainly in the R.S.V. of Matt. 1 : 18 ff. and Luke 1 : 26 ff. as it is in any of our older versions.

Even so, say some critics, it would have been better in Isa. 7 : 14 to retain the form of words which corresponds most closely with the New Testament quotation of the passage in Matt. 1 : 23, seeing that that is a perfectly permissible translation of the passage (as the R.S.V.

footnote recognizes). The unity of the two Testaments would thus become more apparent. There is real substance in this argument, but it does not come well from people who will, almost in the next breath, condemn the R.S.V. for rendering another Old Testament passage in the same way as it is reproduced in the New Testament.

This has been done with Zech. 12 : 10, which foretells a day of great mourning in Jerusalem and the surrounding territory when, as the Massoretic Hebrew text puts it, "they shall look unto me whom they have pierced" (so R.V.). The passage is quoted once and echoed once in the New Testament, and in both places the pronoun is not "me" but "him". This is not so significant in the place where the passage is merely echoed (Rev. 1 : 7, "and every eye will see him, every one who pierced him"), for that is not an exact quotation. Here the predicted looking to the one who was pierced is interpreted of the Second Advent of Christ. But in John 19 : 37 the piercing is interpreted of the piercing of Christ's side with a soldier's lance after His death on the cross, and here Zech. 12 : 10 is expressly quoted: "And again another scripture says, 'They shall look on him whom they have pierced'." It is a reasonable inference that this is the form in which the Evangelist knew the passage, and indeed the reading "him" instead of "me" appears in a few Hebrew manuscripts. The R.S.V. thus has New Testament authority for its rendering of Zech. 12 : 10, "And I will pour out on the house of David and the inhabitants of Jerusalem a spirit of compassion and supplication, so that, when they look on him whom they have pierced, they shall mourn for him, as one mourns for an only child, and weep bitterly over him, as one weeps over a first-born." Why then is the R.S.V. criticized for conforming to the New Testament here? Because, if the reading "me" be retained, the reference would be to the speaker, who is God, and in view of the application of the passage in the New Testament, there are some who see here an anticipation of the Christian doctrine of our Lord's divine nature. The reading "me" is certainly quite early, for it appears in the Septuagint (which otherwise misses the point of the passage); but the New Testament seems to attach no significance to Zech. 12 : 10 as providing evidence for the deity of Christ, although it does elsewhere interpret with regard to Christ a number of Old Testament passages where the original reference is to the God of Israel. And, whoever the pierced one is, the fact that he is referred to elsewhere in the verse in the third person ("they shall mourn for him, ... and weep bitterly over him") suggests that he is Yahweh's representative (probably the anointed king), in whose piercing Yahweh Himself is pierced.

Theological Implications

Criticisms of translations as translations are, of course, perfectly in order, and when the criticisms are sufficiently valid and numerous they may point to a general assessment of a version as a whole. But it is necessary to be very cautious before ascribing theological bias to a version. Sometimes, indeed, a theological bias is openly avowed, and in other cases the circumstances under which a version is issued (as when it is issued by some distinctive sectarian group) make one expect to find such a bias in it. But the committee of revisers which worked on the R.S.V. was sufficiently broadly based to make it unlikely that the version would promote any particular or sectional interest. And in fact it has found widespread acceptance in the years since its appearance in a great variety of Christian communities, theologically conservative as well as theologically liberal. No change in Christian doctrine is involved or implied in the readings and renderings of the R.S.V.; every article of the historic faith of the Church can be established as readily and as plainly from it as from the older versions in whose tradition it stands.

A Test of Intelligibility

According to a report in *The British Weekly* for March 29, 1956, an experiment was made in order to discover whether the R.S.V. was or was not more readily understood by the average American high school student than the A.V. Dr Frank W. Montgomery, a Presbyterian minister of St Clairsville, Ohio, conducted a test of 1,358 high school students in twelve communities which went to show that those who based their Bible reading on the R.S.V. responded more rapidly to questions and generally had a better understanding of what they had read than those whose reading was based on the A.V. But the test also revealed that many passages of the Bible were not generally understood by high school students in either version. In 34 out of 36 test-questions of the multiple-choice variety the R.S.V. proved itself more readily understood, but sometimes not by a wide margin. Those who used the R.S.V. are also said to have completed the tests more quickly and with a higher percentage of correct answers.

The inability of many students to understand a large number of Bible passages in either version raises important questions, which should be made the subject of a further investigation. Is the proper inference that a more idiomatic translation would be more intelligible and remove the difficulties? Or may the trouble not lie in a certain inability to understand some of the things with which the Bible deals, no matter how up-to-date the idiom may be in which they are expressed?

The tenth anniversary of the publication of the Old and New Testaments together in the R.S.V. (1962) was marked by the appearance of new editions, published by other houses than Nelsons, which had the exclusive right of publication for the first ten years. These new editions contained 85 changes from the 1952 edition, authorized by the Standard Bible Committee. One of these changes is of special interest: whereas in 1946 and 1952 the centurion at the cross had been made to say, "Truly this (man) was a son of God!" (Matt. 27 : 54; Mark 15 : 39), in 1962 his words were rendered " ... the son of God". There was no doubt a considerable difference between the centurion's intention and the significance which the Evangelists discerned in his confession: for Mark in particular it is as much the climax of his Gospel—"the gospel of Jesus Christ, the Son of God" (Mark 1 : 1)—as Thomas's confession (John 20 : 28) is the climax of John's, and should therefore be translated so as to convey his fulness of meaning.

In 1962 there was also published (by the Oxford University Press) an annotated edition of the R.S.V. entitled *The Oxford Annotated Bible*, under the editorship of Herbert G. May (for the Old Testament) and Bruce M. Metzger (for the New Testament and Apocrypha). In addition to separate introductions and essays by various scholars, brief exegetical footnotes are supplied on each page of text. There are also tables of weights and measures, chronological tables of rulers, and twelve coloured maps based on the *Oxford Bible Atlas*. A companion to this edition (whether bound in one volume with it or issued as a separate volume) is *The Oxford Concise Concordance to the Revised Standard Version*, compiled by Bruce M. Metzger and Isobel M. Metzger. Proper names are included in their alphabetical order within the main body of the concordance, and the more important personal names and place-names are introduced by brief summaries of the relevant historical and geographical data, so that the work has some of the features of a Bible dictionary as well as of a concordance. *The Oxford Annotated Bible* is a particularly useful edition of the R.S.V.; it is an additional point of interest that it is the first Protestant annotated edition of the Bible to be officially approved for study purposes by a Roman Catholic authority, for Cardinal Cushing, Archbishop of Boston, Mass., gave it his *imprimatur* in 1966. (See also the note on p. 203.)

It might have been expected that in Great Britain and Ireland the publication of the New English Bible would have caused some falling off in the use of the American produced R.S.V. For example, *The Times Literary Supplement* for March 24, 1961, contains this sentence in the course of a review of the New English Bible New Testament:

> The opinion has been expressed that in a few years' time there will be two versions only in normal use in this country—the Authorized Version and the New English Bible: the Revised Version, it is suggested, will quietly disappear (and with it, presumably, the Revised Standard Version).

(The reviewer did not commit himself to this opinion.) So far as the Revised Version is concerned, it is certainly being used less and less. But the use of the Revised Standard Version is increasing, and is continuing to do so several years after the publication of the whole New English Bible. It is a testimony to its qualities that in this country, where it has not enjoyed the intensive "promotion" which it was given in North America, it has made steady headway on the ground of its native merit.

One token of this is the growing number of commentaries, originating in this country, which use the R.S.V. as their basic text. We may mention the second edition of *Peake's Commentary* (1962), the new edition of the *Century Bible* (1966 and following years), the *New Testament Commentary* edited by G. C. D. Howley (1969), the *New Catholic Commentary on Holy Scripture*[1] (1969), the second edition of the Inter-Varsity Fellowship's *New Bible Commentary* (1970) and the later volumes of the *Torch Bible Commentaries*.[2] The *New Clarendon Bible* began in 1963 by using the New English Bible as its basis, but then turned to the R.S.V. The only major commentary based on the New English Bible thus far is the *Cambridge Bible Commentary on the New English Bible* (1963 and following years).

In fact, for the English-speaking world as a whole there is no modern version of the Bible which comes so near as the R.S.V. does to making the all-purpose provision which the A.V. made for so many years.

NOTE. The *Oxford Annotated Bible*, mentioned on pp. 201 f., was reissued in 1977 as *The New Oxford Annotated Bible*. This edition prints the 1971 revision of the R.S.V. New Testament, and to the apocryphal books (which are placed after the New Testament) it adds 3 and 4 Maccabees and Psalm 151. (Psalm 151, included in the Septuagint and in the Psalms scroll from Cave 11 at Qumran, relates in the first person David's anointing by Samuel and his victory over Goliath.) Since the complete canon of the Septuagint as used by Eastern Orthodox Christians is now included, this edition is approved by Orthodox authorities as well as by Catholics and Protestants. Three new special articles are added to those which appeared in the 1962 edition, and there are two further maps, illustrating the Apocrypha. This is probably the best available one-volume annotated edition of the English Bible.

[1] In this case the Catholic Edition of the R.S.V.; see p. 214.
[2] One might add *The Interpreter's Bible* (New York, 1952–57) and the *Broadman Bible Commentary* (Nashville, 1969 and following years), but these were initiated in the United States.

CHAPTER FIFTEEN

Recent Roman Catholic Versions

JUST AS English-speaking Protestants have felt the need in recent years of a revision of the A.V. and R.V., if not indeed a completely new translation, English-speaking Roman Catholics have felt the need of something more adequate than the Douai-Rheims-Challoner version.

The Confraternity Version (New American Bible)

A revision of the Rheims-Challoner New Testament was published in the United States in 1941 under the title *The New Testament of our Lord and Savior Jesus Christ*. The revision was the work of scholars belonging to the Catholic Biblical Association of America and was sponsored by the Episcopal Confraternity of Christian Doctrine. The revisers paid attention to the latest evidence for the Vulgate text, by which quite a number of the readings of the Clementine Vulgate were corrected; they also make mention in their notes of those places where the Latin and Greek texts diverge. In one important place they follow the Greek rather than the Latin: in saying in Heb. 1 : 3 that Christ "has effected man's purgation from sin and taken his seat" they avoid giving the impression (which the Vulgate gives) that the making of purification from sin is what our Lord is now engaged in during His heavenly session. After the publication of the New Testament a beginning was made with the Old Testament side of the work, but the Old Testament was no revision of Douai-Challoner but a new translation, based on the original text. The book of Genesis appeared in 1948, and the rest of the Old Testament was published subsequently in four volumes— Volume I (Genesis–Ruth) in 1952, Volume III (Sapiential or Wisdom Books) in 1955, Volume IV (Prophetic Books) in 1961 and Volume

II (Samuel–Maccabees) in 1969. But it was anomalous that an Old Testament translation from the Hebrew should be accompanied by a New Testament translation from the Vulgate; accordingly, this was remedied with the issue in 1970 of a new version of the New Testament, based on the Greek. At the same time the Old Testament volumes have been revised and brought up to date in various ways: for one thing, proper names no longer approximate to the Vulgate usage as they did in the first edition (where, for example, Volume IV contained the books from "Isaia to Malachia") but take the forms commonly used in the English-speaking world, as also in the Catholic edition of the R.S.V. (e.g. "Isaiah to Malachi"). The work on both Testaments is in the hands of a team of distinguished members of the Catholic Biblical Association of America. The Old Testament commission has as its chairman Professor Louis Hartmann of the Catholic University of America, and the New Testament commission meets under the chairmanship of Mgr Myles Bourke of St Joseph's Seminary, Dunwoodie, New York. In addition to the fifty-nine Catholic scholars engaged on the work, a number of Protestant scholars have been co-opted as editors and translators in its later stages—Professors Frank Cross, J. A. Sanders, and David Noel Freedman for the Old Testament and Professors W. D. Davies and John Knox for the New Testament. Introductions to the books are provided and textual notes are appended. The attempt, maintained in the first edition, to preserve something of the flavour of "Bible English" has been abandoned; the idiom is thoroughly twentieth century. Where the idiom of the original text is of high literary quality, every effort is made to make the translation produce an equivalent effect, but where the original is more pedestrian, "it would be false to attempt to make such parts literary masterpieces in modern English".[1] The format is in conformity with modern standards of book production.

Such an up-to-date and ecumenical version deserves an appropriate title: it is accordingly no longer called the Confraternity Version but the New American Bible. Many editions (mostly in one volume) have been put out by a dozen or more publishers.

[1] Stephen J. Hartdegen, O.F.M., *Confraternity Bible Evaluated* (1965), p. 3.

The Westminster Version

An excellent translation by English Roman Catholic scholars, based on the original texts in both Testaments, is the *Westminster Version of the Sacred Scriptures*, which was launched under the general editorship of the late Cuthbert Lattey, S.J. This version comprised introductions and commentaries to the various books of the Bible, as well as translations. The New Testament was complete by 1935; in 1948 a smaller edition of it appeared, consisting of the translation with very brief introductions and notes by Father Lattey. The first instalment of the Old Testament was the book of Malachi, edited by Father Lattey (1935); other volumes followed in the following years, though the work suffered a sad blow in Father Lattey's death in 1954.

R. A. Knox's Version

The *Westminster Version* is an independent venture; it is not an "official" translation. It is otherwise with a better known Roman Catholic version of the twentieth century—the translation of the Bible carried through by Mgr Ronald A. Knox. This has been given a place alongside the Douai-Rheims-Challoner translation as an official version of the Bible for Roman Catholics in Great Britain, authorized by the Roman Catholic hierarchy of England and Wales and the hierarchy of Scotland. It is described on the title-page of the 1955 edition (the first one-volume edition) as "a translation from the Latin Vulgate in the light of the Hebrew and Greek originals".

The New Testament in this version appeared in 1945, with the authorization of the Roman Catholic Archbishops and Bishops of England and Wales. The Old Testament appeared in 1949, in two volumes; according to the title-page it was "newly translated from the Latin Vulgate by Mgr Ronald A. Knox at the request of the Cardinal Archbishop of Westminster: for private use only". After some revision, however, the Old Testament version too received hierarchical authorization.

About the same time as the first edition of his Old Testament appeared, Knox published a valuable little book entitled *On Englishing the Bible*, in which he brought together eight articles and lectures dealing with his experience as a Bible translator. This book is a most useful handbook to his translation, as it sets forth clearly the principles on which he worked.

The first point to be noticed is that his work is a translation from the Latin Vulgate. The original text has been consulted throughout, but the Latin formed the basis of his version. In his 1949 edition of the Old Testament he included a translation of the Vulgate book of Psalms (the Gallican Psalter)[1] in the appropriate place, but added as an appendix an English translation of the new Latin Psalter, made by members of the Pontifical Biblical Institute directly from the Hebrew. In the 1955 edition his translation of the Gallican Psalter is left out; it is his translation of the new Latin Psalter that appears between Job and Proverbs.

Not only is Knox's version a translation of the Vulgate; it is a translation of the Clementine Vulgate—the edition of the Latin Bible authorized by Pope Clement VIII in 1592, which has remained the standard text for the Roman Catholic Church since that time. Knox felt unable to avail himself of the freedom claimed by the Confraternity revisers of 1941, to go behind the Clementine Vulgate to a purer recension of Jerome's version, even in places where it was perfectly obvious to him that the Clementine text was corrupt. He mentions one such passage: in Acts 17 : 6, where the Jews of Thessalonica describe Paul and his companions as men "that have turned the world upside down", the original Vulgate very properly has *orbem* for "world". But at a later stage in the transmission of the text *orbem* was corrupted to *urbem*, "city"; and *urbem* is the reading of the Clementine Vulgate. What is a conscientious translator to do? The Confraternity revisers, very properly, ignored the corruption and translated "these men who are setting the world in an uproar". But Knox stuck to the Clementine text and rendered "the men who are turning the state upside down"; to be sure, "state" could be a compromise, as the English reader might well take it to refer to the Roman Empire (which is what "world" means here) rather than to the city of Thessalonica. Knox justifies his procedure by saying: "that is how the thing stands in every Vulgate in the world nowadays, and it is no part of the translator's business to alter, on however

[1] See pp. 116 f.

good grounds, his original."[1] As to that, two things may be said: the first Vulgate that I took down from the shelf to check Knox's statement has *orbem*, not *urbem*; and while it may be no part of the translator's business to alter his original, he is doing no good service to his original when he declines to correct a palpable misprint or copyist's error.

Another example of the same thing may be found in 1 John 5 : 7, the passage about the Three Heavenly Witnesses. This passage was absent from the original Vulgate, but later found its way into the Latin text and is present in the Clementine edition. So Knox includes it in his text: "Thus we have a threefold warrant in heaven, the Father, the Word, and the Holy Ghost, three who are yet one"—to which he adds a footnote: "This verse does not occur in any good Greek manuscript. But the Latin manuscripts may have preserved the true text." But the fact is that the best *Latin* manuscripts also lack the verse. More recent Catholic versions omit it.

Even where the basic text is the purest attainable form of the Vulgate, Knox's version inevitably suffers from the limitations inherent in the fact that it is a secondary version—a translation of a translation. Not that any blame attaches to him in this regard; this was the task which he was commissioned to carry out. In fact, time and again our admiration is excited by the skill with which he surmounts these limitations. But the result is that no one will go to his version for help in determining the precise sense of the original.

But Knox's version has the overwhelming advantage of being the work of a man who had an uncanny instinct for getting the right word or the right phrase in any given context. As readers of his other works know, Knox was a master of English style, and not of one English style only. He can adapt the style to the subject-matter and the author's purpose with convincing effect. Equivalence of effect is what he aims at throughout. Quoting Hilaire Belloc, he points out that the translator's task is not to ask himself, "How shall I make this foreigner talk English?"—in which case a foreign-sounding English is bound to result—but "What would an Englishman have said to express this?" Never did a translation read less like a translation. There is no reason, Knox said, why Paralipomena (Chronicles)

[1] *On Englishing the Bible* (London, 1949), p. 2.

should not be made as readable as Froissart; and this is what he has done with it.

> That same night, the Lord appeared to him, bidding him choose what gift he would. Thou hast been very merciful, Solomon answered, to my father David, in granting him a son to succeed him; and now, Lord God, make good thy promise to him. Since thou hast made me king over thy people, a great people countless as the dust, grant me wisdom and discernment in all my dealings with them. How else should a man sit in judgement over such a people as this, great as thy people is great? And the Lord answered, For this choice thou hast made, thou shalt be rewarded. Thou didst not ask for riches or possessions, for glory, or vengeance upon thy enemies, or a long life. Thy prayer was for wisdom and discernment, to make thee a better judge for the subjects I have given thee. Wisdom and discernment thou shalt have; and I will give thee riches and possessions too, and such glory as never king shall have before or after thee (2 Chron. 1 : 7-12).

Or take the story of King Uzziah's clash with the priests (2 Chron. 26 : 16 ff.):

> But this greatness of his made his heart proud, to his own un-doing. He slighted the Lord his God; into the temple he would go, and there burn incense at the censing-altar. Close at his heels the high priest Azarias entered, and eighty priests with him, strong men all, to withstand the royal will. Not for thee, Ozias, they cried, to burn incense in the Lord's honour; that is for the priests, the sons of Aaron, that are set apart for this office. Leave this holy place, and profane it no more; thou wilt win no favour from the Lord God by such doings as these. At this, Ozias turned round in anger, the censer already in his hand with the incense ready for lighting, and began to threaten them. And with that, in the priests' presence, there in the Lord's house, by the censing-altar, the mark of leprosy started out on his brow. No time they lost, Azarias and his fellow-priests, that sign once seen, in thrusting out the leper; he himself, feeling the stroke of the Lord's present judgement, was in haste to be gone.

Knox admitted that, with the best will in the world, no translator would ever succeed in making Leviticus "newsy"; but here is a sample of his rendering of this book (Lev. 17 : 10 ff.):

> Any Israelite, or alien dwelling among you, who consumes the blood when he eats, becomes my enemy; I will sever him from my people. It is the blood that animates all living things, and I have destined it to make atonement for your souls upon the altar, blood for the purgation of your souls. That is why I have warned the sons of Israel that neither they nor the aliens who dwell among them must consume the blood when they eat. Any Israelite, or alien living among you, who hunts down a beast or snares a bird, such as you are allowed to eat, must drain its blood and cover it with earth. Because it animates all living things, I give the sons of Israel this warning: Never, on pain of death, turn it to your own use, the blood that holds the life.

When translating the poetical parts of the Old Testament, Knox felt that it would be unwise to try to preserve the parallelism so characteristic of Hebrew poetry; "to our notions of poetic composition, these remorseless repetitions are wholly foreign; when you have read a page or two on end, they begin to cloy."[1] Thus, the opening words of the prophecy of Amos (rendered in the A.V., "The LORD will roar from Zion, and utter his voice from Jerusalem") become: "Loud as roaring of lion, said he, the Lord will speak in thunder from his citadel at Jerusalem."

Some of the poetical compositions of the Old Testament are acrostics: Psalm 119 is the best-known and most elaborate example of this. Knox has attempted to carry the acrostic pattern over into English; thus in Psalm 119, each of the first eight verses begins with A, each of the second eight with B, and so on.

It is interesting to compare Knox's rendering of the Song of Songs with Moffatt's. Both aim at equivalent effect, but Knox's equivalent effect is of a more literary, and indeed poetical, order than Moffatt's. "What wonder the maids should love thee?" is Knox's counterpart to Moffatt's "the girls are all in love with you". Indeed,

---

[1] *On Englishing the Bible*, p. 97.

the Song of Songs has probably never been rendered into such beautiful English as in Knox's version.

> The voice I love! See where he comes, how he speeds over the mountains, how he spurns the hills! Gazelle nor fawn was ever so fleet of foot as my heart's love. And now he is standing on the other side of this very wall; now he is looking in through each window in turn, peering through every chink. I can hear my true love calling to me: Rise up, rise up quickly, dear heart, so gentle, so beautiful, rise up and come with me. Winter is over now, the rain has passed by. At home, the flowers have begun to blossom; pruning-time has come; we can hear the turtle-dove cooing already, there at home. There is green fruit on the fig-trees; the vines in flower are all fragrance. Rouse thee, and come, so beautiful, so well beloved, still hiding thyself as a dove hides in cleft rock or crannied wall. Shew me but thy face, let me but hear thy voice, that voice sweet as thy face is fair (2 : 8-14).

Knox uses "thou" for the pronoun of the second person singular throughout; he considered the policy of using "you" throughout, but decided that "thou" was preferable. He saw quite clearly the difficulties which were bound to arise if "thou" were used only in addressing divine persons, and "you" in other places. When is our Lord addressed as a divine person, and when not?

His aim, he tells us, is "to secure, as far as possible, that Englishmen of 2150, if my version is still obtainable then, shall not find it hopelessly 'dated'."[1] A version could become "dated" in a generation or two by being too idiomatic in the contemporary journalese sense as much as by being too archaic. And as regards the Old Testament, he has an interesting passage in which he maintains that "an earlier and more vigorous tradition of English", when the language was still fluid and adaptable, is the proper idiom for rendering it in such a way as to produce the right effect.[2]

It is not entirely Protestant prejudice, I think, which suggests that Knox fails to bring out Paul's doctrine of justification by faith in his translation of parts of the Epistle to the Romans. Take, for example, Rom. 3 : 26: "and he [God] has also vindicated the holiness of Jesus

---

[1] *On Englishing the Bible*, p. 52.   [2] *Ibid.*, p. 98.

Christ, here and now, as one who is himself holy, and imparts holiness to those who take their stand upon faith in him." Or the closing words of the fourth chapter:

This, then, was reckoned virtue in him [Abraham]; and the words, It was reckoned virtue in him, were not written of him only; they were written of us too. It will be reckoned virtue in us, if we believe in God as having raised our Lord Jesus Christ from the dead: handed over to death for our sins, and raised to life for our justification.

Where justification is in view—God's pronouncing the verdict of Not Guilty on the sinner and conferring a righteous status on him—the introduction of such words as "holiness" and "virtue" tends to confuse the issue.

In the New Testament especially there are copious footnotes. Many of these discuss points of text and rendering, particularly where the Latin deviates from the Greek (or Hebrew, in the Old Testament). Some are designed to elucidate the sense to a greater degree than the translation in itself can do. For example, on Rom. 12 : 21: "If we avenge ourselves, we Christians are converted to the enemy's point of view, instead of converting him to ours." Others discuss the relation of the text to the teaching of the Church. Thus, Matt. 1 : 25 is translated: "and he [Joseph] had not known her [Mary] when she bore a son, her first-born, to whom he gave the name Jesus." A footnote points out that a more literal rendering would be "he knew her not till she bore a son"; and maintains that even this rendering "does not impugn the perpetual virginity of our Lady."

It is with difficulty that one resists the temptation to go on giving further sample quotations. Suffice it to say that, for all the inevitable limitations of a secondary version, Knox has given us a most readable edition of the English Bible. It may now, as some suggest, have something of the nature of a period piece, but it is none the less attractive for that.

A Common Translation?

In our day biblical study transcends confessional barriers; we find, for example, Protestants and Roman Catholics, and (so far as Old

Testament study is concerned)[1] Christians and Jews, freely making use of each other's work and freely acknowledging their indebtedness to it. This applies to each other's Bible translations as much as to other work in the field of biblical study. But an interconfessional translation was thought until recently to lie beyond the realm of practical politics; the presence of Dr Orlinsky on the committee which prepared the Revised Standard Version of the Old Testament did not make that version a joint Christian–Jewish product. Within the frontiers of historic Christianity no barrier seemed more insurmountable, so far as ecclesiastical relations went, than that between Roman Catholics and those who do not belong to the Roman obedience. We used each other's Bible translations with profit, but any co-operation on an agreed Bible translation appeared to be excluded by considerations of church politics.

All the more interesting, then, was an article entitled "The Bible is a Bond" which appeared in the American Roman Catholic journal *America* in October 1959. In this article the associate editor of the journal, Father Walter M. Abbott, s.j., expressed the view that a common translation of the Bible "would be a great achievement in the history of Christianity". He pointed out that while agreement on the exact wording of a Bible version would by no means settle all doctrinal differences, it could put an end to minor deviations of practice, as in the wording of the Lord's Prayer and the numbering of the Ten Commandments. When all Christians are "talking about the same commandments, there would be hope for better observance of the one great commandment."

Father Abbott mentioned that a group of Roman Catholic scholars in Britain recently made a detailed examination of the R.S.V., and came to the conclusion that with a few changes in wording—some twenty in all—the version could be made completely acceptable for use by Roman Catholic readers.

Father Abbott may have been flying a kite in this article, but it is

---

[1] The parenthetical qualification "so far as Old Testament study is concerned" must be dropped when we think of the *Anchor Bible*. This is a new translation of the books of the Bible (not including the Apocrypha), with introduction and notes, begun in 1964 and to be completed in 38 volumes, published by Doubleday of New York. The editors are W. F. Albright and D. N. Freedman, and the approximately thirty authors include Catholics, Protestants, and Jews.

significant that such a kite could be flown. It is, in any case, not so much the wording of the Bible but the doctrine of the Bible—whether it is or is not in itself the sufficient rule of faith and practice—that keeps Protestants and Roman Catholics apart. On the Protestant side, as might be expected, Father Abbott's overture received a speedy and cordial response. Professor Robert M. Grant of Chicago University, President of the American Society of Biblical Literature and Exegesis, said it would be "hard to overestimate" the importance of such an agreed version of the Bible as a "unifying force" among Christians.

These last three paragraphs have been left standing here in practically the form in which they appeared in the first edition of this book. The reviewer in the *Catholic Biblical Quarterly* concluded his exceedingly generous appraisal of the book with a brief reference to these paragraphs, and ended his review with the words, "the time for kite flying is not yet".

That was 1961. But things moved swiftly in the Roman Catholic Church in the years immediately following, largely, but by no means solely, through the influence of Vatican Council II (1963–65), with its encouragement of just such common versions as Father Abbott advocated. Father Abbott himself was appointed to the Secretariat for Christian Unity in Rome, with special responsibility for cooperative action in the field of Bible translation; he has been popularly called the Pope's "Bible ambassador".[1] In 1965 a "Catholic Edition" of the R.S.V. New Testament was published, and this was followed in 1966 by the whole Bible.[2] For this edition we have to thank the Catholic Biblical Association of Great Britain. The New Testament was commended in a foreword by the Apostolic Delegate to Great Britain (Archbishop Cardinale), the complete Bible by Cardinal Heenan, Archbishop of Westminster. The changes introduced in the Catholic Edition are conveniently listed in an appendix; the most obvious change, to anyone leafing through the volume, is the placing of the books of the Apocrypha in their Vulgate position, interspersed among the Old Testament books, and not as a separate section at the end of the Old Testament. In the Introduction to the

---

[1] He became General Secretary of the World Catholic Federation for the Bible Apostolate.
[2] In the same year the *Oxford Annotated Bible* received Cardinal Cushing's *imprimatur*.

New Testament volume of 1965 it was pointed out that today

the sciences of textual criticism and philology, not to mention others, have made such great advances that the Bible text used by translators is substantially the same for all—Protestants and Catholics alike. Thus, for example, Catholics no longer make their translations from the Latin Vulgate; though it is arguable that before the development of textual criticism it was in certain respects a better way of making a translation than to make it from late and in some places corrupt Greek manuscripts, as was done by some of the Reformers.[1] Today, and indeed since the appearance in 1943 of the Encyclical Letter, *Divino Afflante Spiritu*, encouraging Biblical studies, Catholics like every one else go back to the original languages and base their translations on the same critical principles.

Yet in 1949 Mgr Knox wrote that "for all official purposes a Bible translation must take the Vulgate as its standard".[2]

The Jerusalem Bible

A further landmark in Catholic versions of the English Bible was the publication, in October 1966, of the Jerusalem Bible. This fine work owes its inception to the enterprise of the Dominican *École Biblique et Archéologique* in Jerusalem, which from 1948 onwards produced *La Bible de Jérusalem*, a series of volumes presenting a new and authoritative French translation of the books of the Bible, with textual and exegetical notes. A one-volume edition of the whole work, in which the notes were abridged so as to be less technical, appeared in 1956; the *Jerusalem Bible* is the English counterpart of this. The general editor of the French work is the distinguished head of the *École Biblique*, Père Roland de Vaux; the general editor of the English edition is Fr Alexander Jones, Senior Lecturer in Divinity in

---

[1] The point here is that the early Reformers (e.g. Luther and Tyndale) based their versions on the early printed editions of the New Testament, which were based on quite late manuscripts, whereas the Vulgate was based on very much earlier Greek manuscripts. But by the sixteenth century the Vulgate text was in as corrupt a state as the Greek text; hence the Clementine Vulgate of 1592 and versions based on it were in no better case than the "Received Text" and versions based on it.

[2] *On Englishing the Bible*, p. 1. And he makes it plain that by the Vulgate he means the Clementine edition (see p. 207 above).

Christ's College, Liverpool, who secured the assistance of a considerable number of collaborators in translation and literary revision. Where literary revision is concerned, some very eminent names can be recognized in the list of collaborators.

The *Jerusalem Bible* is not simply translated from the French work. The introductions and notes to the books of the Bible are indeed translated from the French, though they have been revised and brought up to date. But the Biblical text itself is based on the Hebrew, Aramaic, and Greek originals, though the French version was regularly consulted where questions of variant reading or interpretation arose. The work carries the *imprimatur* of Cardinal Heenan.

While the *Jerusalem Bible* is a Catholic version, in the sense that it was produced by Catholic scholars, it is not a version for Catholics in particular, but for Bible readers in general. It could scarcely be otherwise, for there are no more ecumenically minded men in the world than the Dominicans of the *École Biblique*, whose praise is in all the churches. In fact, in 1969 one enterprising publisher issued an edition of the French version under the title *La Bible Oecuménique*. This, however, is a misleading title, because a truly ecumenical French edition of the Bible is in course of production—and, for the matter of that, a truly ecumenical German edition too. By a "truly ecumenical" edition is meant one on which Protestant and Roman Catholic translators collaborate—not in the sense that one does this book and another does that book, but in the sense that every part of the translation is the fruit of such collaboration. This kind of exercise is envisaged by the Constitution *On Divine Revelation*[1] of Vatican Council II, where it is provided that, "given the opportunity and the approval of church authority", translations should be "produced in cooperation with the separated brethren". According to unofficial reports, this form of collaboration runs into no difficulties when it is a question of translating (say) Paul's Letters to the Romans and the Galatians, with their exposition of justification by faith (which was *the* crux in the days of the Reformation and Counter-Reformation). There all that is necessary is to translate what Paul says, and there is no disagreement about his meaning. Such difficulties as do arise are more likely to concern the rendering of terms for

[1] Paragraph 22.

ecclesiastical institutions and offices in (say) the Pastoral Letters, and these difficulties are not of the first importance.

To return to the *Jerusalem Bible*: the notes which accompany the translation are not concerned to reaffirm traditional interpretations but to elucidate the text. An informative note on Genesis 3 : 15, where God says to the serpent with regard to the woman's offspring, "It will crush your head and you will strike its heel", points out that the Greek version ("he will crush") expresses "the messianic interpretation held by many of the Fathers", while the Latin version ("she will crush") has been taken as a reference to Mary: "this application has become current in the church". But there is no suggestion that "she" represents the original meaning, or that (as R. A. Knox's footnote asserts without any obvious basis in fact) it "plainly gives a better balance to the sentence". Matthew 1 : 25 in itself "does not assert Mary's perpetual virginity"—which, however, "the gospels elsewhere presuppose". Thus the brothers of Jesus in Matthew 12 : 46, etc., are said to be "not Mary's children but near relations, cousins perhaps". On James 5 : 16 it is noted that "this mutual confession and prayer for each other, instead of being only recommendations to the sick (v. 15), are here urged on all Christians. Nothing special, however, may be deduced about sacramental confession." The three heavenly witnesses of 1 John 5 : 7 have disappeared; a footnote rightly points out that the passage is "not in any of the early Greek MSS, or any of the early translations, or in the best MSS of the Vulg. itself", and suggests that it is "probably a gloss that has crept into the text".[1]

The idiom of the Jerusalem Bible is contemporary: "thou", "thee", "thy", and "thine" are jettisoned completely, no matter who is addressed. "The first duty of a translator," says the general editor, "is to convey as clearly as he can what the original author wrote." Jacobean phraseology is rejected, together with that form of "poetic language" which is sometimes used to lend "artificial dignity to plain statements" (p. vi). In the Old Testament the personal name of the God of Israel appears as Yahweh—a form commonplace among scholars, but rare in Bible translations intended for a wider public.[2]

---

[1] Contrast R. A. Knox, quoted on p. 208.
[2] See pp. 133, 170 f., 231, 281

The editor acknowledges that in the Psalms especially this form may be unacceptable, but points out that anyone who prefers may substitute "the Lord" for "Yahweh".

Here and there a different translation might be preferred. For example, when it is said in Ezekiel 21 : 27 that the crown of Judah must remain desolate "until he comes whose right it is" (R.S.V.), we should probably recognize an echo of Genesis 49 : 10, where Jacob, blessing the tribe of Judah, says that it will retain the kingship "until he comes to whom it belongs" (R.S.V.).[1] In a marginal reference at Ezekiel 21 : 27 the Jerusalem Bible mentions Gen. 49 : 10, but the actual translation imports an allusion to Nebuchadrezzar: "To ruin ... am I going to bring it, to such ruin as was never known before this man came who is appointed to inflict the punishment which I am determined to impose on it." In Daniel 9 : 25 it would probably have been better to follow the Massoretic punctuation, which puts a fairly heavy stop between "seven weeks" and "sixty-two weeks", as the R.S.V. does (" ... there shall be seven weeks. Then for sixty-two weeks ...").[2] This makes sense when compared with the actual chronology of the events in question, whereas it is difficult to make such good sense of the "seven weeks and sixty-two weeks" of the *Jerusalem Bible*.

The apocryphal books are included in their Septuagint or Vulgate positions, except that the books of Maccabees, instead of coming at the end of the Old Testament, are placed with the other historical books, following on from Esther. The Greek additions to Esther are set in italics to distinguish them from the Hebrew book.

The Psalm numbers follow the Hebrew arrangement and not that of the Septuagint and Vulgate; this arrangement is more familiar to Protestant than to Catholic readers. Similarly, as in the New American Bible (the new edition of the Confraternity Version), the proper names have the form more familiar in Protestant versions: in both Testaments we find Isaiah, Jeremiah, Hosea, etc., and not Isaias (Esaias), Jeremias (Jeremy), Osee, etc.

The work throughout reflects the text and interpretation generally

[1] The *Jerusalem Bible* translates identically, apart from the subjunctive "come" instead of the indicative "comes".
[2] The N.E.B. rendering is in line with that of R.S.V.

accepted in the interconfessional world of Biblical scholarship. The introductions and notes make due appraisal of current critical research: on the Pentateuch, for example, it is observed that the classical form of the documentary theory is giving way to a new approach, reckoning with the light thrown by archaeological discovery on the pre-literary stage of the material, which "is less artificial and literary; it is closer to realities and to the conditions of life" (p. 7).

Among other "helps" at the end of the volume is an index of Biblical themes, calculated to be very useful to Bible students, and reflecting the interest of Fr Alexander Jones, whose advocacy of the thematic study of the Bible is well known.

A work like the *Jerusalem Bible*, whose acceptance takes no account of old party lines, encourages us to look forward to the day when it will be thought as odd and anachronistic to talk of Catholic versions and Protestant versions as it would be now to talk of Anglican versions and Free Church versions. There could be no more important or welcome manifestation of the ecumenical spirit than co-operation in the production and study of the Bible and in the receiving and practising of its message.

CHAPTER SIXTEEN

Other Recent Versions

MANY TRANSLATORS have felt urged to respond to the special challenge presented by the Pauline Epistles. Paul's style is none of the easiest, and anyone who wishes to get to grips with his thought is almost compelled to try to put Paul's argument into his own words, in order to make it plain to himself first, and then to others.

A. S. Way's version of the Epistles

Arthur S. Way (1847–1930), a classical scholar, published the first edition of a translation of *The Letters of St Paul* in 1901. Five years later he produced a second edition, which represented a thorough revision of the first, and also included a translation of the Epistle to the Hebrews.

Paul's epistolary style no doubt owes something to his habit of dictating his letters instead of writing them himself. At times one can picture Paul, set on fire by his subject, walking up and down pouring out the words of inspiration, while his amanuensis does his best to get them all down in whatever system of shorthand he used. But, swiftly as Paul's words flowed, swifter still was the current of his thought, and every now and then his words, as though they despaired of keeping pace with his thought, seem to overleap the intervening gap and make a fresh beginning abreast of his thought, only to fall behind once again. These gaps make it difficult for the modern reader to follow the course of Paul's argument. Way fills them up for us, so that we may keep track of the apostle's line of thought more easily. This procedure calls, of course, for a good measure of insight and interpretation; but these are qualities which are called for in any good translation.

Another noteworthy feature of Way's translation is the printing as poetry of those passages where he believes Paul was quoting well-known snatches of early Christian hymnody—a feature which he is inclined to overdo.

St Paul from the Trenches

St Paul from the Trenches, by Gerald Warre Cornish, is a work with a personal interest of its own. Cornish, a Cambridge graduate, was Lecturer in Greek in Manchester University when the First World War broke out in 1914. He joined the fighting forces, and was killed in action in September 1916. Among his effects was a muddy copy-book containing "in minute but perfectly legible script" a translation of the two Epistles to the Corinthians and part of the Epistle to the Ephesians. It was not until 1937 that this work was published; then it went rapidly into several editions. The apostle's language is considerably expanded so that the sense may be brought out more fully: here, for example, are the opening sentences of 1 Cor. 6:

> Now another matter—the Greeks are devoted to litigation, it is a passion with them, but what has that to do with you? Are you going to haunt the law-courts of Corinth and with cases which you bring against one another! This has little to do with the true judgment and justice which your faith exemplifies. That is capable of judging angels, and if you have it are you not even capable of settling these business disputes which arise amongst yourselves? Have you no one wise enough for that, but must you go to law with one another, and invoke the methods and assistance of a corrupt judicial system to get the better of your brother? Questions of everyday life then cannot be settled by the Church, but you must needs take them before those who know nothing of your faith, and whom the Church on that account esteems as of no account. Yet you bring your quarrels and disputes before them!

Bishop Wand

When Dr J. W. C. Wand was Archbishop of Brisbane, he produced a translation of *The New Testament Letters* (1943), which was reissued in a revised edition in 1946, after he had become Bishop of London. "I have tried," he says in the preface, "to put the Epistles into the kind of language a Bishop might use in writing a monthly letter for his diocesan magazine." A sample of his work may be given by quoting his rendering of these same opening verses of 1 Cor. 6:

> When you have a case against another member of the Church, how dare you take it before a pagan court? Don't you realize that Christians will judge the whole world? If you are to judge the universe, are you incapable of judging the smallest matters? Don't you realize that we shall even judge the fallen angels? Much more then shall we judge human affairs. Well, when you have such affairs to adjudicate upon, do you set those who are of no account in the Church to act as arbitrators? I am saying this to arouse in you a sense of shame. Isn't there a single intelligent person among you who can act as arbitrator for the brotherhood? Has it come to this, that brother must drag brother into court and that before unbelievers? You have already lost your case by the very fact that you have lawsuits with one another.

Where Paul quotes passages from the Old Testament poetical books, or pieces of Christian hymnody, Bishop Wand likes to turn them into verse, much as a modern bishop might quote a hymn in his diocesan letter. So Gal. 4 : 27 is rendered:

> The empty house resounds with joy,
>   The childless wife breaks into song;
> To her who was bereft of all
>   Unnumbered children now belong.

And the doxology of Rom. 16 : 25–27 appears thus:

> To God all-wise be glory
>   Who strength hath given to men
> By making known His secret
>   Long hid from human ken.
>
> Prophetic voices told it
>   To ears that closed again,
> But now to faithful Pagans
>   He makes the mystery plain.

Let us hope that the readers of the diocesan magazine would get the apostle's point, and realize that they are among the "faithful Pagans" referred to!

J. B. Phillips

Of all translations of the New Testament epistles, none has attained such immediate and lasting acceptance as J. B. Phillips's *Letters to Young Churches*, first published in 1947. This version, undertaken in the first instance to relieve the tedium of civilian duties in war-time, was introduced to publishers and readers with a warm commendation from C. S. Lewis. "It would have saved me a great deal of labour," wrote Dr Lewis, "if this book had come into my hands when I first seriously began to try to discover what Christianity was."

Undoubtedly, of all modern English translations of the New Testament epistles, this is one of the best—perhaps actually the best—for the ordinary reader. The reader who has never paid much attention to Paul's writings, and finds them dull and sometimes unintelligible in the older versions, would be well advised to read them through in Dr Phillips's version. He will find them (possibly to his surprise) interesting, and (more surprising still) remarkably relevant to the present day and its problems. He will be helped to understand the arguments by the brief introductory notes which precede each Epistle, and by the cross-headings at the beginning of each section. In fact, he will share something of the translator's own experience as he proceeded with his task: again and again, he tells us, he "felt rather like an electrician re-wiring an ancient house without being able to 'turn the mains off'."

Some would call Dr Phillips's work a paraphrase rather than a translation. Such terms call for definition, and it is not too easy to determine where translation ends and paraphrase begins; let us say that what he gives us is a meaning-for-meaning translation. And what is the purpose of a translation if it does not communicate the meaning? The flavour of his work may be conveyed by two sample quotations:

I have made a fool of myself in this "boasting" business, but you forced me to do it. If only you had had a better opinion of me it would have been quite unnecessary. For I am not really in the least inferior, nobody as I am, to these extra-special Special Messengers. You have had an exhaustive demonstration of the power God gives to a genuine Messenger in the miracles, signs and works of spiritual power that you saw with your own eyes. What makes you feel so inferior to other churches? Is it because I have not allowed you to support me financially? My humblest apologies for this great wrong! (2 Cor. 12 : 11-13).

I am appealing for my child. Yes I have become a father though I have been under lock and key, and the child's name is—Onesimus! Oh, I know you have found him pretty useless in the past but he is going to be useful now, to both of us. I am sending him back to you: *will you receive him as my son, part of me?* I should have dearly loved to have kept him with me: he could have done what you would have done—looked after me here in prison for the Gospel's sake. But I would do nothing without consulting you first, for if you have a favour to give me, let it be spontaneous and not forced from you by circumstances! (Philemon 10-14).

From translating the Epistles, Dr Phillips went on to translate the Gospels into modern English, and this part of his work appeared in 1952. It might be thought (by those who have never tried to do it) that the Gospels would be easier to translate, but in fact, as Dr Phillips points out at the beginning of his preface to *The Gospels in Modern English*, there is a peculiar difficulty in turning these documents into modern English, and that for a number of reasons. His own procedure, he says, was "to 'forget' completely the majesty and beauty of the Authorised Version" and "to translate the Greek text as one would translate any other document from a foreign language, with the same conscientiousness but also with the same freedom in conveying, as far as possible, the meaning and style of the original writer."

It may be thought that his rendering of the Gospels is less happy than his version of the Epistles. But if his rendering is intended primarily for those readers who have no previous acquaintance with the

Gospels, it may be just what the modern pagan needs to bring him into vital touch with the Life of lives. One may wonder, however, if the statement, "At the beginning God expressed Himself", conveys even to the modern pagan the sense of the opening clause of St John's Gospel. ("From the beginning God has been expressing Himself" would be better, though still far from adequate.)

But to pick out points for criticism alone would be ungracious. It is only by comparison with the translator's own standard in *Letters to Young Churches* that his version of the Gospels appears to suffer. We should pay tribute to the solid worth of great areas of the work, especially the parables in the Synoptic Gospels.

Dr Phillips continued his translating work with a rendering of Acts, *The Young Church in Action* (1955), and *The Book of Revelation* (1957). To his rendering of Acts he appended an expanded version of four of the speeches which are summarized in the course of the narrative—an interesting and successful exercise. The peculiar difficulties of Revelation he decided were not of the sort which could be removed by paraphrase, because they inhere in the apocalyptic symbolism of the book. The difficulties of this symbolism remain, but the language in which Dr Phillips expresses the symbolism will help the reader to appreciate not only its unearthly power but also the glory of the triumph of Christ which it symbolizes.

In 1958 a one-volume edition of Phillips's completed *New Testament in Modern English* was published.

The "Penguin" Translations

The Penguin Classics, which were published under the editorship of Dr E. V. Rieu, a distinguished classical scholar, include a new translation of *The Four Gospels*, by Dr Rieu himself (1952), and one of *The Acts of the Apostles*, by his son, C. H. Rieu (1957). In an introduction Dr Rieu discusses some of the problems of Gospel translation, and describes his own experiences and impressions as he carried through his work. The fact that "we have for long been preoccupied with subjects other than religion, and our daily concerns are reflected in our daily speech" is the fact which more than any other "makes it impossible to translate *everything* in the Gospels into the normal idiom of 1952. However, the translator must accept this limitation as a challenge rather than a handicap, blending the old wine with the new in such a manner that the skins hold both."

A most interesting discussion was broadcast on December 3, 1953, between Dr Rieu and Dr Phillips on this subject of Gospel translation, on which both men had earned the right to be heard; it is reproduced in *The Bible Translator* for October 1955. Both translators were in perfect agreement about the principle of equivalent effect, and Dr Rieu made an important point here with regard to the translating of our Lord's words. Our Lord often spoke paradoxically, and His original hearers did not always find it easy to grasp His meaning; a translation, therefore, which aims at making everything He said crystal-clear is not producing the equivalent effect—and could, indeed, reflect the translator's own failure to grasp His meaning. Another point made by Dr Rieu is that a recognizable rhythm runs through the Greek Gospels; in his attempt to reproduce it in his translation, he found that the best plan was to read it aloud first to himself and then to competent critics sitting with paper and pencil in hand. Dr Phillips declared himself to be very largely in agreement with him.

Dr Rieu's remarks on Gospel translation deserve all the more respect because his experience as a translator from Greek into English is not confined to the biblical field. It is not appreciated to-day as much as it should be that a man whose knowledge of Greek is confined to the Greek New Testament, or even to the New Testament together with the Septuagint, does not really know Greek—not well enough, at any rate, to translate it with any authority.

Where Dr Rieu and Dr Phillips criticize each other's work, as they do to some extent in this discussion, there is substance in both sets of criticisms. Dr Rieu, for example, suggests that Dr Phillips's translation of John 1 : 1, "At the beginning God expressed himself", lands him in difficulties later on, as when he has to say in verse 14, "So the Expression of God became a human being." Dr Phillips agreed that that was not one hundred per cent accurate, but mentioned that to a number of people who had spoken to him this rendering did mean something, whereas "word" (whether capitalized or not) was too ambiguous, and the retention of the Greek term *logos* unacceptable— on this last point Dr Rieu (who himself retains the rendering "the Word") agrees: "I don't think we want Greek words".

Dr Phillips, for his part, criticizes Dr Rieu's practice of relegating to footnotes those passages where the Evangelists turn aside in the course of their narration to tell us that these things happened in order that such-and-such an Old Testament prophecy should be fulfilled. Dr Phillips would feel quite happy about this in all the Gospels but Matthew's; but he feels that to Matthew these quotations are "part of the fabric of his style". He is right; they are, as he says, "part of the stuff of Matthew", playing an essential rôle in the fulfilment of his aim as he makes his Gospel.

But Dr Rieu was able to cap this criticism by pointing out that Dr Phillips omitted the genealogies of Matt. 1 : 2-17 and Luke 3 : 23-38. What Phillips has actually done is to condense each of these genealogies into a single short sentence. Matt. 1 : 1-17 is rendered thus:

> The genealogy of Jesus Christ may be traced from Abraham, through forty-two generations, to Joseph the husband of Mary, Jesus' mother—fourteen generations from Abraham to David, fourteen more from David to the Deportation to Babylon, and fourteen more from Babylon to Christ himself.

And here is the telescoped version of Luke 3 : 23-38:

> Jesus himself was about thirty years old at this time when he began his work. It was assumed that he was the son of Joseph whose ancestry may be traced back through the generations past Abraham, to Adam and back to God.

Dr Phillips defends himself by appealing again to the principle of equivalent effect. The effect produced on first-century readers by a string of Jewish names was very different, he suggests, from that which it would produce on twentieth-century readers. While it was important to emphasize that the genealogy of Jesus went right back through Jewish history, the actual list of names as such was not now so important. In Matthew's genealogy, however, one thing is emphasized which Dr Phillips's condensed version does not bring out—that Jesus was the legal heir to the throne of David.[1]

---

[1] In the one-volume edition (1958) the genealogies are given in full.

Both translators agreed that the work of translating the Gospels made a profound impression on them. At the end of his introduction to *The Four Gospels* Dr Rieu says:

> Of what I have learnt from these documents in the course of my long task, I will say nothing now. Only this, that they bear the seal of the Son of Man and God, they are the Magna Charta of the human spirit. Were we to devote to their comprehension a little of the selfless enthusiasm that is now expended on the riddle of our physical surroundings, we should cease to say that Christianity is coming to an end,—we might even feel that it had only just begun.

And at the end of his broadcast discussion with Dr Phillips he said: "My work changed me."

C. H. Rieu's translation of Acts in the Penguin Classics is preceded by thirty pages of introduction and followed by over sixty pages of notes—all of which enhances the value of an excellent piece of work.

H. J. Schonfield

The Authentic New Testament (1955) is a translation by a distinguished Jewish scholar, Dr Hugh J. Schonfield, who approaches the documents "as if they had recently been recovered from a cave in Palestine or from beneath the sands of Egypt, and had never previously been given to the public." Dr Schonfield has an intimate mastery of the Jewish environment of New Testament times, and agrees with Mr Victor Gollancz in wondering "whether a Gentile, however imaginative, can really live as a Jew can in the New Testament atmosphere." Since the significance of the word "authentic" in the title of his translation has been misunderstood, he points out that it does not refer to his translation (as if no other translation were genuine) but to the quality of the New Testament itself, which he endeavours to bring out. The introduction and notes supply much helpful information on the Jewish references in the New Testament documents. The translation itself is of a high quality, although inevitably one finds things here and there that might have been better expressed: "no one esteems the Son except the Father" (Matt. 11 : 27; Luke 10 : 22) says something less than the Evangelists intend by the verb which they use in this statement.

The Berkeley Version

Among recent English translations of the whole Bible which have been sponsored by private groups none is more worthy of special mention than *The Holy Bible: The Berkeley Version in Modern English*.

In 1945 a translation of the New Testament, the work of Dr Gerrit Verkuyl, appeared under the title *The Berkeley Version of the New Testament* (from Berkeley, California, where the translator lived). During the following fourteen years a staff of twenty scholars worked on a similar translation of the Old Testament under Dr Verkuyl's direction as editor-in-chief, and in 1959 the complete work was published in Grand Rapids, Michigan, and in London, England.

The general format of this version reminds one forcibly of the Revised Standard Version, and it might not be too wide of the mark to describe it as a more conservative counterpart to the R.S.V. As in the R.S.V., the older use of italics to denote words added to complete the sense has been abandoned, and direct speech is indicated by quotation-marks. But where God is the speaker, or (as regards the New Testament) where Christ is the speaker, quotation-marks are not used; for the whole Bible (and not only the express utterances of God) is viewed as the Word of God, and Christ Himself is the personal Word of God. Thus in the book of Job the speeches of Job and his friends are marked off by quotation-marks, but not so God's own contribution to the debate; and in Christ's conversations with His disciples and others, their words are so marked, but not His. Accordingly, there is no punctuation in the third chapter of St John's Gospel to show where our Lord's words to Nicodemus come to an end and the Evangelist's comments on the conversation begin, as there is in R.S.V. after verse 15.

Divine persons are addressed as "Thou", but otherwise "you" is used for the pronoun of the second person in the singular and plural alike. Pronouns referring to divine persons are regularly capitalized; this is a departure from traditional usage in Bible printing. But in the Gospels Christ is addressed as "you", not "Thou", in those passages "where His disciples are still unaware of His deity, and ... where His enemies accost Him"; and in such passages pronouns referring to Him are not capitalized. Thus, in Mark 4 : 38 the disciples wake Him up and say, "Teacher, do you not care that we are sinking?" but a few verses further on the Gadarene demoniac cries to Him: "What dealings hast Thou with me, Jesus, Son of God Most High! I adjure Thee to God, do not torment me" (Mark 5 : 7). Such transitions are decidedly awkward, and confirm our conviction that it is best to use "thou" throughout or "you" throughout where Christ is spoken to in the Gospel narrative.

It was a conservative complaint against the R.S.V. that it rendered a number of familiar messianic prophecies in the Old Testament in such a way as to obscure their messianic application. The Berkeley translators, on the other hand, declare themselves to be "in tune with the 'Authorized Version' of 1611 in fidelity to the Messianic Promise, first made as soon as man had sinned, renewed to Abraham, Isaac and Jacob, narrowed to Judah's offspring and later to David's descendants." Their use of capitals in pronouns referring to divine persons makes the messianic sense of a number of those prophecies explicit. Thus the identity of the woman's seed in Gen. 3 : 15 is made clear by the capitalized "He" in the clause "He will crush your head" (but surely the non-capitalization of "his" in the following clause, "and you will crush his heel", is an oversight). Capitals, together with the use of the pronoun "Thou", similarly mark out the royal bridegroom of Psalm 45 as the expected Messiah, in agreement with the interpretation found in Heb. 1 : 8 f., according to which it is Christ, the Son of God, who is addressed in verse 6 of the psalm: "Thy throne, O God, is for ever and ever." A footnote to Psalm 45 in the Berkeley version tells us that this psalm summarizes The Song of Songs. But when we turn to The Song of Songs in the Berkeley version, we find that it is not interpreted messianically; instead, we are told that it speaks "the love-language of a young woman and her lover" and expresses "the joyful exaltation of that love which sanctifies marriage". So the maiden is not made to address her lover as "Thou", and pronouns referring to him are not capitalized, as would have been the case had this version followed the tradition of the A.V. chapter-headings and understood the book to set forth the mutual affection of Christ and the Church.

The use of capitalized pronouns makes it quite plain how the prophecy of the "seventy weeks" in Daniel 9 : 24-27 is interpreted. The anointed one who is cut off in verse 26 is identified with Christ: "Messiah shall be eliminated, although there is nothing against Him". So also in verse 27 it is evidently Christ who is to "make the covenant to prevail for many" and "cause sacrifice and offering to cease". It may be argued that what is ambiguous in Hebrew should have some of its ambiguity preserved in English, so that the English reader may make up his mind about the meaning, uninfluenced by capitalization. One edition of the A.V. (*The Englishman's Bible*, edited by Thomas Newberry), which capitalizes pronouns referring to divine persons, gives quite a different interpretation to these closing verses of Daniel 9 by capitalizing pronouns which the Berkeley version leaves without capitals, and *vice versa*. The standard versions, which leave all such pronouns without capitals, have chosen the more satisfactory way.

The various translators have evidently been left to use their own judgment in rendering divine names, and no editorial consistency has been imposed. The name Yahweh is reproduced at least once ("YAHWEH His name", Hosea 12 : 5); occasionally it appears as "Jehovah" (as in Ex. 15 : 3, "Jehovah is His name"); but it is usually rendered "the LORD" (as in Amos 5 : 8, "the LORD is His name"). Whereas the spelling of "the LORD" with four capital letters (or of "GOD" with three) should be reserved for those places where the name Yahweh appears in the Hebrew text, the Berkeley version exhibits inconsistencies. Thus in Ezek. 2 : 4 and elsewhere we find "the LORD God" where we should expect "the Lord GOD" as the rendering of *'Adonai Yahweh*. In Amos 7 : 1 we find the correct rendering "the Lord GOD", but elsewhere in Amos *'Adonai Yahweh* is simply reproduced as "the Lord God". In Psalm 45 : 11 "He is your LORD" should appear as "He is your Lord", for the word used there is not *Yahweh* but *'adon* with the appropriate inflection.

The Berkeley version further resembles the R.S.V. in that the

Old Testament part is a better piece of work than the New. Passing over some doubtful translations (such as "made righteous" for "justified" in Rom. 5 : 1 and "May your spirit be without a flaw and your soul and body maintained blameless" in 1 Thess. 5 : 23), the New Testament in this version contains too many stylistic oddities. "Pattern after me, as I pattern after Christ" (1 Cor. 11 : 1) sounds rather strange, on the European side of the Atlantic at any rate, and so does "the leftovers shall be saved" (Rom. 9 : 27). The Old Testament section of the work is not completely free from such infelicities—"my face-saver and my God" (Psalms 42 : 11; 43 : 5), "Thou didst sell Thy people dirt-cheap" (Psalm 44 : 12), and "My insides!" (Jer. 4 : 19) are renderings which make one rub one's eyes—but they are less frequent than in the New.

Little fault can be found with the translation on the score of accuracy. "Many who sleep in the Adamic dust" (Daniel 12 : 2) is a curious mistranslation; the Hebrew expression ('admath 'aphar) means "the dusty ground", not "the Adamic dust".

There are copious footnotes, which contain not only information intended to make the sense plainer to the reader, but also moralizing observations. For example, at Gen. 3 : 12 there is a note on our first parents' attempts at self-exculpation after they were convicted of eating the forbidden fruit: "Passing the buck is as old as humanity; it shows lack of repentance." Sometimes, unfortunately, the information given is apt to mislead the reader instead of helping him, as when the footnote to Esther 1 : 1 says that Ahasuerus is "a Persian title for 'king', rather than a name" (it is in fact a Hebrew reproduction of the same personal name as the Greeks represented by Xerxes, whereas the Persian word for "king" was khshayathiya—which has become considerably simplified in the modern Persian word Shah).

From Gen. 12 : 1 onwards chronological dates are given. No authority has been claimed for these, but it is a pity that for the age of Moses and Joshua dates should be given which, although they are those suggested by the late Professor John Garstang, have been rendered untenable by more recent archaeological research. Weights, measures and sums of money have to a large extent been expressed in terms of modern American currency.

The Berkeley version was revised as *The Modern Language Bible*, and many of the above-mentioned "stylistic oddities" were happily replaced by more acceptable renderings (1969).

Today's English Version, otherwise entitled *Good News for Modern Man* (1966), was prepared by the American Bible Society for people who speak English either as their mother tongue or as an acquired language. It is a translation of the New Testament from the Greek text edited by an international committee of scholars working under the sponsorship of five member-societies of the United Bible Societies and published in 1966.[1] The translator is Dr Robert G. Bratcher of the American Bible Society; the idiom is contemporary, not "timeless", and aims at producing "dynamic equivalence" i.e. producing the same effect in the reader to-day as the Greek text produced in those who first read it. Its format is popular, and the text is attractively illustrated with line drawings by Mlle Annie Vallotton. There is a word list at the end explaining proper nouns and technical terms, and the book is indexed like any modern book. In some degree its policy is similar to that of the Basic English and Plain English versions, except that there is no arbitrary limitation of its vocabulary. It is well designed for widespread circulation; the general idea has caught on, and comparable versions in other modern languages have been prepared. Many competent critics of Bible versions will agree with Fr Walter Abbott, who describes it as "not only clear and accurate, but also a masterpiece of modern linguistic study". If a query may be voiced, is it clear that "he was the same as God", the last clause of John 1 : 1, is any improvement on "the Word was God"? May this rendering not introduce a confusion of its own?

Lastly (for we must stop somewhere) we greet William Barclay's new translation of *The New Testament*, which has been published by Collins in two volumes: *The Gospels and the Acts of the Apostles* (1968) and *The Letters and the Revelation* (1969). Professor Barclay is a prince of communicators, and he has never exercised this gift of his to better purpose than in communicating the content of the New Testament. Not only does he give us his translation; he tells us how, in his judgment, this task must be undertaken and prosecuted in his forty-five-page Appendix to Volume I entitled "On Translating the

[1] The Old Testament has now been translated: see chapter 18.

New Testament". If God speaks to us in our own language, so (as Professor Barclay puts it in a discussion of the second personal pronoun at the end of this Appendix) "we must speak to God ... in the ordinary language of a child to his father, and not in an archaic Elizabethan language which no one has used in a person-to-person way for centuries".

CHAPTER SEVENTEEN

The New English Bible[1]

FROM TYNDALE'S New Testament of 1525 down to the Revised Standard Version of 1952 we have traced a sequence of English versions of the Bible belonging to one dominant tradition. The Geneva Bible, the Bishops' Bible, the Authorized Version, the Revised Version (in its British and American recensions) and, most recently, the Revised Standard Version all represent revisions of earlier stages of this traditional sequence. When we speak or think of the English Bible, it is usually these successive versions—or, more probably, one of them—that we have in mind. Together they constitute a crowning glory of English-speaking civilization. The part played by the English Bible in the world is well summed up in the words addressed to the Queen at her coronation when she was presented with a copy of the Authorized Version: "Our gracious Queen: to keep your Majesty ever mindful of the Law and the Gospel of God as the Rule for the whole life and government of Christian Princes, we present you with this Book, the most valuable thing that this world affords. Here is Wisdom; This is the royal Law; These are the lively Oracles of God."

But it may be questioned whether successive revisions of earlier revisions are adequate for the needs of the present day. It is widely felt that what we require to-day is a completely new translation, based on the most accurate and up-to-date findings in all the relevant fields of knowledge—linguistic, textual and historical—and carried out by men who themselves hear the voice of God speaking to them in Holy Scripture. In 1940 the late Cecil John Cadoux stated that "all serious Christians are fundamentally at one in needing a version of the Scriptures which is as truthful as human skill, aided by the divine grace, can make it."[2] This view was shared by very many Christians in the British Isles, as subsequent events were to show.

[1] Quotations from the New English Bible in this chapter are published by permission of the Oxford and Cambridge University Presses; this kindness is gratefully acknowledged.
[2] *The Bible in its Ancient and English Versions* (ed. H. W. Robinson), p. 274.

The Genesis of the New English Bible

At the General Assembly of the Church of Scotland in 1946 the suggestion was made, and eagerly adopted, that a completely new translation of the English Bible should be undertaken. The Church of Scotland approached the Church of England and the principal Free Churches, and the suggestion won their approval. Accordingly a joint committee was set up in 1947. It included representatives of these Churches, of the Oxford and Cambridge University Presses, of the British and Foreign Bible Society and the National Bible Society of Scotland. Its terms of reference were to prepare a new translation of the Bible into modern English. After hearing reports from advisory and consultative panels which had been set up for this purpose, the committee met in the Jerusalem Chamber of Westminster Abbey under the chairmanship of Dr J. W. Hunkin, Bishop of Truro, and appointed three panels of translators—for the Old Testament, New Testament, and Apocrypha respectively—and a fourth panel of advisers on literary and stylistic questions. The many criticisms levelled against the Revised Version of the New Testament on stylistic grounds were not forgotten. Good scholars are not always good stylists, and the decision to set up a literary panel was a wise one.

When Dr Hunkin died in 1950 he was succeeded as chairman of the joint committee by Dr A. T. P. Williams, Bishop of Winchester. On Dr Williams' death in 1968, his place was taken by Dr F. D. Coggan, Archbishop of York, who contributes the preface to the New English Bible of 1970 as Dr Williams contributed the preface to the New Testament of 1961. The first secretary of the joint committee was Dr G. S. Hendry, who on behalf of the Presbytery of Stirling and Dunblane presented to the General Assembly of 1946 the overture which launched the project. When he crossed the Atlantic in 1949 to occupy a Chair in Princeton Theological Seminary, he was succeeded in the secretaryship by Dr J. K. S. Reid, now Professor in the University of Aberdeen.

Each book, or part of a book, was at first entrusted to an individual translator. He produced a first draft, which might bear little resemblance to the finally approved translation. (Professor T. W. Manson was a member of the New Testament panel until his death in 1958;

some readers may find it interesting to make a comparison between his translation of Mark in *The Beginning of the Gospel* [1950] and that in the New English Bible.) The first draft of a book was sent to all members of the appropriate panel, who worked through it along with the translator in the course of their next meetings. When the draft had been thoroughly discussed in the panel, it was revised and the revision was submitted to the literary panel. The suggestions of the literary advisers were then considered by the appropriate translation panel, who adopted such of them as they approved. When the translation panel had completed all its work on a book and reached final agreement, the agreed text was laid by until such time as it was submitted to the joint committee, with whom the responsibility for the ultimate decision lay.

The Principles of the Translation

At an early stage in the work the following memorandum was drawn up by Professor C. H. Dodd (General Director of the whole enterprise from 1949 onwards):

> It is to be genuinely English in idiom, such as will not awaken a sense of strangeness or remoteness. Ideally, we aim at a "time-less" English, avoiding equally both archaisms and transient modernisms. The version should be plain enough to convey its meaning to any reasonably intelligent person (so far as verbal expression goes), yet not bald or pedestrian. It should *not* aim at preserving "hallowed associations"; it *should* aim at conveying a sense of reality. It should be as accurate as may be without pedantry. It is to be hoped that, at least occasionally, it may produce arresting and memorable renderings. It should have suffi-cient dignity to be read aloud. ... We should like to produce a trans-lation which may receive general recognition as an authoritative second version alongside the A.V. for certain public purposes as well as for private reading, and above all a translation which may in some measure remove a real barrier between a large proportion of our fellow-countrymen and the truth of the Holy Scriptures.[1]

[1] Quoted from an article on "A New Translation of the English Bible", by T. H. Robinson in *The Bible Translator* 2 (1951), pp. 167 f.

On March 20, 1959, Professor Dodd contributed an informative article to *The Times Literary Supplement* on "The Translation of the Bible: Some Questions of Principle", in which he amplified several of the points touched upon in the above memorandum. The translation, he says, is bound to be a faithful one, but wherein does faithfulness consist? A word-for-word rendering may be the most faithful rendering where the terms used are capable of scientific definition, where they are more or less like the agreed symbols of mathematics; it may also be the most faithful rendering where scholarly or specialist readers require to be given some idea of the structure of a newly deciphered language. But where living languages are concerned (and the books of the Bible were written in living languages) the idea that faithfulness can best be preserved by a word-for-word rendering is fallacious. The idea that one word in the original can be uniformly represented by one word in the translation is exploded by a consideration of the wide range of meaning covered by such important biblical Greek words as *logos* ("word", "reason", "account", etc.) and *pneuma* ("wind", "breath", "spirit", etc.). The unit in translation cannot be the word, but at the very least the clause or sentence, and "it may be much more extensive". But in saying this, Professor Dodd to a large extent is echoing the language of a much earlier translator of the Bible into English, John Purvey, who laid it down "that the best translating out of Latin into English is to translate after the sentence and not only after the words."[1] "The overruling principle is intelligibility."

Professor Dodd concluded his article by reminding us that complete success is hardly to be expected in so formidable an undertaking as producing a translation which shall read like an original composition and not like a translation—a translation "which will in some measure evoke in the reader a response corresponding to that which was evoked in the minds of the first readers by the original. ... It is a first qualification for a translator that he should know that he practises an impossible art. Yet it is permissible to hope that from time to time the ideal may be realized in part. But the proof of the pudding is in the eating; the new translation will not be published until 1961."

This last clause applied to the New Testament part of the work, of

[1] See p. 19.

238

course. When it appeared, various views were expressed about its English style. "It's quite good," a little girl is said to have remarked, "but it's not so *holy* as the old one, is it?" This absence of a hieratic quality from its diction was noted also by Mr Robert Graves, who is credited with the judgment that the new version lacked *baraka* and that he would not feel that an oath sworn on it was so binding as one sworn on the A.V. Professor Henry Chadwick described it as "the Bible for the beat generation".[1] But, so far as its style was concerned, the severest criticism came from T. S. Eliot. "So long as the *New English Bible* was used only for private reading," he wrote, "it would be merely a symptom of the decay of the English language in the middle of the twentieth century. But the more it is adopted for religious services the more it will become an active agent of decadence."[2] But much of this kind of criticism arises from comparison of the new version with the older versions in the Tyndale tradition, culminating in the A.V., which maintained a level of uniform literary excellence not always present in the Hebrew and Greek texts which they translated. One may justly regret, nevertheless, that T. S. Eliot was not included on the literary panel.

The New Testament panel, working under the convenership of Professor Dodd, completed its task in March 1960, when this part of the translation was accepted by the joint committee at a meeting in the Jerusalem Chamber of Westminster Abbey. It was published on March 14, 1961, by the Oxford and Cambridge University Presses, and was an immediate best seller: four million copies were bought in the first twelve months, and at the end of nine years the figure had risen to 7 million (of which about 2,750,000 had been distributed in the United States).

For the Old Testament, which is three times as long as the New and considerably more difficult to translate, it was necessary to wait much longer. The first Old Testament book (Ruth) was presented to the joint committee in 1952, and the last (Ecclesiastes) in 1965. But in 1970 we were given the whole completed work, comprising the product of the Old Testament panel (under the convenership of Sir Godfrey Driver, Joint Director) and of the

---

[1] In the *Daily Telegraph*, March 14, 1961.
[2] In the *Sunday Telegraph*, Dec. 16, 1962, reprinted in *The New English Bible Reviewed*, ed. D. E. Nineham (London, 1965), pp. 96 ff.

Apocrypha panel (under the convenership of Professor W. D. Mac-Hardy, Deputy Director), together with a slightly revised edition of the 1961 New Testament.

New Testament

One thing that Bible translators have to make up their minds about before they start translating is the text that they are going to translate. The men who gave us the Authorized Version of 1611 did not concern themselves about this; so far as concerns the New Testament, they simply followed the text of the early printed editions of the Greek Testament. The Revised Version, largely under the influence of Westcott and Hort, paid chief respect to the ancient Alexandrian text, represented principally by the Sinaitic and Vatican Codices. This policy marked a great advance on the Authorized Version; and one of the abiding virtues of the Revised Version of the New Testament is the great superiority of its underlying Greek text over that which underlay the older version. Today, however, the Alexandrian text, reliable as it is, would not be accorded the same solitary pre-eminence as was given it by Westcott and Hort. The Introduction to the New English Bible New Testament says:

> There is not at the present time any critical text which would command the same degree of general acceptance as the Revisers' text did in its day. Nor has the time come, in the judgement of most scholars, to construct such a text, since new material constantly comes to light, and the debate continues. The present translators therefore could do no other than consider variant readings on their merits, and, having weighed the evidence for themselves, select for translation in each passage the reading which to the best of their judgement seemed most likely to represent what the author wrote. Where other readings seemed to deserve serious consideration they have been recorded in footnotes.

This decision in favour of an eclectic text is inevitable and wise in the present situation; although one might wish that the footnotes sometimes, instead of merely saying that "some witnesses read" something different from what appears in the text, could have given a little indication of the relative support given to variant readings. But then it was no part of the translators' responsibility to provide an *apparatus criticus* to their text.

Rarely if ever has conjecture been resorted to. There is one reading which used to be called the only certain conjecture in the New Testament. That is the reading "javelin" for "hyssop" (or "marjoram") in John 19 : 29. The advantage of adopting this reading in such a context is fairly obvious. It was first suggested by a scholar in the sixteenth century, on the ground that an original *hyssō perithentes* might have become *hyssōpō perithentes* by the accidental dittography of two letters. More recently the reading *hyssō* ("on a javelin") has been identified in the first hand of a mediaeval manuscript, in which, however, a later hand changed it to *hyssōpō* ("on hyssop") in accordance with the general text.

This reading was examined some years ago by Professor G. D. Kilpatrick, who pointed out that, for all its attractiveness, "this plausible conjecture lands us in improbabilities and difficulties greater than those of the text of our manuscripts".[1] His main reason for saying this was that the Greek word *hyssos* was used as the equivalent of the Latin *pilum*, not of any kind of javelin without distinction. Now the *pilum* was the weapon of Roman legionary troops, not of auxiliary troops; but until A.D. 66 no legionary troops were stationed in Judaea. In that case, no *hyssos* would have been available at the time of our Lord's crucifixion to be used for putting the vinegar-soaked sponge to His lips. Yet the New English Bible gives the rendering: "they soaked a sponge with the wine, fixed it on a javelin, and held it up to his lips." A footnote on "javelin" says: "*So one witness; the others read* on marjoram." In preferring "javelin" in the text the new translation follows Moffatt, the Basic Bible, Goodspeed, Rieu, Phillips, and Kingsley Williams; but on Dr Kilpatrick's showing this reading cannot be accepted, unless indeed we hold that John used the word in a looser sense than any other Greek writer who uses it. As for the word used in the footnote, it may be asked whether "marjoram" is more intelligible to most readers of the English Bible than the traditional "hyssop".

As regards the translation, it must be reiterated that it is an utterly

1 "The Transmission of the New Testament and its Reliability", *Journal of Transactions of the Victoria Institute* 89 (1957), pp. 98 f.

new translation, not a revision of any existing version. This being so, it does not lend itself to comparison with, say, the Revised Standard Version, which was simply a revision and therefore retains much of what the English-speaking world has come to regard as "Bible English". Still less does the new version lend itself to comparison with the Authorized Version, although its sponsors make it plain that it is not intended to supersede the Authorized Version but rather to be used alongside it. Yet, because throughout the English-speaking world the Bible is best known in the Authorized Version, the New English Bible is bound to be compared with it, and many people will come to their own conclusions about the new version in the light of such a comparison, and express their "like" or "dislike" of it accordingly.

The sonorous English of the Authorized Version, which in essence we owe to William Tyndale, and which makes the Authorized Version so eminently suitable for public reading, will probably be missed from the New English Bible. Yet the new translators have achieved some noble passages. The Canticles in Luke's nativity narrative, for example, do full justice to the poetic quality of the original; here is the beginning of the *Magnificat* (part of which has already been set to music):

> Tell out, my soul, the greatness of the Lord,
> rejoice, rejoice, my spirit, in God my saviour;
> so tenderly has he looked upon his servant,
>   humble as she is.
> For, from this day forth,
> all generations will count me blessed,
> so wonderfully has he dealt with me,
>   the Lord, the Mighty One.

In some respects the new translation follows the Authorized Version rather than the Revised Version: for example, it does not imitate the Revised Version in using the same English word, as far as possible, to represent the same Greek word throughout the New Testament. This feature of the Revised Version is one which makes it so admirable as a student's version, and no doubt exact students of the New Testament, who wish to have the vocabulary of the original represented as precisely as possible by English equivalents, will continue to value the Revised Version for this reason. But the 1970 edition of the New English Bible imposes some greater measure of uniformity in this regard than the 1961 edition did. For example, the Greek word *xylon* (literally meaning "wood") is used five times in the New Testament in reference to the cross (which elsewhere is indicated by another Greek word, *stauros*). For those five occurrences the older versions have "tree", in conformity with Deut. 21 : 23, which underlies them all. But the 1961 edition of the New English Bible had "gibbet" in Acts 5 : 30; 10 : 39; 13 : 29; "tree" in Gal. 3 : 13 (quoting from Deut. 21 : 23); "gallows" in 1 Peter 2 : 24. The 1970 edition, however, has "gibbet" in all five places. (In Deut. 21 : 23 the N.E.B. renders "gibbet".)

Sometimes the new translation goes back to even earlier models than the Authorized Version. The translators of the Authorized Version claim to have avoided "the scrupulosity of the Puritanes, who leave the old Ecclesiastical words, and betake them to other, as when they put ... *congregation* instead of *Church*". But whether it was Puritan scrupulosity or some other consideration that moved the new translators, they have shown a preference for "congregation" over "church" where a local church is in view. In Matt. 16 : 18 they make Jesus say, "on this rock I will build my church"; but in Matt. 18 : 17 we find "report the matter to the congregation; and if he will not listen even to the congregation, you must then treat him as you would a pagan or a tax-gatherer". So Tyndale comes into his own again.

Some books on the English Bible have quoted for its quaintness the rendering of 1 Cor. 16 : 8 in most of the older English versions from Wycliffe to Geneva: "I will tarry at Ephesus until Whitsun-tide." Now the New English Bible can be added to the list: "I shall remain at Ephesus until Whitsuntide." When I first saw this, I looked up Revelation 1 : 10 in pleasurable anticipation, wondering if John might be made to say (as in Tyndale and Coverdale) that he was in spirit "on a Sunday", but no: "It was on the Lord's day." Nor has Passover reverted to Easter in Acts 12 : 4. The preceding verse says: "This happened during the festival of Unleavened Bread." But the translators' propensity for using now one phrase and now another to represent the same original appears when we compare Acts 20 : 6;

here "after the days of Unleavened Bread" is relegated to a footnote as the literal rendering, while the text reads: "after the Passover season".

Great care is taken to distinguish between the present and aorist tenses of such a verb as "believe" by the use of such phrases as "have faith in" and "put faith in"; phrases like these have the additional advantage of making the relation between the verb "believe" and the noun "faith" immediately apparent. This is specially helpful in the Epistle to the Romans. In John 20: 31, where the manuscripts vary between the present and aorist tenses of this verb, the New English Bible adopts the present tense for the text ("in order that you may hold the faith ...") and refers to the aorist in a footnote ("that you may come to believe ...").

As regards the pronoun of the second person singular, the N.E.B. follows the precedent of the R.S.V., regularly using "thou" and so forth only where God is addressed[1] and where Christ is consciously addressed as a divine being. Quotation marks are used as in the R.S.V., although the new translators' judgment on where quoted speech begins and ends does not always coincide with the judgment of the R.S.V. team. Thus in John 3 our Lord's words to Nicodemus do not come to an end with verse 15 but are continued to the end of verse 21. Later in the chapter, however, John the Baptist's reply to his disciples ends with verse 30, the following paragraph (verses 31–36) being the Evangelist's comment; this is in agreement with the R.S.V.

"The public in view", says the sixteen-page *Handbook to the New English Bible* published by the Oxford and Cambridge University Presses simultaneously with the complete Bible itself, "was that large section of the population which has no effective contact with the Church in any of its communions; people sufficiently educated to understand a good deal of the Bible, but to whom the language of the current versions is in part unintelligible or misleading, and has an air of unreality; those young people now growing up for

---

[1] Curiously, however, Adam in Genesis 3: 10–12 addresses God as "you", whereas in the following chapters Cain, Abraham, and others address Him as "thou". In the prologue to Job, Satan addresses God as "you", whereas in the epilogue Job addresses Him as "thou"; but (according to a report in the *Daily Telegraph* of Aug. 20, 1962) Satan was intended to appear as a "bumptious person".

whom the Bible, if it is to make any impact, must be 'contemporary'; intelligent church-goers for whom the traditional language is so familiar that its phrases slide over their minds almost without causing a ripple" (p. 7).

In the years since its publication, the New English Bible has commended itself for private and also for public use. Not only the language but the format draws the reader on; he cannot be content with a small portion as enough to be going on with, but finds himself reading further to see what comes next. This has no doubt been partly due to the novelty of the version. How have they translated this? What will they make of that? From time to time he is pulled up with a jerk. The last clause of John 1 : 1 reads: "what God was, the Word was". Is that what the clause really means? Or have the translators perhaps been moved by an unconscious desire to give a rather different rendering from the Authorized Version? On reflection, this is probably excellent exegesis of the words literally rendered in the older versions as "the Word was God". Sometimes the idiom is positively homely: "This is more than we can stomach!" say the offended listeners to our Lord's discourse about the bread of life (John 6 : 60). "Why listen to such talk?"

This last quotation illustrates the occasional stylistic revision which the 1961 edition of the New Testament has undergone; there the question appeared in the form: "Why listen to such words?" But the speakers meant to be disparaging, and "talk" reflects their mood better than "words". Another example of such unobtrusive improvement appears in Acts 11 : 30, where "This they did, and sent it off in the charge of Barnabas and Saul to the elders" (1961) becomes "This they did, and sent it off to the elders, in the charge of Barnabas and Saul" (1970). In view of the delicate touch with which this kind of improvement has been effected, it is surprising that nothing has been done in 1 Cor. 5 : 9 to remove the stumbling-block presented to people with an inopportune sense of humour by the rendering: "you must have nothing to do with loose livers".

When the 1961 edition appeared, considerable debate was stirred by some passages in the nativity narratives of Matthew and Luke relating to our Lord's virginal conception. The one really inept rendering in this connexion has now been changed to something much more satisfactory: in Luke 1 : 34 Mary no longer says "I have no husband" but "I am still a virgin".

Much of the criticism of the 1961 edition, as has been mentioned, was directed at its diction. In his introduction to *The New English Bible Reviewed* (London, 1965), in which a number of assessments are brought together, Professor D. E. Nineham observes that "those written by New Testament specialists are on the whole favourable, while those written by literary critics are markedly less so" (p. x).[1] In some degree he sympathizes with the literary critics, and suspects that in some places "the translators were seduced by the delusive ideal of a timeless English style into using expressions which are not genuinely current usage with any contemporary group" (p. xii).[2] He comments further on the "small number of reviews ... which attack the new version on grounds of doctrinal bias or error" (p. x).

There were some reviewers who did just this, however, though rarely with the exuberance with which their American counterparts belaboured the R.S.V. More in sorrow than in anger, the Secretary of the Trinitarian Bible Society contributed a review to *The English Churchman* of March 17, 1961, in which (over and above stylistic criticisms) he found doctrinal deficiencies with regard to Christology and soteriology.[3] While some of his points called for serious consideration, others were really concerned with the underlying Greek text and not the translation, while the implied disapproval of the rendering "priestly service" in Rom. 15 : 16 (which "will ... doubtless be of interest to R.C.s and Anglo-Catholics") comes to grief on the hard fact that this is precisely what the Greek word (*hierourgeō*) means. Later issues of *The English Churchman* carried a further critique by N. A. E. Earle which was reprinted as a pamphlet entitled *Spiritual Losses in the New English Bible*. These "spiritual

---

[1] A few lines below he puts it thus: "it is a fair generalization to say that reviewers whose chief criterion was fidelity to the original Greek have fairly consistently given this translation better marks than those who judged primarily by aesthetic criteria". Other literary assessments in *The New English Bible Reviewed* are by Charles Garton, Henry Gifford, Martin Jarrett-Kerr, F. L. Lucas, and C. L. Wrenn.

[2] He adds, however, that "it is a perfectly possible criticism of the Authorized Version that it muffles the wide variety of styles to be found in the New Testament ... under the single blanket of a sonorous, but undifferentiated, English prose".

[3] T. H. Brown, *The New Translation of the New Testament: A Detailed and Critical Examination of the Text* (reissued as a four-page pamphlet by the Trinitarian Bible Society and reprinted in part in *The New English Bible Reviewed*, pp. 143 ff.).

losses" affect a wide range of Christian belief and practice alike. But Mr Earle's most telling criticism has to do with what is scarcely a "spiritual loss"; he is certainly right in deploring the translation of *daimonion* (or *daimōn*) and *diabolos* alike as "devil", instead of reserving "devil" exclusively for the latter. In the New Testament there are many demons, but only one devil; the N.E.B. (like the A.V. and R.V.) obscures this distinction, whereas the R.S.V. makes it plain.

A blunderbuss attack came from Northern Ireland in the shape of a pamphlet by Dr Ian Paisley: *The New English Bible—Version or Perversion?* It missed fire, however, in the introduction by suggesting that the inclusion of the Apocrypha in a Protestant Bible was an innovation ("Rome can rightly rejoice that at last her view of the canon of Scripture has displaced that of the Apostolic Church")—as though the Apocrypha had not been included, as a matter of course, by the Geneva and King James translators, to mention no more.[1]

A more sober and extended critique came from across the Atlantic, from the pen of the veteran Dr Oswald T. Allis,[2] who had some years previously published similar critiques of the R.S.V.[3]

But when all has been said by way of criticism of the work in relation to Christian doctrine,[4] the fact remains that the great verities of the faith can be established from the New Testament in the New English Bible (in both its 1961 and 1970 editions) as firmly as from any other English version.

Old Testament

When one turns to the Old Testament the first impression is that probably Sir Godfrey Driver's influence has been even more pervasive here than Professor Dodd's was in the New Testament. This

---

[1] Dr Paisley also issued an eight-page folder (*The New English Bible—A Corruption of the Word of God*) which lists "222 passages in which the Scriptures of Truth are corrupted through ALTERATIONS–ADDITIONS–DELETIONS by the translators of the New English Bible". The standard by which alterations, additions, and deletions are detected is the A.V.; the majority of the criticisms are basically criticisms of the Greek text, not of the translation.

[2] *The New English Bible: The New Testament of 1961* (Philadelphia, 1963).

[3] *Revision or New Translation?* (Philadelphia, 1948); *Revised Version or Revised Bible?* (Philadelphia, 1953).

[4] To a severe Scottish critic it was suggested that the new version could not be so bad as he maintained, since Professor Tasker was one of the translators and Professor Bruce had spoken well of it. "On the contrary," replied the critic, "we do not think better of the New English Bible for that; we think the worse of the two professors."

was inevitable, since we gather that the original draft translations of the Old Testament books did not go immediately to the appropriate panel (as those of the New Testament books did) but were submitted in the first instance to Sir Godfrey Driver, who examined them in the light of his expert linguistic and textual knowledge and suggested modifications which the respective translators might adopt or not as they saw fit; after this the drafts were submitted to the members of the Old Testament translators' panel. One major source of strength of the Old Testament part of the New English Bible is that it has been able to draw, in unstinted fashion, on the scholarship of such a master in Semitic philology.

The next impression made by the Old Testament version is that conjecture has been resorted to much more freely than in most of the older English versions—or even in others of more recent date. The conjectural element may take the form of emendation of the Hebrew text (either with or without the support of the Septuagint and other ancient versions) or reinterpretation of the Hebrew text by the aid of other Semitic languages—whether surviving languages such as Arabic or dead languages like Akkadian and Ugaritic.

Both these forms of conjectural restoration must be submitted to the discipline of strict and generally accepted rules of procedure if they are not to become excessively subjective; of both it may be said, as it has often been said of conjectural emendation, that the conjecture should be adopted only where, once it has been proposed, it imposes itself on all qualified judges as unmistakably right. In particular, the reinterpretation of classical Hebrew by reference to cognate languages requires to have procedural rules laid down: this subject is dealt with by Professor James Barr in his important work *Comparative Philology and the Text of the Old Testament* (Oxford, 1968), which was published too late to be available to the translators of the New English Bible.

It is not always easy to determine whether we are being offered a conjectural emendation or a conjectural reinterpretation, except that the former is normally indicated by a footnote saying "*prob. rdg.*" (i.e. "probable reading") followed by a remark that the Hebrew is obscure, or corrupt, or omits something given in the new version, or adds something not given in the version, or the like. Where the

Hebrew text as it stands makes no sense to the reader, this could be the result of textual corruption in the course of transmission, or it could be due to the fact that all clue to the meaning of the words used has been lost. Not so long ago it was customary to postulate large-scale corruption in the Hebrew text and to indulge in lavish emendation. To-day Old Testament scholars, including the translators of the New English Bible, are far more cautious and conservative—partly because the access of knowledge about Semitic languages has shown that much that was once thought to be corrupt or meaningless is perfectly sound and intelligible Hebrew.

Even so, the degree of conjectural emendation in the Old Testament rendering of the New English Bible is considerably greater than in the R.S.V. (which perhaps erred on the side of conservatism in this matter). The textual situation is set out in an interesting introduction to the Old Testament by Sir Godfrey Driver, in which he discusses the present state of the question in the light of the latest discoveries—the Biblical scrolls from Qumran, for example.[1] We are now able to trace the history of the Hebrew text back not only to the Massoretic manuscripts of the ninth to the eleventh centuries A.D., preserving a consonantal text which had been handed down practically unchanged from the second century A.D., but still farther back to the second century B.C., and possibly earlier. But the oldest parts of the Hebrew Bible had a history stretching back about 1,000 years earlier still. "The Hebrew text as thus handed down," says the introduction, "is full of errors of every kind due to defective archetypes and successive copyists' errors, confusion of letters (of which several in the Hebrew alphabet are singularly alike), omissions and insertions, displacements of words and even of whole sentences or paragraphs; and copyists' unhappy attempts to rectify mistakes have often only increased the confusion." While scholars will recognize the facts thus described, this description of them may give the ordinary reader of the English Bible the idea that the scale of confusion and uncertainty is far greater than it actually is. Indeed,

---

[1] It is not only in the sphere of textual criticism that the Qumran scrolls have been helpful. The rendering "with streets and conduits" at the end of Daniel 9 : 25 is confirmed by the occurrence of the last word in the famous "Copper Scroll" (3Q 15).

considering the antiquity of the Old Testament text and the vicissitudes which it has undergone, we may say that it has been preserved in quite astonishingly good condition.

Since, as Sir Godfrey says, the third edition of Kittel's *Biblia Hebraica* (1937) is the basis for the present translation, it has not been necessary to publish a volume for the Old Testament corresponding to Professor R. V. G. Tasker's edition of *The Greek New Testament, being the text translated in the New English Bible 1961* (Oxford and Cambridge, 1964). A handbook of another kind, however, has been provided in *The Hebrew Text of the Old Testament*, by L. H. Brockington (Oxford and Cambridge, 1973). This volume sets out the Hebrew and Aramaic readings adopted by the translators in places where they deviated from the Massoretic text, and gives some indication of the authority behind those preferred readings. It would be a further boon to have a volume indicating the places where the Massoretic text has been retained but has been given a different meaning from that found in other contemporary scholarly versions. The Hebrew text of Song of Songs 1 :7, for example, has not been changed, but readers might like to know where the unparalleled translation "picking lice" comes from. A handbook explaining such phenomena would be very helpful.

The help of Ugaritic has apparently been enlisted in Ps. 89 : 19b, which now reads:

> I have endowed a warrior with princely gifts,
> so that the youth I have chosen towers over his people.

Similarly, as in R.S.V., the word for "glaze" has been recognized in Prov. 26 : 23:

> Glib speech that covers a spiteful heart
> is like glaze spread on earthenware.

But in several other places where revised renderings have been confidently recommended on the strength of Ugaritic the New English Bible goes its own way. Thus the "wide house" of Prov. 21 : 9 and 25 : 24 is not a "beer house" but a "brawling household"; the unintelligible "fields of offerings" of 2 Sam. 1 : 21 (A.V.) become not "upsurging of the deep" (R.S.V.) but "showers on the uplands", and he who "rides upon the clouds" according to the best Ugaritic analogy in Ps. 68 : 4 (R.S.V.) is the one "who rides over the desert plains".

The ineffable name of the God of Israel is usually represented by "the LORD" (occasionally "GOD"), as in the older versions, but in the few places where a personal name is required the traditional form "Jehovah" is used, although it is pointed out in the introduction that this is based on a mediaeval misunderstanding of the relation of the vowel-points attached to the consonants YHWH in the Hebrew text. As scholars, the translators would no doubt have preferred to use the form "Yahweh", for which the Jerusalem Bible has set a highly reputable precedent—but "Yahweh" has not yet naturalized itself in liturgical usage. Even so, if the New English Bible had ventured to break with tradition here, the process of naturalization might have been expedited.

On the first page of the Old Testament some interesting renderings present themselves. The first clause is subordinated to what follows: "In the beginning, when God made heaven and earth ..." In the phrase traditionally rendered "the spirit of God" in Gen. 1 : 2 the word "God" is taken (as in some other places in the Old Testament) to be a way of expressing a superlative: "a mighty wind that swept over the surface of the waters". Where A.V. has "firmament", the new version has "vault". The first creation narrative ends with the recapitulatory words of Gen. 2 : 4: "This is the story of the making of heaven and earth when they were created."

In the creation narrative which immediately follows, the "mist" of Gen. 2 : 6 (A.V.) is rendered "flood"—probably rightly. The garments which Adam and Eve make out of fig-leaves (Gen. 3 : 7) are neither "aprons" nor "breeches" but "loin-cloths". The Creator's words to Cain in Gen. 4 : 7 are rendered:

> If you do well, you are accepted;
> if not, sin is a demon crouching at the door.
> It shall be eager for you, and you will be mastered by it.

But the footnote alternative for the last clause, "but you must master it" (cf. R.S.V.), is preferable. In verse 8 Cain's words to Abel, lost from the Massoretic Hebrew, are restored (as in R.S.V.) from the

Samaritan, Greek Septuagint, and Latin Vulgate: "Let us go into the open country."[1]

The heavenly beings of Gen. 6:2, 4, are called "the sons of the gods"; the same expression in Job 1:6 is rendered "members of the court of heaven" and the similar expression in Ps. 29:1 is simply rendered "gods".

The story of the Tower of Babel opens engagingly with the words, "Once upon a time all the world spoke a single language ..." (Genesis 11:1); but this obscures the probable intention of the author of Genesis, to treat this story as the sequel or amplification of the last clause of chapter 10: "from them [i.e. the sons of Noah] came the separate nations on earth after the flood". At the end of the story the play on words in the original is brought out well: "That is why it is called Babel, because the LORD there made a babble of the language of all the world" (Genesis 11:9).

In the Blessing of Jacob in Gen. 49 the enigmatic reference to "Shiloh" in verse 10 appears as "so long as tribute is brought to him"; "tribute" presumably is taken as the interpretation of "that which is his" (cf. R.S.V., "to whom it belongs").[2] In verse 22 the blessing pronounced on Joseph begins, traditionally, "Joseph is a fruitful tree"; J. M. Allegro's rendering, "Joseph is a fruitful ben-tree" (i.e. Euphratean poplar), is mentioned in a footnote, but might well have been promoted to the text.[3]

In 1 Sam. 14 not only is the fuller Septuagint reading followed in verse 41 (with its reference to Urim and Thummim), but the Septuagint reading is also appropriately adopted in verse 18: "Saul said to Ahijah, 'Bring forward the ephod', for it was he who carried the ephod at that time before Israel." At the beginning of Solomon's prayer of dedication (1 Kings 8:12) the fuller Septuagint reading is also followed, but in the second person, not the third:

> O LORD who hast set the sun in heaven,
> but hast chosen to dwell in thick darkness.

[1] See p. 192.
[2] See p. 218; the rendering of the R.S.V. and *Jerusalem Bible* is preferable. On the other hand, the N.E.B. rendering of Ezek. 21:27, "until the rightful sovereign comes", could not be bettered; it is a pity that the prophet's allusion to Gen. 49:10 is obscured. No doubt Genesis and Ezekiel were translated by two different scholars.
[3] Cf. J. M. Allegro, "A Possible Mesopotamian Background to the Joseph Blessing of Gen. xlix", *Zeitschrift für die Alttestamentliche Wissenschaft* 64 (1952), pp. 249 ff.

But, with the R.S.V., the N.E.B. omits the further note of the Septuagint indicating that the narrator derived the quotation from the book of Jashar.

Where R.S.V. has "Kue" in 1 Kings 10 : 28, N.E.B. has "Coa", the form used in the Latin Vulgate; it is not any more intelligible than "Kue".[1]

The astronomical vocabulary of the Old Testament—more particularly, of the book of Job—is enriched. In Job 9 : 9 and 38 : 32 "Arcturus" of A.V. or "the Bear" of R.S.V. appears as "Aldebaran", but chapter 38 now contains an astronomical passage unknown to the older versions:

In all your life have you ever called up the dawn
    or shown the morning its place?
Have you taught it to grasp the fringes of the earth
    and shake the Dog-star from its place;
to bring up the horizon in relief as clay under a seal,
    until all things stand out like the folds of a cloak,
when the light of the Dog-star is dimmed
    and the stars of the Navigator's Line go out one by one?

This rendering of verses 12–15 has one conspicuous merit, for which it compares favourably even with the R.S.V.: it makes sense.

A handful of samples from various books will illustrate some further features of the new version. In Psalm 22 : 16 the problematic Hebrew which A.V. renders "they pierced my hands and my feet" is rendered "they have hacked off my hands and my feet". This is described in the footnote as the probable reading, but in fact it is rather improbable; whatever be the picture which the speaker intends to convey of his affliction, this kind of mutilation is difficult to fit into it.

The fourth Servant Song (Isa. 52 : 13–53 : 12) is marked by a minor transposition: the second part of 52 : 14 is inserted after 53 : 2, with which it has a close affinity in sense:

---

[1] For the R.S.V. renderings of 1 Sam. 14 : 18, 41; 1 Kings 8 : 12 f.; 10 : 28 f., see p. 193.

> he had no beauty, no majesty to draw our eyes,
>   no grace to make us delight in him;
> his form, disfigured, lost all the likeness of a man,
>   his beauty changed beyond human semblance.

The Servant is distinguished from the people of Israel in that he is referred to in the third person while Israel is addressed in the second person (52 : 14a):

> Time was when many were aghast at you, my people.

"My people" is no part of the Hebrew text here; it is added presumably to make it plain who are being addressed. In 53 : 8, however, both the Servant and "my people" are mentioned in the third person:

> he was cut off from the world of living men,
>   stricken to the death for my people's transgression—

where "to death" represents a very probable emendation of the Hebrew in conformity with the Greek Septuagint version. The Greek version also supports the opening words of 53 : 11:

> After all his pains he shall be bathed in light.

Here the footnote appeals to higher authority than the Greek version: "*so Scroll*", it says—referring presumably to the complete Isaiah scroll found over twenty years ago in Cave 1 at Qumran. In fact, an incomplete Isaiah scroll found in the same cave at the same time also has the word "light" in this verse. The "Scroll" is also cited as authority for "a burial-place" instead of "in his death" in 53 : 9:

> He was assigned a grave with the wicked,
>   a burial-place among the refuse of mankind.

The rendering " the refuse of mankind" (first suggested, it seems, by the late Professor Alfred Guillaume) involves no emendation of the Massoretic text; it is based on the derivation of the Hebrew word from another Semitic root than that meaning "rich"—and one which fits the poetical parallelism better.

Many readers will probably prefer the new rendering of 53 : 10:

> Yet the LORD took thought for his tortured servant
> and healed him who had made himself a sacrifice for sin—[1]

although this does involve some emendation of the Hebrew.

[1] See p. 50 for another translation.

254

If we move from the Isaianic Suffering Servant to the Suffering Servant of Zech. 12 : 10 the first person singular of the pronoun in the Hebrew and Septuagint texts is skilfully combined with the third person of other Greek versions in the rendering:

They shall look on me, on him whom they have pierced.

There is probably justification for this in the original context: the God of Israel is the speaker, but the pierced one is his anointed representative, in whose piercing Yahweh himself is pierced.[1] The oracle "O sword, awake against my shepherd ..." (Zech. 13 : 7–9) is transposed to follow 11 : 17; this raises in a specially acute form the question of the relationship of this shepherd to the "worthless shepherd" of 11 : 17.

The protest of the man in Zech. 13 : 5 who is charged with being a prophet contains a surprising deviation from the customary translation:

He will say, "I am no prophet, I am a tiller of the soil *who has been schooled in lust* since boyhood."

The italicized words, which may suggest his association with the Baal cult, represent no emendation.   However, they do not suit the context so well as R.S.V., "the land has been my possession" (which involves a slightly different word-division from that of the Massoretic text). The New English Bible, like the Syriac version early in the Christian era, derives the word not from the root which signifies "possession" but from that which it renders "passion" in Song of Songs 8 : 6—"passion cruel as the grave" (where A.V. and R.S.V. have "jealousy").

Another surprising translation—this time, however, in the footnotes and not in the text proper—occurs in Hosea 11 : 4, where Yahweh, like a father bringing up infant children, says of Israel:

they did not know that I harnessed them in leading-strings
and led them with bonds of love.

The footnote says: "bonds of love: *or* reins of hide". This makes one look back to the first sentence in this chapter to see whether "I loved him" has appended to it as an alternative rendering, "I gave him a good hiding"—but no.

[1] See pp. 199 f.

On p. 146 we animadverted on the R.V. replacement of A.V. "desire" by "caper-berry" in Eccles. 12 : 5. The A.V. rendering was restored by R.S.V., but now the new version, like R.V., gives the literal sense of the Hebrew word by translating the clause: "caper buds have no more zest". Another passage in the same book to which reference has been made above is Eccles. 3 : 11, where the R.S.V. rendering, "he has put eternity into man's mind", has much to commend it. The N.E.B., however, translates the clause: "he has given men a sense of time past and future".

In the Song of Songs, where the sex of the speaker or of the person addressed is commonly indicated in Hebrew by the gender of pronouns and other forms which have no corresponding distinction in English, the identity of the speaker has been indicated by such captions as *Bridegroom*, *Bride*, and *Companions*. This is one of the ways in which the Old Testament translators, as their convener says, "have had in mind not only the importance of making sense, which is not always apparent in previous translations, but also the needs of ordinary readers with no special knowledge of the ancient East; and they trust that such readers may find illumination in the present version".

Apocrypha

The translation of the apocryphal books, which comes as an appendix to the Old Testament, has been the work of the panel convened by Professor MacHardy, whose help with the New English Bible, on the testimony of the preface by the Archbishop of York, has by no means been confined to the Apocrypha. Among various interesting features of this translation, we observe that the dragon in the story of "Bel and the Dragon" has been demythologized: the story is now entitled "Daniel, Bel and the Snake". One of the most helpful things that the translators have done in this part of the work, however, is to translate the entire Greek Esther, with the "Additions" coming in their proper contexts, instead of appearing as unrelated fragments; those parts of the Greek Esther which are not usually printed in the Apocrypha (because their counterparts are included in the Hebrew Bible) are here placed within square brackets.

Study Edition

Honourable mention must now be made of *The New English Bible with Apocrypha: Oxford Study Edition*, published by the Oxford University Press in 1976. For this a distinguished Jewish scholar, Dr Samuel Sandmel, has served as general editor, with Dr M. Jack Suggs as editor for the New Testament and Dr Arnold J. Tkacik for the Apocrypha. Thirty other scholars—Protestant, Catholic and Jewish—have collaborated in the work. There are introductions to the various divisions of the Bible and to each of the books, with interpretative annotations at the foot of the pages, a substantial sketch of the history and geography of Bible lands, and special articles on reading the Bible, on literary forms of the Bible, and on the reckoning of time. The volume is equipped with a select index to people, places and themes in the Bible and ends with nine maps (with their own separate index). It might be said that it goes far to providing for the New English Bible what *The New Oxford Annotated Bible* (see pp. 201–203) does for the Revised Standard Version; but it is a completely independent work, produced by quite different editors and contributors.

CHAPTER EIGHTEEN

The English Bible in the Seventies

THE STORY of the English Bible has continued to unfold since 1970.

The Common Bible

One welcome development has been the publication in 1973 of the Common Bible—an ecumenical edition of the R.S.V. which supersedes the need for separate Catholic and Protestant editions (see p. 214). The day looked forward to on p. 219, when the idea of separate Catholic and Protestant Bibles would be as odd and anachronistic as the idea of separate Anglican and Free Church Bibles, has thus arrived.

This edition, indeed, has the blessing of Eastern Orthodox as well as Catholic and Protestant churchmen. Those books of the Apocrypha which were recognized as canonical by the Council of Trent appear as a first appendix to the Old Testament ("The Deutero-canonical Books"); then 1 and 2 Esdras and the Prayer of Manasseh come as a second appendix. As in the N.E.B. Apocrypha, the Greek Additions to Esther are placed in the framework of the Hebrew narrative (with appropriate distinction of type), apart from which they have no context. The Persian king of this book is called Ahasuerus throughout, for the sake of consistency, although in the Greek text he is called Artaxerxes.

The New American Standard Bible

The New American Standard Bible (completed 1971) was sponsored by the Lockman Foundation of La Habra, California—the foundation which had already produced the *Amplified Bible* (see p. 183). In conformity with the principles of the Lockman Foundation, the members of the editorial board are not named.

This is a revision and modernization of the American Standard Version of 1901 (see p. 138). As such, it retains many of the virtues of that version, notably the precision in rendering which made it in its day so valuable as a handbook for the student. Like the R.S.V., the N.A.S.B. (as this version is regularly abbreviated) has wisely reverted to the use of "the Lord" in place of "Jehovah" of the A.S.V. It makes use, especially in marginal notes, of the latest available textual knowledge; at Isa. 40:12, for instance, it notes the reading (attested by a Qumran manuscript of Isaiah) "who has measured the waters *of the sea* . . .?"—a reading which, indeed, might well have been incorporated in the text.

Some of its features, however, are less commendable. The use of capitals for pronouns referring to divine persons is an unfortunate departure from traditional practice in printed Bibles. It leads, moreover, to inconsistencies. Thus in the Old Testament pronouns believed to refer to the coming Messiah are sometimes capitalized (as in Isa. 52:13–53:12) and sometimes not (as in Isa. 61:1). The forms "Thou", "Thee" and so forth are retained for addressing divine persons "in the language of prayer", but there are curious anomalies, as when Peter in Matt. 16:16 says to Jesus, "Thou art the Christ", but in verse 22: "This shall never happen to You."

The editors have given careful thought to the accurate rendering of tenses, which makes it the more surprising to find in Matt. 16:19 and 18:18, "whatever you shall bind on earth shall have been bound in heaven, and whatever you shall loose on earth shall have been loosed in heaven." The ineptitude of this use of the English future-perfect to translate a Greek future-perfect has been noticed above on p. 180.

If the R.S.V. had never appeared, this revision of the A.S.V. would be a more valuable work than it is. As things are, there are few things done well by the N.A.S.B. which are not done better by the R.S.V.

The Good News Bible

The Old Testament part of *Today's English Version* (see p. 233) has now been completed: the whole work was published in October

1976 as the *Good News Bible*. Because of differences in English idiom on either side of the Atlantic, separate British and American editions were prepared. The British edition is published by the British and Foreign Bible Society and Messrs Collins; in little over three months a million copies were issued. The millionth copy was presented to the Queen in mid-January 1977.

One distinctive feature of the British edition is the metrication of weights and measures. Thus Emmaus is now said to have been "about eleven kilometres from Jerusalem", whereas in *Good News for Modern Man* the distance was "about seven miles" (Luke 24:13). Each of the water-jars at Cana was "large enough to hold about a hundred litres", whereas in the earlier edition it held "between twenty and thirty gallons" (John 2:6). This will make older readers engage in frequent mental arithmetic in order to discover the "real" dimensions. They can immediately picture to themselves three pounds weight or three miles distance, but reckonings in kilograms or kilometres create no such immediate pictures, and have to be transposed into standard weights and measures before such a picture can be formed. The editors, however, have had their eye on rising generations, not on those which are on their way out.

Special attention has been paid to a suitable idiom in the preparation of this version. The idiom is described as "common English"— that is, the idiom which is used in common by all strata of English-speaking society as a means of communication, a spoken idiom rather than a literary one. But where this idiom has been used to translate all the biblical writings, the result is that the diversity of style exhibited by the highly poetical parts of Scripture in contrast to the more prosaic parts cannot be appreciated. Where a literary idiom is replaced by one that is conversational, the sense may be reproduced accurately, but the ideal of "dynamic equivalence"— the attempt to produce the same varieties of impression as were produced by the original text—must be sacrificed. The sponsors and translators may have judged that this sacrifice was necessary and worthwhile for the sake of the end they had in view—"to give to-day's readers maximum understanding of the original texts"—but something has been lost. According to the wording on the dust cover, "the translators have used all their expertise to create the same reaction in the readers of today as the authors brought to the minds of the original readers of the Greek and Hebrew". It is doubtful if the translators themselves would make this claim.

Even in the New Testament the literary elegance of the Letter to the Hebrews, with its well-constructed periods, makes a different impression from Paul's more fractured style or the more colloquial passages of the Gospels. More clearly still in the Old Testament the poetry of the Psalms, "or rapt Isaiah's wild, seraphic fire", made a different impression in its day (as it does in our day in any rendering which achieves dynamic equivalence) from the narrative prose of (say) Judges or Ruth.

For example, the opening words of Isaiah 40 are best known in the English-speaking world in the A.V. form (perhaps as reproduced in Handel's *Messiah*):

> Comfort ye, comfort ye my people,
>   saith your God.
> Speak ye comfortably to Jerusalem,
>   and cry unto her,
> that her warfare is accomplished,
>   that her iniquity is pardoned:
> for she hath received of the LORD's hand
>   double for all her sins.

In the *Good News Bible* these words are rendered:

> "Comfort my people", says our God. "Comfort them!
> Encourage the people of Jerusalem.
> Tell them they have suffered long enough
>   and their sins are now forgiven.
> I have punished them in full for all their sins."

(Presumably "our God" is a misprint for "your God".)

The *Good News* rendering is both accurate and intelligible, but something of the original impact is lost. The poetical diction and rhythm of the Hebrew contribute to the majesty of the message of consolation. The forms of Hebrew poetry cannot be reproduced as they stand in an English translation, but the prose rhythms of the

A.V. (the two opening dactyls, for example) provide a worthy dynamic equivalent, probably as worthy as has been attained in any translation.

Or take another passage from the same chapter (verse 28) in the A.V.:

> Hast thou not known? hast thou not heard,
> that the everlasting God, the LORD,
>   the Creator of the ends of the earth,
> fainteth not, neither is weary?
>   there is no searching of his understanding.

The *Good News* rendering is:

> Don't you know? Haven't you heard?
> The LORD is the everlasting God;
>   he created all the world.
> He never grows tired or weary.
> No one understands his thoughts.

If it be said once again that the *Good News* rendering, while intelligible and accurate, is prosaic, this is not intended to be mere captious depreciation of a modern translation because it differs from the A.V. It is simply the recognition that, if we are looking for a translation dynamically equivalent to the original text of literature at the level of Isaiah 40, we shall find it in the A.V. rather than in the *Good News Bible*. In other words, where the goal of "common English" is incompatible with the ideal of dynamic equivalence, the former has prevailed.

Figures of speech, native to the original languages but naturalized in English through their reproduction in the older versions, have been replaced by expressions felt to be more current or direct. The "spirit" (Gen. 1:2), "arm" (Isa. 51:9), or "hand" (Luke 1:66) of God becomes at times his "power". The cherub on which the God of Israel flew to David's relief remains "a winged creature" in Psalm 18:10 but becomes "his heavenly chariot" in the parallel passage in 2 Sam. 22:11.

Sometimes straightforward expressions have been made more

vague than necessary: the Philippian jailer, for example, having thrown Paul and Silas into the inner cell, "fastened their feet between heavy blocks of wood" (Acts 16:24). But the common reader today knows what "stocks" are. Again, one had hoped that the dysphemism "to have sex" was a passing fashion; by using it repeatedly in a version of Holy Writ the translators of the *Good News Bible* have unfortunately helped to perpetuate it.

A few random samples will illustrate the quality of the work. Noah's ark is a "boat" (Gen. 6:14, etc.); Moses' ark of bulrushes is "a basket made of reeds" (Exod. 2:3); the ark of the covenant is the "Covenant Box" (Exod. 25:30; Heb. 9:4), and the mercy-seat is "the lid on the Covenant Box" (Lev. 16:2) or "the place where sins were forgiven" (Heb. 9:5).

The kings of Midian, begging to be killed by Gideon himself and not by his young son, say, "It takes a man to do a man's job" (Judg. 8:21).

In Ezek. 21:27 the expression which appears in older versions as "he whose right it is" is rendered "the one whom I have chosen to punish the city". The author is probably harking back to Gen. 49:10 ("he to whom it belongs"), where the *Good News Bible* finds the "Hebrew unclear" and renders (conjecturally): "Nations will bring him tribute." The meaning of "my servant David" in Ezek. 34:23 f. and 37:24 f. is clarified by the rendering "a king like my servant David". (There is the further implication that the coming king is a descendant of David, but a translation should not be overloaded.)

The Ethiopians of Psalm 68:31 became "the Sudanese", who "will raise their hands in prayer to God". This is an improvement; it discourages readers today from thinking of the Abyssinians. So also Jeremiah's benefactor is "Ebedmelech the Sudanese" (Jer. 38:7), but another "Ethiopian eunuch", the one to whom Philip preached the gospel, remains such (Acts 8:27).

The statement about the ships of Kittim in Dan. 11:30 reads, "The Romans will come in ships." This is historically correct, although it obscures the probable allusion to Num. 24:24, where a similar reference to ships of Kittim is rendered: "Invaders will sail from Cyprus." The kings of the north and the south in the same chapter of Daniel become, more intelligibly, the kings of Syria and Egypt.

In Dan. 12:4 the command to Daniel to "close the book and put a seal on it until the end of the world" is perhaps rather too final; the last phrase probably means "until the time of fulfilment". The following clause runs: "Meanwhile, many people will waste their efforts trying to understand what is happening"—a change from the older and inappropriate "many shall run to and fro", although the sense may be that when the book is unsealed "many will diligently peruse it, and so knowledge will be increased".

The Semitic idiom, "For three transgressions of Damascus, and for four" (Amos 1:3), becomes: "The people of Damascus have sinned again and again." Ecclesiastes is aptly explained as "The Philosopher" (Eccles. 1:1, etc.) instead of "The Preacher".

In the New Testament misgivings have been voiced about the rendering of Phil. 2:5, according to which Christ "did not think that by force he should try to become equal with God"; this, it has been felt, might give rise to christological error. In its context, however, the rendering can scarcely be misunderstood. There may, moreover, be a contrast here with Adam, who was caught by the bait, "you will be like God" (Gen. 3:4), not to speak of Lucifer, the "bright morning star", as he is called in this version, who was precipitated from heaven because he tried to seize cosmic supremacy and "be like the Almighty" (Isa. 14:12–14). Christ had no need to make any such effort, for "he always had the nature of God"; instead, "of his own free will he gave up all he had" and was accordingly raised by God "to the highest place above" and given "the name that is greater than any other name" (Phil. 2:6–9).

Whatever criticisms are expressed about the *Good News Bible*, they must be outweighed by appreciation. The translation has been carried out according to the standards of up-to-date linguistic science, and the meaning is clear throughout. Aids to understanding the text have been unobtrusively supplied here and there, as when the identity of the speakers is indicated in the Song of Songs or the "thirty sayings" mentioned in Prov. 22:20 are numbered serially from Prov. 22:22 to 24:22. The line drawings of Annie Vallotton greatly enhance the charm of presentation; above all, the good news is plainly communicated to readers who are concerned to pay heed to it.

The Translator's New Testament

A more specialized work to which honourable tribute should be paid is the *Translator's New Testament*, published by the British and Foreign Bible Society in 1973. This was produced by a team of thirty-five scholars, working under the direction of Professor W. D. McHardy. It is designed to provide help for translators of the New Testament to whom the sources of biblical scholarship are accessible only through the medium of English. The English wording of this version is carefully chosen so as to help them in the task of translation, to serve as a bridge between the Greek text and their modern idioms or cultures. The essential meaning of the original has been put into the plainest and most straightforward English, which thus provides a base for translation into other languages. The underlying text is the United Bible Societies' *Greek New Testament* first issued in 1966, which is itself intended primarily to be a handbook for translators.

A Greek-English Diglot

The *Translator's New Testament* has in large measure replaced an earlier enterprise entitled *A Greek-English Diglot for the Use of Translators*, several slim volumes of which, covering about eighteen books of the New Testament, were issued for private circulation by the British and Foreign Bible Society between 1958 and 1964. The director of this project was Professor McHardy. Each volume contained the Greek text with an English translation on facing pages, and proved useful to students and teachers in general, and not only to translators. It is a pity that the project had to be abandoned unfinished.

The New International Version

Another Bible Society—the New York Bible Society—has sponsored yet another translation, the *New International Version*. The adjective "international" in its title indicates that the translators are drawn from many parts of the English-speaking world. The New Testament was published in 1973. Its sponsors claim that it is "written in the language of the common man". This is a rather more literary language than the "common English" of the *Good News Bible*. Like the *Good News Bible* (together with the *Jerusalem Bible* and the *New American Bible*) it uses "you" throughout for the second personal pronoun, whether singular or plural, no matter who is being addressed. The language is dignified, readable and easily understood. The underlying text is that on which at the present time there is a general consensus of scholarly opinion. The translators would all be described as evangelical, but there is nothing in their work that reflects a sectarian or partisan bias. They have approached their task with the seriousness that might be expected to mark men who acknowledge the Bible as God's Word written, and their aim has been to express faithfully in modern English what the biblical writers meant. In this they have already achieved very considerable success.

A team of scholars has been working for some years now on the Old Testament part of the enterprise: it is hoped that this may be complete in 1979. A preliminary translation of the book of Isaiah was produced in 1975, and it promises well for the quality of the work as a whole. The *New International Version* is published in the United States by Zondervan of Grand Rapids and in Britain by Hodder and Stoughton. It has commended itself to the Gideons for placing in hotels and other public places as an alternative to the A.V.

The Revised Phillips

In addition to their publication of the *Common Bible* in 1973, Messrs Collins also issued a completely revised edition of Dr J. B. Phillips' *The New Testament in Modern English* (see p. 223). This revision represents over two years' labour. The text was adapted to the United Bible Societies' *Greek New Testament*, and every Greek word, we are assured, was considered afresh. Colloquialisms which were current in the 1940s but had become obsolete were removed or replaced (the "little tin gods" of 1 Peter 5:3 became "dictators"), and most of the conversationally worded additions to the text in Paul's letters disappeared. The translator realized that for many readers "Phillips" had become an authority, and this imposed on him a sense of greater responsibility.

The Living Bible

A paraphrase which has enjoyed a quite spectacular circulation is *The Living Bible* (1971), the work of one man, Dr Kenneth N. Taylor. Like Dr Phillips before him, Dr Taylor began with a paraphrase of the New Testament epistles, *Living Letters* (1962). The readers for whom he initially prepared it were his own children, and it is not surprising that his paraphrase is specially popular with young people. Much of the biblical narrative is paraphrased in simple language, the earthier phraseology of certain Old Testament stories being rendered by the euphemisms current in polite families, as when King Eglon's servants thought "that perhaps he was using the bathroom" (Judg. 3:24). There are, however, some exceptions to this policy. Some conventionally minded readers have been shocked by King Saul's furious retort to Jonathan, "You son of a bitch!" (1 Sam. 20:30), but probably that is an excellent dynamic equivalent of the Hebrew expression which the A.V. renders, "Thou son of the perverse rebellious woman," (the *Good News Bible* has, more tersely, "You bastard!").

The more theological passages of the *Living Bible* tend to be expressed in the idiom of Sunday School piety, as in Rom. 3:21, where "the righteousness of God" (i.e. God's way of justifying sinners) becomes "a different way to heaven". ("Going to heaven" plays a more prominent part in traditional religious language than it does in the New Testament.) In general it might be said that the *Living Bible* makes Paul use the terminology of a twentieth-century American evangelist. Nevertheless, many readers for whom Bible English is almost a foreign tongue find that the *Living Bible* brings the message of Scripture home to them in terms which they can readily understand. Alongside the edition in American English published by Tyndale House Press, Wheaton, Illinois, there is one in British English, overseen by Dr J. Hywel-Davies and issued in Britain by Kingsway Publications; there are also counterparts in other modern languages.

Other Versions

The number of new translations of the Bible in whole or in part keeps on increasing to a point where it becomes more and more difficult to keep up with them all. Some in particular are aimed at a special subculture with an idiom of its own, like that catered for in Carl Burke's *God is for Real, Man* (1967) and *Treat Me Cool, Lord* (1969). The second of these titles corresponds to the A.V. "Have mercy upon me, O LORD" (Psalm 6:2). Others are designed to give currency to the insights of a particular religious group, like the *New World Translation of the Holy Scriptures* (1961), sponsored by Jehovah's Witnesses. A recent compilation called *The Gospel* (1975) comprises new translations of the four canonical Gospels and of some other Gospels and similar gnostic works found among the Nag Hammadi treatises; in it the familiar first clause of Matt. 11:30 appears in the unfamilar form "my yoga is natural" (an etymological but hardly a dynamic equivalent).

The Picture Bible

A Bible version of a different kind is the *Picture Bible for All Ages*, issued in six paperback volumes by Scripture Union (1974). This strip cartoon version takes us back to the earliest days of English Christianity, when the Bible story was brought home to the people by wall-paintings and relief-carvings in churches and by carved panels, representing scenes from the Gospels, like those on the Ruthwell Cross and similar monuments. Have we thus, in the course of the centuries, come full circle from pre-literacy to post-literacy?

BIBLIOGRAPHICAL NOTE

Of many works which might be recommended (some of which have been cited in the preceding pages), it will suffice here to mention three:

Historical Catalogue of Printed Editions of the English Bible, 1525–1961, edited by A. S. Herbert (British and Foreign Bible Society and American Bible Society, 1968). This revision and expansion of the 1903 *Catalogue* of T. H. Darlow and H. F. Moule lists every printed English version of the Bible from Tyndale's fragmentary Cologne quarto to the first edition of the New English Bible New Testament.

The Cambridge History of the Bible (Cambridge University Press). Volume I: *From the Beginnings to Jerome*, edited by P. R. Ackroyd and C. F. Evans (1970); Volume II: *The West from the Fathers to the Reformation*, edited by G. W. H. Lampe (1969); Volume III: *The West from the Reformation to the Present Day*, edited by S. L. Greenslade (1963). This encyclopaedic project naturally includes much more than the history of the English Bible, but the English Bible receives specially full treatment, and there are ample bibliographies.

The Bible as Literature, by T. R. Henn (Lutterworth Press and Oxford University Press (New York), 1970), is a distinguished study of the literary style of the K.J.V. and an assessment of the Bible's place in English literature.

Index